EST.

ESTABLISH YOURSELF

BRAND, STREAMLINE, AND GROW YOUR GREATEST BUSINESS

ANNIE FRANCESCHI

ESTABLISH YOURSELF

BRAND, STREAMLINE, AND GROW YOUR GREATEST BUSINESS

ANNIE FRANCESCHI

DURHAM,
NORTH CAROLINA

The events and conversations in this book have been set down to the best of the author's ability, with great respect for those referenced. Some names and details have been changed to protect the privacy of individuals who are, perhaps, not ready to be super famous by way of this book.

The advice provided herein is meant to be seasoned with however many grains of salt you feel necessary to make the best decisions in your own life and business. Remember you're in the driver's seat of what you do before, during, and after picking up these pages. When you think about it, that's a pretty great thing. Your business is your business.

While the author plans to provide access to the book-related online resources (companion workbook, templates, etc.) referenced throughout the text for some time, she makes no claim that these resources will always be available to the reader. This is for various reasons including the peculiar nature of the internet and the possibility that we all may live on Mars, where one day such resources may become too expensive to host. The author is not responsible for the availability or any other aspect of external referenced content such as video links, other book titles, etc.

Lastly, while all "free resources" noted in the text are available complimentary/without financial charge, to request and receive access to any such resource, you will be required to subscribe to the author's/Greatest Story Creative LLC's email mailing list using a valid email address. Enjoy your resource(s) and note you can unsubscribe from such list at any time if you don't find value in the communications sent from the author and Greatest Story Creative LLC. For questions, please contact us at info@greateststorycreative.com.

Published in Durham, North Carolina by Greatest Story Publishing, an imprint of Greatest Story Creative®. Greatest Story Creative® is a federally registered trademark of Greatest Story Creative LLC.

This book may be purchased in bulk at special pricing for educational, business, or personal use, and the author is available for speaking, events, and interviews. To purchase multiple copies or to connect with the author for press, speaking engagements, and more, reach us at info@greateststorycreative.com.

Cover and book design by Annie Franceschi
Edited by Jodi Brandon
Photography (unless otherwise noted) by Faith Teasley Photography, faithteasley.com

ISBN: 978-1-7326859-3-2

Library of Congress Control Number: 2022900968
Printed in the United States of America

I think a book should be dedicated to the person
without whom it wouldn't exist.

To Sarah: for always believing in this book,
cheering me on at every stage of a messy journey,
and for all the joy you bring to my life and business
as a friend, partner, and client.

CONTENTS

Introduction: Everything Is How You Tell the Story 1

How to Establish Yourself 9

Be Ready to Take Action with My Free Workbook 10

When Getting By Isn't Good Enough 11

Defining Your Greatest Business 14

EST: The Establish Yourself™ Framework 21

Building Reverse Revenue in Six Areas of Business 24

The 4 Key Cs to Unlocking Your Greatest Business 30

Step One: Embrace Your Story 37

BRANDING 41

Courageous Confidence in Your Story and Value 43

Choose to Focus Where You're Most Valuable 55

Equip Yourself with a Branding Toolkit 81

Your Branding "Key C" Check 107

Step Two: Shape Your Business 111

OPERATIONS 117

Simple Goals, Clear Data, and Courageous Decisions 119

Navigating Boundaries, Bad-Fit Clients, and Brain Pickers 137

Pricing and Profit 157

Systems, Strategy, and Support 173

Your Operations "Key C" Check 201

Step Three: Translate Your Value 205
SALES AND CLIENT EXPERIENCE 209
Confidently Sell Your Value 211
Your Sales "Key C" Check 225
Welcoming and Working with Clients 229
Reviews and Building Lifelong Client Relationships 245
Your Client Experience "Key C" Check 259

REFERRAL RELATIONSHIPS 263
Be Clear (Not Creative) 267
Be Considerate 287
Be Committed 295
Your Referral Relationships "Key C" Check 303

MARKETING 307
Avoid Tactic Tornadoes with Sexy Strategy 311
Simplified Systems for Magic Marketing 319
Your Marketing "Key C" Check 343

Conclusion: The Real Key to Establishing Yourself Now 347
Reveal Your "Greatest Business Plan" 350
Ready to Establish Yourself? 359
Chapter Notes 361
Acknowledgments 363
About the Author 400

INTRODUCTION

Everything Is How You Tell the Story

I haven't lost faith in myself and my business—
but maybe other people have?

Maybe there isn't a market that wants me?

Is the ride over already?

It was spring 2016, and I was taking a walk. Big things were on my mind. At that time, I'd been in business for three years. Up until that point, I'd had no trouble getting clients. Through the magic of Google, they would just find me and I'd get by.

But by that spring, it was suddenly crickets. I looked around and realized that I only had two project clients at the time: my cousin and one of my best friends from high school. Yet there wasn't a shortage of interest in my work. I was doing a lot of consultations and estimates. I put a ton of effort into these proposals to make them custom, thoughtful, and beautifully designed. But then I'd email the quote and never hear back. Ghosted, time and time again, for months on end.

What was happening?

I felt lost and heartsick.

Am I not good enough?
Was my proposal not up to snuff?
Was the quote too high?
Why is my business falling apart in front of me?

I knew deep-down why this was happening. I just didn't want to say it out loud. **I hated selling.**

Maybe you do, too. Do you ever get exhausted by all the business and marketing gurus that flood your inbox daily? Everyone who is selling "just do this and you'll get millions of followers!"? The online posts that can make you feel *less than* and play to your fears and insecurities? It's the *worst*.

As much as I desired having a passionate *and* profitable business, I never wanted to do it at the expense of the clients who I sincerely wanted to help. I was terrified of coming off like the sleazy sales guy. So, my natural inclination was to run fast in the opposite direction. But this led to one very hard-to-admit truth: I wasn't selling myself *at all.*

At the time, in a typical sales conversation or email, I would come off more like your best friend than the doctor you're seeking out for advice and treatment. I was afraid to show up as the expert. So when things dried up in spring 2016, this fear of selling was about to cost me my business and my life as an entrepreneur.

As that possibility grew, I knew I needed to face another fear: asking for help. As a young business owner living off my husband's salary, I felt so much pressure to do everything scrappy and never ask for (or pay for) help to grow. I'm lucky that I happen to be a weird "jill-of-all-trades." There's much I can do on my own—graphic design, marketing writing, technical wizardry, and so on. As a result, I'd gotten by for quite some time. But this problem was different. It was beyond me. I'd tried everything and hadn't cracked it. I wasn't even sure if there was a solution. I remember thinking:

> *Can I learn to sell better and save my business?*
> *And is it even possible to sell in ways that feel good—not slimy?*

If anyone might have the answer, I had a hunch that it was Adele. Not the singer. Even better: business mindset coach Adele Michal. I'd met Adele just a few months prior when she spoke at a local networking event. Of my parents' generation, Adele is tall, graceful, and captivating when she speaks. She is kind and engaging, and she has a heart for helping entrepreneurial women. All of this came through quickly in her presentation. Her talk was all about presence and selling with confidence and authenticity. At the end of the event, something in the universe compelled me to introduce myself. I didn't know that what followed next would change the entire course of my life and business.

A few months after that first meeting is when I reached my selling crossroads. I hadn't booked any new clients. I had begun wondering if I should go back to a traditional job/career path. I was feeling desperate and entertaining the idea of accepting failure. I was *that* afraid of selling that I'd let it all go rather than seek help.

But then I remembered Adele, and what she clearly said she helped women do. After that walk when I considered quitting, I mustered up the courage to call her. Adele answered, and from there I said *yes* to the biggest (and only) investment I'd made in my business to date: a VIP day to work on my selling skills (or lack thereof)!

We got together for two half-day sessions on Zoom *(years before Zoom was a household way of life!).* Going into it, I thought I'd get some sales coaching and tips. I got so much more: a guided introspective experience that helped me do what I couldn't do on my own. Adele helped me to see that my problem wasn't "sales," rather it was owning my experience and expertise.

You see, at that point, I had been running my business, Greatest Story Creative® for three years. I was offering branding for coaches, consultants, and service business owners in a creative way that included writing, graphic design, and strategy . . . but *I* didn't go to art school. *I* wasn't a certified brand strategist. *I* wasn't a trained copywriter. I was new to this as a professional, and I'd invented my company and what it offered out of nowhere. Who was *I* to be writing someone's tagline or designing their business cards? Was I really an expert *yet?*

These were the stories I was telling myself. And as I'll share with you in this book, ***everything* is about how you tell the story.**

That's what Adele helped me see. I wasn't afraid of selling so much as I was afraid of having an unorthodox background in branding and business. While I didn't go to art school, I am a self-taught graphic designer who'd been doing creative projects for decades. Though I'm not a certified brand strategist, I learned branding at the highest levels of The Walt Disney Studios, where I worked for five years at the start of my career. Despite the fact that I'm not your traditional copywriter, I'd been the "writer" all my life—with a degree in literature from Duke University and a lifelong passion for writing stories, parodies, and other pieces. And though at the time I was fairly new to entrepreneurship, both my parents were business owners, as were my grandparents.

But I was afraid to own each of these stories, and I realized that this was showing itself in *every single sales conversation* I was having! Consciously or subconsciously, I was terrified that I wouldn't be as helpful to a client as someone else who was better. I was worried that I couldn't deliver the best possible work, so I wasn't conveying confidence when I presented what I offered. In some cases, I even talked prospective clients *out of working with me* and doing it themselves! *Oy!*

I couldn't see any of this until I faced my fear and finally hired the expert. Adele and I worked through it together. I took steps with her that I couldn't have taken without a supportive guide to explore my own thoughts. And while I gained practical skills for selling in a confident, value-minded way (versus sleazy selling tactics), I got something far more valuable from my coaching with Adele.

I discovered how to give myself permission to be in business as *myself.* I gained the ability to trust that I have value to offer someone else, even if I didn't have the "perfect story" of how I got there. I found a new respect for and worth in my story and how it informs my work. I claimed the approval I was seeking to show up confidently as the expert in every conversation from sales to networking. Ironically, it turned out that being my best business self *was* the path to helping the clients I wanted to help! I like to say that it's like I'd always had in the "key" in the lock, but Adele showed me how I could finally turn it.

Shortly after my VIP day with Adele, I co-hosted my first series of four local business seminars called "Small Business Gut Check." As a result, my practice exploded *(in a good way!).* I had dozens of successful consultations. I got my first *yes* on the spot in a video proposal. I booked two best friends for projects.

(Hi, Michele and Mary Ann!) Soon after, I was booked out for months. Suddenly, I had a new challenge: too much business and no systems to keep up with it. Generally, a better problem to have!

I'm sharing this with you now, six years after facing that pivotal crossroads in my business. At that moment, I faced a fear, asked for help, and learned a critical lesson about confidence. It led to me create "Batch December," my month-long, annual sabbatical for business development. It helped me more than triple my annual revenue and become a consistent six-figure business. Fueled by this kind of confidence, I've been asked to speak for thousands, I've advised hundreds of entrepreneurs, and I've created clear, consistent branding for more than 120 businesses. I wrote my first book about giving yourself permission to try. And I've been able to feel proud of every single one of those things.

Looking back, what I've learned is that lacking confidence can cost us so much: money, time, joy. We know deep-down that it's hurting us and holding us back. We all struggle with this, and I still do in various seasons of my life. It's powerful and all-consuming to face alone.

I was actively considering quitting rather than trying to address my business crisis of confidence. If I had done that, it breaks my heart to think what could have happened. I would have given up on that popcorn about to pop—all the things I'd been building in business for years—because I was afraid to embrace my story and ask for help. I was afraid to choose confidence and commit to the things I'd need to do to build my greatest business possible. But finally facing my fears and asking for help unlocked that.

How to do that—how to build your greatest business from here so you love it and it loves you back—is what I want to share with you.

> If you're wondering if you have what it takes to get to the next level . . .
> If you're feeling inadequate and like you don't have the best story . . .
> If you're not sure if you have value worth paying for . . .
> If you're thinking of asking for help but afraid to raise your hand . . .

This book is for you. This is the book I needed to read when I was a 31-year-old business owner and lost. It's the book I want you to have when you need confidence, permission, and support on this sometimes-lonely journey of entrepreneurship. Let it be your rocket fuel to finally face the fears, turn the key, and start building.

While I founded Greatest Story Creative in 2013, I like to say that I "established myself" in 2016. That was the year that I intentionally chose to grow my greatest business. It's when I decided to embrace my story, shape my business, and translate my value—and to do so confidently, clearly, consistently, and with a continued commitment. Choosing to establish myself allowed me to create and grow the profitable, passionate business I'd always wanted and hoped was possible. It was a choice that changed everything. That's what I want for you, too.

Are you ready to establish *yourself?* Read on. What follows will help you do exactly that.

Working with Adele

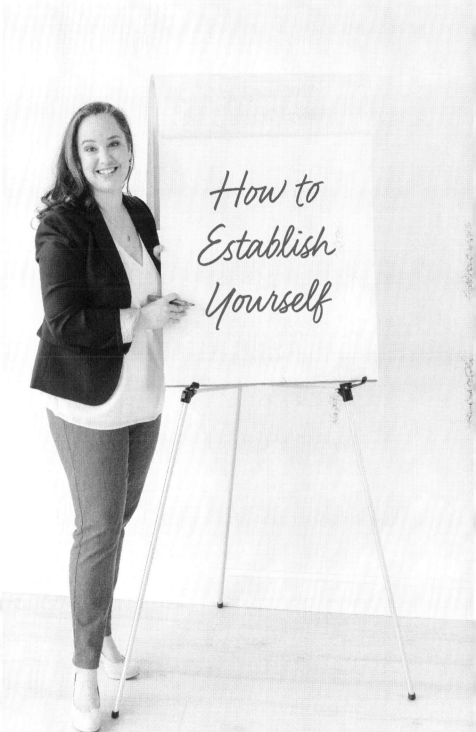

How to Establish Yourself

Be Ready to Take Action with My Free Workbook

Early readers of this book agree: This won't be something you read in one sitting, or even two.

Establish Yourself isn't a beach read. It's a practical business book that will light a fire under you—probably several. It will likely inspire you to take immediate action on areas of your business and have you scribbling notes in the margins, doing the exercises, and returning to review passages, processes, and more over time.

To help you do this important work as you read, **I've created a free, printable workbook for you.**

The Establish Yourself Companion Workbook
is a 60+ page PDF that includes:

- **Every exercise** in the book with space to complete them/take notes.
- **At-a-glance visuals** for the book's main frameworks.
- **Key links** to access/invest in additional referenced resources, tools, trainings, and templates.

FREE RESOURCE

To get the most value out of this book and all that it can help you do to grow your business, **download and print your FREE copy right now at greateststorycreative.com/workbook.**

When Getting By Isn't Good Enough

There comes a time when getting by isn't good enough anymore. That's where I was in 2016. Are you there now?

Maybe you started your business a few years ago and you've had some clients along the way. You've been using a thrown-together logo and an okay website, and you've seen a bit of success. I'm sure you're good at what you do, but every time you go to talk about it . . . or launch a new service . . . or make more money—*ugh. Stuck.*

Over the years, you've become better at what you do. Your business has evolved, your work has changed, you prefer some types of clients over others—yet your pricing, marketing, and more don't reflect that story. So to stay afloat, maybe you feel like you've got to do that icky self-promotion stuff, get thousands of people on your email list, and post a ton more on social media? That thought alone is pretty paralyzing, right? Because generally, business social media is the *worst!*

Have you ever felt embarrassed to show people your website and its lack of branding? Or have you felt like you're relying on other people to sell and share your business through word of mouth? I get it. When marketing feels uncomfortable, you barely do it. *(But then you sit at your computer and feel jealous of other people's websites and branding! Awful!)* Of course, every time you talk to potential new clients, you struggle. You worry about how to share what you do clearly. The list goes on and on, right?

These are feelings that swirl when you've reached a plateau. So many of us do, especially if you're a woman in business. Did you know that the overwhelming majority of women entrepreneurs struggle to break past the six-figure mark? In 2018, American Express reported that 88% of all women-owned businesses generated annual revenues less than $100,000.[1] So, you might be one of the nine in every 10 women who knows what *this* kind of stuck really feels like. (If you want to read an excellent book on making more money as a woman, scope out Rachel Rodgers's *We Should All Be Millionaires.)*

Stagnation is a deep hole and no matter what you've tried on your own, you're still there. Stuck at the same level, with no way to turn the key and reach any heights beyond where getting by has gotten you. You know it's time to do something different—but *what?*

What if I told you that you could get past this point, but you didn't have to become a social media maven to do it? What if moving forward wasn't about following any one particular marketing "guru" or uncomfortable strategy, but instead was about finding *your* best strategies?

That's what I want to help you do. As I share in this book, I tried the ways that "everyone" teaches for years. I wrote *all* the newsletters and posted on *all* the social media. I sold things I didn't believe in and paid a guru thousands for that bad advice. When none of it got a good return on my time or my money, I felt disappointed and dejected, and lost faith in myself.

So, I let it all go. I chose to do what made more sense for me. Then I did what few do: I committed to it and hung in there for more than a few weeks or months. I served my clients first before my marketing leads. Only when I figured out how to do this hard work of building my (not anyone else's) *greatest* business did I find the lasting, meaningful success I wanted. That's what you deserve, too.

Let's figure this out together. This book is here to help you find your next step. We're going to walk the entrepreneurial journey together to get there. But I'll go ahead and tell you now,

this book *can't* help you:

- Gain thousands of followers,
- Become the internet darling of Instagram, Facebook, or LinkedIn,
- Sell a million coffee cups,
- Get 10,000 people to join your email list next week,
- Become the next Oprah, Amy Porterfield, Jenna Kutcher, or *whoever,*
- Reach $1M in revenue overnight,
- Be featured on *Huffington Post, Forbes,* or *Inc.,*
- Become an epic designer/writer/website builder to DIY your branding and website,
- Learn absolutely everything you need to start and market a business from scratch,
- Create the ultimate sales funnel to sell all the things, or
- Build an unstoppable LadyBoss Empire of some sort. *(Side note: I really hate the terms* LadyBoss *and* BossLady. *Just* "boss" *is good.)*

However, this book *can* help you:

- Reach six figures (or other financial goals) if you've been making money but you're stagnant now,
- Become known in your area/sphere/network as a go-to person with a valuable solution,
- Make both your time and your business more profitable,
- Work with more ideal clients/companies,
- Say goodbye to bad-fit clients/companies,
- Get better referrals,

- Make your good reputation *great,*
- Sell with more confidence and comfort,
- Learn the keys to clearly and consistently market and brand your business,
- Spend less time on marketing/operations and more time serving clients/growing,
- Find your balance by setting up systems for social media, email lists, and content creation,
- Take a month (or two) off, if you want to,
- Love what you do *more,*
- Dread the "business stuff" less,
- Get more work/life balance that aligns with your values and dreams, and
- Go from getting by to growing with confidence.

In short, it can help you grow *your* greatest possible business, however you choose to define that. And yes, that can be a business that doesn't have to have 40K followers on social media! *Whew!*

If this feels like what you need, I'm so glad you're here. I can't wait to work through this with you. Let's do it. Your greatest business awaits.

Defining Your Greatest Business

When I had my confidence breakthrough with Adele in 2016, it fueled a season of growth that took me from "getting by" to running my most passionate and profitable business ever.

That season kicked off by embracing a radical idea: taking an annual month-long sabbatical. When I was busier than ever in 2016, I decided to take an entire month off from the business to work *on* it, not *in* it, and it was an eye-opener.

At the time, the incredible increase in clients and my suddenly glaring lack of systems had me feeling massively behind, disorganized, and not ready to serve clients well. I had a wild idea: If I had a month off, I could have enough time to focus and create some clear, strategic systems. Though it meant saying *no* to clients, I closed completely for all of December 2016. I called this business development experiment Batch December and dedicated it to one thing: getting my head around how to better organize my business so it could grow profitably without burning me out.

In 160 dedicated hours that month, I did everything from document every client process to tighten my branding toolkit to set new boundaries in my contracts. I created templates, committed to goals and decisions, and focused on setting myself up for success in the year ahead. It was exhilarating, but it also felt like a big risk. What was I doing taking off an entire month from paying clients to work *on* the business instead of in it?

Well, I started January 2017 with real systems for the first time across my entire business. Supported by the intention I'd just poured into my work, I emerged more confident, clear, consistent, and committed than ever to myself, my expertise, and the business I wanted to run. The rewards came with time, and I still benefit from daily from the thinking, organization, and decisions I made during that first sabbatical.

Taking a Batch December was so successful that I've taken one every year since then. Six Batch Decembers later (2016–2021), I've used this dedicated time to do everything from write my first book to finish this second one. While I've missed out on a client or two, I've gained many more who not only love the concept of Batch December but want to learn how they can do it themselves.

Looking back on those sabbaticals, I've cracked what it takes to finally have a passionate, profitable business that plays to my strengths, lets go of what doesn't work, and continues to grow and evolve along with me. This is what I call the Establish Yourself Framework: three upward steps to brand, streamline, and grow *your* greatest business possible. Notice I didn't say my greatest business, I said *yours.*

Before I teach you the framework, it's important for you to begin thinking about what *your* greatest business might look like. Your greatest business only needs to reach two things: being **passionate** and **profitable**.

- **Passionate:** At its core, being passionate means your business involves something that you love to do, that you're greatest at, and that others find immense value in (something *they* can be passionate about and invest in).
- **Profitable:** Your business also has to be profitable to sustain your passion for your work long term. What good is something you love if it burns you out and/or bankrupts you? Helping others is such a beautiful driving value—but you can't help others for long if you can't afford to keep your business afloat or your lights on.

But the good news here is that *you* get to define what passionate and profitable look like for you, and it can be different from mine or anyone else's definitions.

For one person, it's a seven-figure consulting empire with major companies as clients, a team of associates, books, paid speaking, and a three-week trip to Mexico every year. For someone else, it's profit to fund your children's college tuition and pay for family vacations. For another, it's having a meaningful impact on individual women's lives and helping them heal after traumatic grief and loss through coaching work. There's no right or wrong answers here—only *your* answers.

What's most essential is to define it in the first place, and take action to make it a reality. To provide some inspiration and share with you what a business aligned to your value and needs can look like, **here's what my greatest business looks like today:**

- Working an average of 10 months of every year (about 30 hours a week, plus holidays/vacations).
- Taking the entire month of December annually to have business development and family time.
- Earning six figures or more in annual revenue while taking home 60% or more in profit/salary.
- Having a bestselling book *(Permission to Try)* that helps others.
- Never having to pitch myself in cold "prospecting" for new clients.
- Instead, having a waitlist of ideal clients ready to work with me and invest in my value/services.
- Clients I love working with who are easy and fun to work with.
- Nobody picking my brain for free, unless I'd like to offer that value to help someone in need.

- Being paid and asked to speak regularly.
- Deeply enjoying the work I do and finding it meaningful.
- Enjoying marketing the work I do, and only doing the most essential marketing so my time isn't wasted.
- Never worrying about my business's social media, and spending only one or two days of time on it every year, *max!*
- Working less time but making more money each year.
- Having my family and work life in harmony and sync so I can be a good business owner, spouse, and parent and enjoy what's most important to me: my family.
- Being well-known, respected, and consistently referred in my network.
- Coaching/consulting for hundreds of incredible coaches, consultants, and service business owners.
- Speaking to thousands on branding, marketing, and living your greatest story.

If I had to simplify it down to a guiding mission, it'd look something like this:

> ***My greatest business looks like*** *working less, making more, loving my clients, and being known for being excellent at what I do* ***because*** *spending quality time with my family, being paid well for what I do and offer, being able to save/invest in what brings me joy, and doing legacy work that brings happiness and meaning to others* ***are deeply important and valuable goals for me.***

As you can see, my greatest business has a lot to do with being profitable (with my time, my resources, and my energy), loving my work and clients, and not having business be my entire life. It's not about being famous, having a zillion followers, or becoming an overnight millionaire. None of that other stuff really matters as much as I used to think it did.

When I stopped to really think through what matters most—for me—my business has become about loving what I do, being financially able to do it and keep our family afloat while my husband has been in physical therapy school, and being proud of what I'm creating as a legacy that helps others. *Someday, I'm sure I'll add "getting the Disney World vacation house of my dreams," too.*

So what about you? Why don't you take a stab at this now, while it's fresh in your mind?

EXERCISE

What Does Your Greatest Business Look Like?

Use the *Establish Yourself Companion Workbook* (free to download at greateststorycreative.com/workbook) or your own notebook to do a brainstorm for the next five to 10 minutes, dreaming up what your business would look like if you really loved it and it was thriving in the ways that matter most to you.

You may want to imagine what type of work you're doing most, the time you want to be spending in and away from your business, and the types of goals you'd want to reach—financial, professional, and even personal. You decide, and feel free to take some inspiration from the examples shared in this section.

When ready, look over your brainstorm and summarize your vision for *your* greatest business using the prompt provided.

MY GREATEST BUSINESS VISION:

My greatest business looks like

(As a list, briefly describe 3–4 of its major attributes, like how you spend your time, what types of clients you serve, how many of them you have, how much annual revenue you make, what you'll be most known for, and so on.)

because

(Note your top 3–4 values. These could be financial security, freedom, health, doing work I love, putting my child or loved one through school, having time to spend with family, etc.)

are deeply important and valuable goals for me.

When you feel ready, head to the next page to reveal the Establish Yourself Framework and how its three steps can get you there.

EST: The Establish Yourself Framework

Meet the Establish Yourself Framework: a journey of three steps to establish yourself and grow your greatest business. This approach is a repeatable method to help you build up to a new level of growth and satisfaction by elevating three biggest needle-moving elements of it: you, the *business* part of your business, and how you market what you do.

The Establish Yourself Framework comes to life in the easy-to-remember abbreviation EST.

E | Embrace Your Story
S | Shape Your Business
T | Translate Your Value

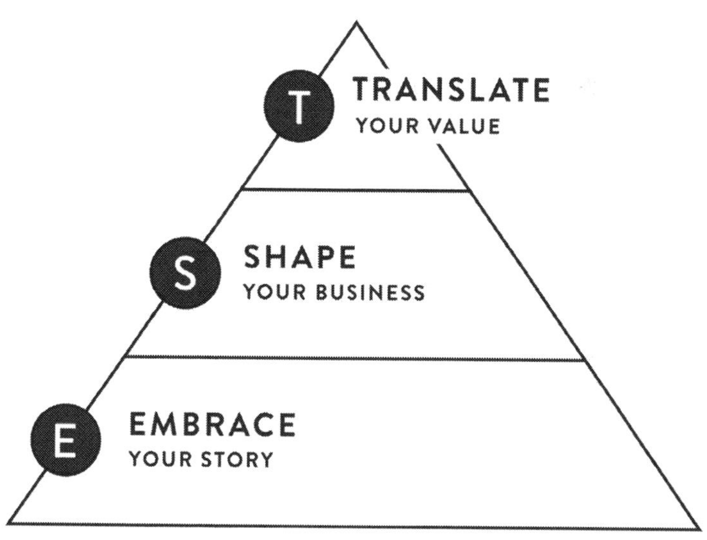

The Establish Yourself Framework Pyramid

I've found that doing all three of these things in order, well, and over a committed period of time has helped me design, run, and grow my greatest business, and they can lead you to realize yours. Here's how the steps work and build upon themselves, upward, forming a pyramid.

STEP ONE: EMBRACE YOUR STORY

Too often, people think that a problem in their consulting or coaching practice is related to their website, social media, or 10 trendy marketing tactics. However, having consulted on brands for hundreds of entrepreneurs, I've seen that typically both the biggest challenge and biggest opportunity is staring at you in the mirror: *you.*

To make the most of your business, the best place to start is with *you.* Your journey begins with learning new ways to embrace confidence—in your expertise, in the main solution you offer, and in the primary clients or companies you've chosen to help. This kind of clarity will be critical and foundational to anything else you're doing to grow into the future. If you hate self-promotion or being the "face of your business," this step is about facing that block, too. Because if you're not feeling strong about what you're doing and you're uncomfortable owning your path to your expertise, people will sense that and your business won't go any higher from here. So we start by embracing your story.

STEP TWO: SHAPE YOUR BUSINESS

You might expect the next step has to be knocking out social media, email lists, and more. But it's not. Surprisingly, the next biggest block to moving to a new level is not marketing, it's the underlying business itself.

Once you're clearly committed to being the expert you are and the value you bring to your clients, the next step has to be ensuring that your business is organized and set up to consistently deliver that value—passionately and profitably. It's about quantifying the success that matters most to you, without chasing just the "holy grail" of six-figure income. That means defining goals, setting boundaries and systems in alignment with them, and committing to those choices—even if you have to turn away red-flag clients or set office hours. Ultimately, this step is all about being more strategic to set up the back end for your larger success as a business.

So we focus on shaping your practice, making sure you put intention (and attention) on the areas that need to change in order for it to be its greatest—not only for you, but also for your clients.

STEP THREE: TRANSLATE YOUR VALUE

Before we tackle traditional marketing best practices, I show you why getting clients and repeat business can encompass so much more than what many marketing gurus would have us believe. In fact, translating your value—taking your expertise and putting it into language, activities, and visibility that your ideal clients can connect with and invest in—can and should be done in many different ways beyond the click of a mouse.

As we complete "Translate Your Value," you'll feel more empowered to market yourself in your own ways—ready to connect the confident expertise you have to great-fit ideal clients who can't wait to work with you (and tell all their friends).

—

Taken together, and worked through step-by-step, embracing your story, shaping your business, and translating your value will be an investment you're invited to undertake—one you'll make with both your heart and your head. So let's make that investment now, building our way upward through six of the most valuable parts of your business.

Building Reverse Revenue in Six Areas of Business

Through the three steps of the Establish Yourself Framework, I guide you through six essential areas of business in a specific order, one that I call reverse revenue. This is an approach that flips business growth and marketing in a reverse, less-overwhelming order from how most people teach it.

In my work with coaches and consultants, I've seen two big ways they approach marketing: what I call "under-marketing" and "over-marketing." People who are "under-marketing" aren't doing much at all to market themselves. If you're an "under-marketer," your only real marketing is having clients who refer you. You may not even have a website, or if you do, it's not one you really want to share with people. You don't know what to say in your own marketing, so you feel overwhelmed by the marketing guru world of a million options, thousands on an email list, and the latest webinar strategy. What's the effect? You don't attempt it at all (and your growth stops or slows).

Conversely, if you're "over-marketing" you're chasing every "tactic tornado"—every new app, strategy, big hot marketing idea. Much of your time is spent worrying about what to post on social media and monkeying with the words on your website. Before you know it, you're down a black hole of internet marketing. I dive more into this later, but if you spend most of your time marketing and aren't seeing results, you might be an "over-marketer."

Whichever you are, the juggernaut of gurus out there teaching all the things you "have" to do to get clients have done a major brainwash on us all. All the stuff out there has generally convinced us that marketing is *everything*—when it's but one of many components. The question has been framed wrong altogether.

If your business growth has stalled, the question too often is "Well, what should I do for marketing?" I want to change that question to "Where can I *more easily* find passion and profit in my business?"

In my experience, the answer lies in what I call reverse revenue: focusing on optimizing your existing clients and network *first*—working *backward* from how most people teach marketing and business optimization.

Traditional marketers and trainings often teach you to worry most about and cater to ice-cold connections first (or solely). Yet, cold connections are the people who are totally brand new to knowing about you and your business. They don't know, like, or trust you yet. Despite this, most traditional marketers recommend spending a lot of your limited time, resources, and energy on trying to get someone who's never heard of you before to quickly feel a strong-enough connection to you to invest hundreds to thousands of dollars in your services. This creates what I call the "stuck in marketing mode" triangle.

The "Stuck In Marketing Mode" Triangle

You end up chasing tactics that almost always keep you stuck on step one of marketing constantly across a ton of different platforms with a gazillion messages, while never reaching the promised gold rush of sales, fans, and clients. This is how you stay at the same level (or sink lower) when you work harder than ever on that "marketing is king" mentality.

Seem hard? Yep, it is. The reason connecting to cold leads is always so hard is that it's the challenging work of relationship building—no matter how you slice it. That's what social media or blogging, for example, when done well, can do: create a new relationship. But while nurturing and converting cold prospective clients through marketing tactics can certainly be worthwhile, if all you focus on is them, you miss huge, profitable opportunities to maximize the relationships you've *already* established.

If that sounds like a breath of fresh air, I invite you to do what I've done and what I've led my clients to do: focus your efforts in reverse revenue order. Flip the script!

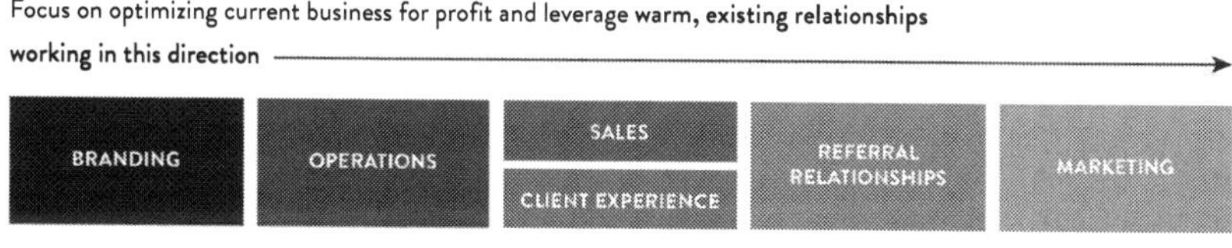

Instead of catering to cold connections first, the Establish Yourself way is to start with your *warmest* connections and *existing* relationships: your current clients, past clients, referral partners, and network. What can you do to sell more or be more profitable with your existing clients, whether they're individuals or represent companies with opportunities? Are you staying top of mind with your past clients? Are you fostering strong referral relationships (or could you be)? And are you even selling services as valuable as they could be?

These questions don't get answered by attending a million free masterclasses. Rather, they get answered by working from a foundational perspective. I personally solidified this reverse revenue approach to business after asking a coach of mine how she tackled adding a new offer to her practice. She'd found that her best practice was to create the offer backward: developing the pieces in the opposite direction of how her clients would journey through her process. This way, no one would get stuck in the system at any point and could flow smoothly once she marketed the service. Doing it backward was so valuable that she'd even pause client work altogether to get a specific program or offer "just right," rather than try to do it on the fly or develop in the other, more popular direction.

When I soon had a new service to develop, it was tough to fight the instinct to do it in the "traditional" way of working from marketing to operations. But I took her advice and worked backward. I focused, created an incredible program and all I'd need to execute it well, and then sold it to existing clients only (that's right: no marketing). A month of behind-the-scenes, focused work delivered on a new personalized strategy service that brought in $20,000 from a handful of past clients in just six weeks' time!

This success had me looking back across my business and led me to realize that I am the most successful when I'm strategic, and I've seen that the most sound strategy starts from working backward from the prospective client's journey. Not only can it be a path to optimize how you launch a service, but—far more big picture—it's a powerful approach to maximize your entire business, which is what I'm inviting you to do using this book.

Every system and process that keep my business running smoothly and growing to new levels every year rely on that principle of prioritizing maximizing warmest connections first—versus obsessing and spending too much time and resources trying to convert cold ones. Taking this big picture, the reverse revenue approach has become my go-to way to both rejuvenate my business and to guide others in bringing new life to theirs.

So, here are the six essential areas of business in reverse revenue order:

1. Branding
2. Operations
3. Sales
4. Client Experience
5. Referral Relationships
6. Marketing

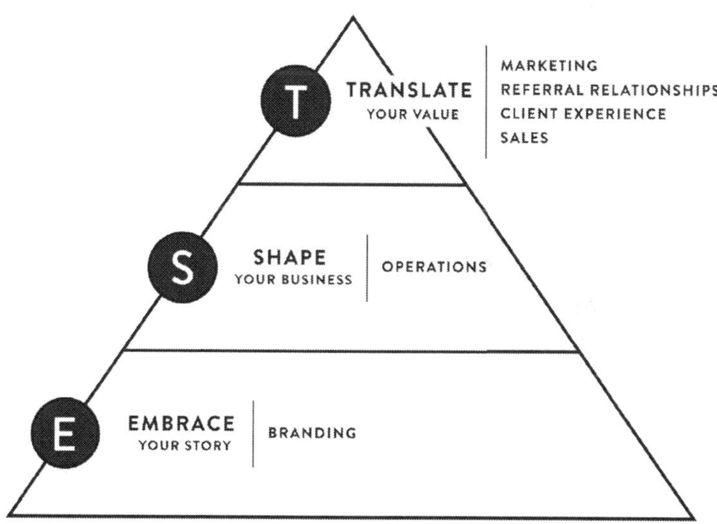

Together, we explore embracing your story through **branding,** both the overall branding choices you make and the tools you need to tell the story. Then, we shape your business through **operations**—goals, boundaries, pricing, and systems of behind-the-scenes success.

We're able to translate your value by working first through inviting, sleaze-free **sales** and an elevated **client experience** that turns those new clients into lifelong fans. We make the most of your network, creating even more fans through **referral relationships,** and, finally, we look at how to build a smart, efficient **marketing** strategy that will foster as many warm connections as it will introduce you to cold ones.

This is what I take my Establish Yourself clients through when they're ready to grow beyond what they can see and they don't want to waste their time. We let go of the expectations to have the perfect funnel or marketing strategy and instead focus on the reverse revenue—optimizing each area, in order, and more quickly capturing profit and passion in the work they do.

Now, here's your guided opportunity to find reverse revenue as you work to establish yourself and grow your greatest business. You're going to make that happen with the help of what I call the Four Key Cs.

The 4 Key Cs to Unlocking Your Greatest Business

Imagine your current practice like a pyramid, with great levels growing higher and higher—but often feeling out of reach. Sometimes, it may feel like you've been stuck on one level forever, unsure of what you need to do to unlock others. For this reason, the Establish Yourself Framework is designed as a pyramid-building process, with three big-picture, inspiring steps to reach new, sustainable growth.

But to transform *your* business, how can you know exactly what to change and improve? What and how do you choose to level up, especially when you're not sure what's had you stuck where you are?

The answer lies in making sure you've got all of the Four Key Cs on your side. Having spent more than eight years in business and having consulted on branding and business growth for hundreds of coaches and consultants, I've identified the Four Key Cs as the four most important factors to building a passionate, profitable practice, while establishing yourself as a known expert in your network and beyond.

When business owners are lacking one or more of these Cs, they typically stay stuck at the same level for a long time. In their inefficient efforts to grow, they are likely to change their message about 100 times in six months, and they let their business ultimately disappear (or rebrand) when they don't see instant results. In chasing quick wins, in trying to figure out how to master every social media network, and in losing touch with their network while trying desperately to turn new people into paying clients, they burn out.

Conversely, those who succeed keep an eye on the Cs, and are willing to invest their time, resources, interest, and patience in realizing the meaningful, lasting success the Cs can foster. When these thriving business owners reach plateaus, they hire experts to help them keep growing upward to new levels that once felt impossible. They hold tight to the decisions they make, do the hard work, get feedback, and keep polishing. They nurture relationships over time and show their clients they care about them as they grow. Over the course of months and years *(never days and weeks),* they become an "overnight" success.

After trying what the gurus teach, burning out, and choosing to go my own way, I discovered that maximizing the Four Key Cs is exactly what has worked for me, and what observably works for every successful entrepreneur I know in real life (not just those luminaries I follow online). You easily know these when you see them in action. Imagining them together as one physical key, these four factors unlock your next levels, building up meaningful success to whatever heights you want to go. But these components are also useful in that they can point to why and where you're stuck on your current level. They can work like a diagnostic, helping you understand the reasons you haven't been going anywhere, no matter how hard you've been trying to make the climb.

These are the 4 Key Cs, and using them can be critical to your growth from here:

1. *Courageous* confidence
2. *Crucial* clarity
3. *Conscious* consistency
4. *Continued* commitment

COURAGEOUS CONFIDENCE

Confidence in business comes down to believing in yourself, the work you do, the solutions you provide, the people you help, and the way you present the value of your work through marketing. Like all of the Cs, confidence often comes down to a series of choices we have to continually make. Believing in yourself and all the hard things about being in business—that really does takes courage.

So we look at your business through the lens not only of confidence, but of having *courageous* confidence. Choosing to be confident is brave. It's critical to your success and survival to be brave enough to do wild things like call yourself an expert, even when you worry about your experience.

CRUCIAL CLARITY

Clarity is incredibly important to branding any business. *Who are you? Who are your ideal clients? How can we clearly communicate what you do so those clients get it and want to work with you?* However, the C here isn't only clarity, it's *crucial* clarity.

According to Oxford Languages, *crucial* means "decisive or critical, especially in the success or failure of something."[2]

Decisive. Business, again, is about making decisions. If you are a solopreneur or have a small team, you do not have all the resources, money, time, team members, or a marketing department to throw at your business, so you must act with crucial clarity.

This means that whether you are working on embracing your story, shaping your business, or translating your value, you must focus on what is most essential to accomplishing those steps. In *Marketing Made Simple* by Donald Miller and Dr. J.J. Peterson, they recommend that your marketing always be related to your customer's "survival."[3] But this survival mindset extends way beyond marketing.

As I share, being "crucial" has greater impact when you expand its application to your whole business, not only how you market it. The stakes are high and your crucial focus impacts what you communicate to your client and to yourself, and what you do and don't do behind the scenes of your business (like boundaries, pricing, and more).

In this book, we look at how you might focus on what is most crucial, not just possible—in other words, what is most important to make decisions about, further define, and take action on across all three steps and six areas of business we dive into. Let it be said here, and many times before this book is over: Your business is much bigger than your marketing. To borrow from *The Princess Bride,* anyone who says otherwise is selling something (likely a marketing course).

CONSCIOUS CONSISTENCY

Often overlooked and abandoned for many reasons, consistency is just as important as clarity. They go hand-in-hand. The clearest message that isn't consistently shared will be useless to you. The unclear message shared everywhere consistently is also useless. They need each other, and you need both.

What good is having clarity about what you do or a great color palette if you don't consistently use either in how you run and market your business? How worthwhile is writing a newsletter every week if that newsletter is confusing your ideal clients?

I cover the value of consistency throughout your business, and also the importance of that consistency being intentional or *conscious.* While you may *think* you're being consistent, if you are not practicing awareness in how you are both running and marketing your business, how do you know that for sure? The game-changer is having a system—a thought-out, strategic process to ensure you are consistent and to make that consistency easier. That starts with being intentional about it, rather than being hopeful.

CONTINUED COMMITMENT

Maybe we don't even realize how often we're doing it. Nevertheless, even when we do all the work to be confident, clear, and consistent, we are often too nervous to put those things into action long enough to see real results. We change what we're doing because it's easy to edit and far harder to hang in. But if I had only one thing I could teach other business owners like me, it would be the value of keeping your eyes on the big picture and practicing continued commitment to make it a reality.

—

***Not a single C stands for* creative, capital, *or even* competitive advantage.** The Four Key Cs don't require you to be constantly reinventing yourself or being unbelievably magical or special. In fact, quite the opposite is true.

Instead, they require you to hang in there. To do your best possible work. To persevere. To focus. To streamline. To commit to a message, and an audience, and a solution (to their problem) that you really believe in. Those things are in some ways harder to do because you can't hide from them: There's no way to do them but to act, and act with confidence.

So while each of the Four Key Cs is important, you can't unlock new levels of success unless they're *all* there, doing their part to make up *one* complete key. Only having all four of these elements in play can give you access to that next level (and the ones beyond that), getting you building upward again to your greatest business.

So this is what we look for throughout the book as we navigate the six areas of business in the Establish Yourself Framework. Through a "Key C" exercise at the end of each area, I give you an opportunity to use the Four Key Cs as a gut check—a chance to see what may be keeping you stuck and where your next action step coming out of this book may lie. Exploring the Four Key Cs will help us zero in on where you need to take the most action, and where your time, resources, and investment would be best spent.

As you begin your path, I encourage you to be thinking about that first C: courageous confidence. In my first book, *Permission to Try,* I talk about confidence through the lens of changing careers and chasing your dreams. But once your dream has been to become a business owner and you've been selling your consulting, coaching, or service abilities to others, now comes the time for that next level of permission: permission to confidently embrace your story, shape your business, and translate your value.

Business building and thriving are deeply connected to confidence. Get it, give it to yourself, and invest in the expert or the course or the thing you need to give yourself permission to be confident. In her TED talk, activist, author, and podcaster Brittany Packnett boldly proclaims, "Confidence needs permission to exist."[4]

So will you give yourself permission? To own what you do, how you do it, everything that led you to it, and all the lives you're going change with it—including your own? Because that will be the lynchpin. That permission is going to change everything.

STEP ONE
Embrace Your Story

Did you know that there's no such thing as a "lost child" at Walt Disney World? There are only "lost parents." If a kid gets separated from their parents at the theme park, walks up to any cast member, and tells them they're lost, the cast member will do a curious thing. They'll say something like, "Don't worry. You're not lost, you're right here! We know where *you* are! It's just *your parents* who are *lost!* Let's find them!"

Everything is about how you tell the story. Everything is branding—how you choose to position this story—both for yourself and others.

Your business, and especially your life as an expert and entrepreneur, are no exceptions. But often, I see a lot of business owners struggle with the most core part of being in business: believing in yourself and your expertise. If you haven't clearly defined what you do (and don't do), if you haven't committed to doing it, if you don't show up as the expert for yourself—well *why* would other people invest in you?

In her book *The Gifts of Imperfection,* Brené Brown shares, "[O]wning our story and loving ourselves through that process is the bravest thing that we will ever do."[5] It does take courageous confidence to show up every day and make your expertise available in the form of a business. It takes summoning a ton of belief in yourself. As evidenced in my experience with Adele, and a lesson I've learned over and over in my work as I've launched new programs and products, my business succeeds when I *choose* to believe in it, and it doesn't when I don't. So before I can impart any best practices to you, everything we do together has to start with checking in with you. To root out imposter syndrome (or at least slide it to the side as best we can), we have to be our own first "investors," "followers," and "clients." We have to find our way to not just *own* our story as Brené suggests, but moreover, we need to *embrace* it.

Embrace (verb)
To accept or support (a belief, theory, or change) willingly and enthusiastically [6]

The time has come to support yourself—willingly, enthusiastically. To lead the way that you want others to follow. To reframe and rebrand how you tell the story. To embrace it, *so others can too,* is the only way to love what you do and be able to consistently and profitably do it for years to come.

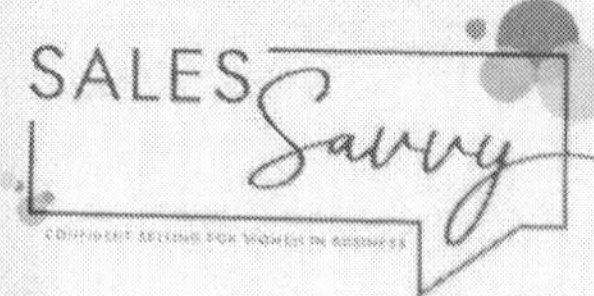
SALES
Savvy
Brand Story Guide

Branding

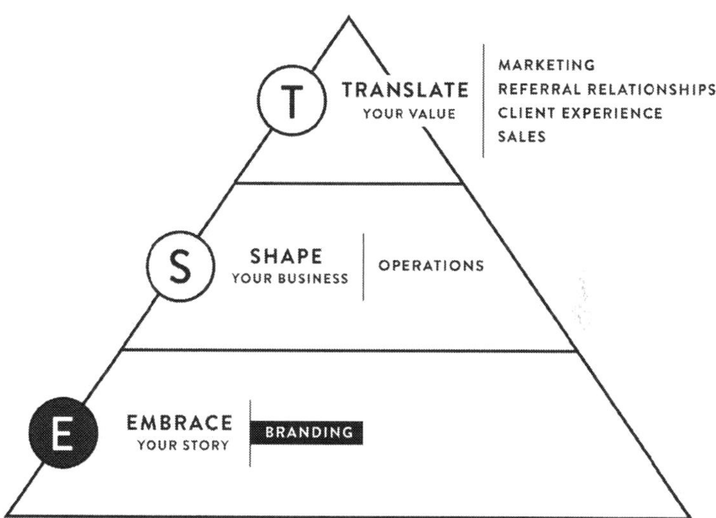

In this first step of embracing your story, I share with you the most critical aspects of branding to your success: how you tell the story to yourself *and* the tools you use to confidently tell it to clients.

To cleanly define it for us, to brand means to "mark indelibly."[7] Today, in this moment, you and your business already have a "brand"—just as you personally have a reputation. Your brand is how people think and feel about you and what you do. That impression has been forged by every client experience, email, website page, post, and comment you've made in passing along the way. Your brand is a living thing that grows and changes as you grow and change. It is something you can positively impact, if you choose to.

With how you choose to shape every one of the experiences you have with clients and your network, and the tools you use to tell the story and share your value (your logo, website, tagline, etc.)—*aka* your business's brand identity—you have the incredible opportunity to push through to a new season.

As we explore branding together as our means to embrace your story, I begin by sharing the three biggest things that have attacked my confidence and made it hard at various times in my business to embrace my story: having an imperfect path to the work I do now, struggling to give myself credit, and worrying about being "self-promotional." I share how to find more permission to embrace your story. We then look at where you can find crucial clarity in how you embrace that story as well as the story you tell clients, from your most valuable service to your most ideal client.

Lastly, we work on identifying the biggest thing you'll need to brand your new chapter—a branding "toolkit"—and the most important assets you need to define and/or have created to shape your business and translate your value successfully.

Let's start with the core work of branding yourself at this crossroads moment, a process that starts with acknowledging how you got here.

BRANDING

Courageous Confidence in Your Story and Value

For your new chapter, branding begins with bravery. It starts with choosing to be courageously confident about how you became the expert you are, seeing yourself as a valuable guide, and giving yourself the credit that's likely long overdue. It's a walk with permission and discovering that you have a light that others need. It's time to allow yourself to shine.

Permission to Have Pivoted

Who do you think of when I reference Dwayne "The Rock" Johnson?

Powerhouse actor?
Top film producer?
Tequila maker?
Maui from *Moana*?
WWE wrestler?

How about *professional football player?*

Well, not that. "The Rock" is many things, but we don't typically think football when we think of Dwayne Johnson. Yet, would it surprise you to know that, growing up, his biggest dream was to play in the NFL? Or that, as a young man, he actually got partway down that path by playing in the Canadian Football League (CFL)?

It's true. And after pushing hard for his dream for many years, Dwayne got cut from a professional Canadian team after just two days of play. On his Instagram, he often shares this story and refers to this turn in his career as "the best thing that never happened" to him. If Dwayne hadn't had this dream fall apart, he wouldn't have created the unbelievably successful, fulfilling life (and businesses) he has now.

Did you arrive at the work you do now from a twist or a turn? Rather than feel shame or concern that you don't have the perfect story that led you to your work now, what if we change that narrative today? What was the "best thing that never happened" to you? What are the forks in the road—those you chose and those that were thrust upon you—that led you here? Is it time to reframe your story?

For me, it wasn't until I partnered with Adele that I realized how much emotional baggage and how many limiting beliefs I was carrying into my daily work and how I sold and marketed expertise. I'd been creative all my life, self-taught at graphic design, and trained as a creative writer in my education, but I didn't *feel* like an expert. I was keenly aware that there were so many other people who did branding, copywriting, and web design who were "true professionals." There were people who had degrees in what I was doing, 20 years of time on me, or both! To my mind, I was never going to be good enough, and I was carrying that around like an enormous weight around my neck.

I also had a dream that didn't pan out: becoming a major film producer (and maybe even screenwriter). As I share in my book *Permission to Try*, my first dream wasn't to be an NFL player, it was to make it in Hollywood, developing major movies. I got close—even earning a "dream job" at The Walt Disney Studios writing and designing storytelling presentations for major upcoming films like *Maleficent* and the live action *Cinderella*. For me, that dream job didn't add up to the life I wanted. So I wasn't "cut from the team" like the Rock, but I did choose to quit when I saw that my "one path" wasn't what I wanted most for my life.

Maybe you've had a similar road to getting here and the work you do. The question to start with is: How much baggage might you be bringing with you because your path to where you are was unorthodox?

As a branding consultant, one of the biggest things I do is write "brand voice guides." As I create them, they are powerful wording toolkits that include 10 of the most foundational messaging pieces you use to communicate your value to ideal clients and your network. One of those pieces is the "about" story. Having written more than 100 "about" stories for entrepreneurs, I can tell you that my own is just one of many stories about reframing and reinvention.

I often say that I make people cry for a living, because that's what tends to happen when I read a client their new "about" story. It's a phenomenon that's happened to dozens of my clients, of all ages and backgrounds. After it happened the first time, I realized why. It's not that my writing's so incredible. It's simply that when you get to hear your own life story told in a way that celebrates your expertise, it presents your story as "making sense" and leading you to being the absolute best person to help your clients. Finally seeing that clearly can be deeply moving.

If you worry about the validity of your path and your value to others, I can tell you for a fact that I've worked more than 100 people who've felt the same you do now. When they finally had a chance to reposition the story—to see the value in all that they've done and how it's led them to be the exact expert their clients need to change their lives—it's breathtaking. It's powerful. When it's *your* story, it can make you cry.

When you doubt yourself, I want you to know about Sarah Potts, an operations consultant who became a patient, organized partner to business owners after a path to become a social worker didn't work out. I'd like you to discover Marcey Rader, whose career in clinical research led to developing three autoimmune diseases and so much burnout that she gave it up and later became a health and productivity expert. I wish you could sit down with Janice Smith, a teacher and instructional leader who channeled her passion for teaching and education into videography for business owners. I'd love for you to meet Tricia Russo, whose long path to becoming a Hollywood executive got interrupted by cancer but led her to create a nonprofit organization and feature documentary about navigating cancer and infertility.

You could also have coffee with Teri Rogowski, whose personal tragedy of losing her husband at a young age guided her path to becoming a daily money manager for people. Or perhaps, you could take a walk with *the* Adele Michal. For all the wisdom she shared with me, she was originally a trained counselor and, later, a documentary producer. These were two careers she thought would be "it" before realizing life had more adventures in store for her (lucky for me).

These incredible women each had (and I'm sure still do have) dark moments when they doubted themselves, even though their stories and vulnerability in not having it all figured it out from the get-go are so inspiring to those they help.

It seems that gone are the days of our parents and grandparents who worked for one company for the majority of their lives. With the rise of the gig economy, the impact of the pandemic, and the incredible access the internet provides us, so many of us are turning our unique stories into something of value as a business. But in order for our stories to have true, lasting, and visible value, we have to embrace them. We have to believe that the value exists *first*.

When I look back, I'd gotten by in those first three years of my business just by winging it. But I couldn't get to the consistent six figures, high demand, and high satisfaction of *my* greatest business if I didn't—once and for all—accept and embrace my story.

I'm not a cookie-cutter brand strategist. I don't have a fancy certification. I learned Adobe Illustrator because I had to design my wedding invitations on a deadline when my printer backed out. I've spent two decades doing creative writing. I learned how branding works at the highest levels of The Walt Disney Company, and I've learned how to apply those lessons by advising hundreds of entrepreneurs and branding more than 120 of their businesses along the way.

How I got here isn't something I need to apologize for; it's something I need to use. The same goes for you. You don't have to apologize for your path here; you need to celebrate it and use it to help others. Your story doesn't just add value, it *is* the value you bring to the table.

Will you embrace your story so far, even though it's not the one you thought you'd write in your career or your business?

Will you embrace your . . .

Expertise?
Experience?
Perspective?
Time invested in yourself and others?
Character?
Incredible value?

In the central book of Judaism, the Talmud, it is written, *"If not now—when? If not me—who?"* To you, I say: If not now, *when?* If not *you*, who?

Claiming Your Expertise and Credit

Growing up, I was definitely an "arts" kid. I was most definitely not a sports kid. I'd get hit in head with the ball, even in Wiffle ball. If you're an arts kid and a terrible athlete, you may know: There aren't a lot of trophies for "best art" or "most creative."

I'm not sure why this annoyed me, but it did. When I was 11, I wanted more credit for my value, even though I wasn't a "success" in what my school most valued: athletics. I don't remember whose idea it was, but one day, my mom took me to the local trophy business and paid for me to design a custom trophy for myself.

As I'm writing this, I'm cringing. It feels super embarrassing. But yes, as a kid, I actually had a trophy made just for me, *engraved* with "Most Creative And Talented." *Ughhhh!*

As silly as this was, it helped my confidence tremendously at that time. When I initially got that trophy on my 11th birthday,

Photo by Annie Franceschi

it felt deeply satisfying to have some kind of recognition (that I gave myself). It sat on my bedroom shelf for years and I've only recently dug it out. Though I find this story embarrassing in many ways, I share it because it underscores an important point: Sometimes you just really need to give yourself a damn trophy.

To confidently embrace your story means to finally give yourself credit, even if you find that hard to do. I've observed throughout my career that many of us don't give ourselves enough kudos for what we've accomplished, nor do we use our track records to fuel what we're capable of creating in the future.

It's been my experience that women especially struggle with this. There's an oft-cited, famous internal report that was done by Hewlett-Packard in 2014. It's since been referenced in several books, and *Forbes* wrote about the study, sharing that "women working at HP applied for a promotion only when they believed they met 100% of the qualifications listed for the job. Men were happy to apply when they thought they could meet 60% of the job requirements."[8]

One hundred percent versus 60%. When I was a woman in Corporate America, I'd hesitate to apply always if I didn't think I was a complete fit. Like the women at Hewlett-Packard, I was much less likely than my male contemporaries to throw my hat into the ring for jobs I could have done and could have been considered for. In this way, I was opting to bench myself and wasn't even realizing it.

What I've also learned is that, if we wait for others to give us credit, affirmation, positive reviews, and so forth, or if we depend on others to do that, we may wait forever or give up when that praise falls short. Simply, we can't base our actions and our confidence on the shoulders of others. Those people are likely struggling to give themselves credit, too. It's very human.

When I'm working on a client's clear marketing message (a brand voice guide), I make sure to ask them to quantify their work in my questionnaire, literally forcing them to give themselves credit. Many of my branding clients have never stopped to count how many years they've been in their field, or how many clients they've helped, or how many people they've spoken for until we are working together.

Through this exercise, one of my branding clients, leadership coach Dawn Potter Sander, realized that, although her private practice was only a few years old, across her 25-plus-year career in training and coaching, she's guided and taught *thousands* of people at all levels of leadership. So while new to an entrepreneurial setting, Dawn can bring the value and credibility of her deep experience transforming leaders to her corporate and individual clients easily, especially by quantifying that in her messaging and on her website.

But what if Dawn had never paused to count? Similarly, what can *you* give yourself credit for?

EXERCISE

Give Yourself Credit

Pull out your *Establish Yourself Companion Workbook* (or your own notebook) and brainstorm these questions:

- *How many clients have I helped?*
- *How many people have I trained or taught?*
- *How many speaking engagements have I done?*
- *How many people could I have spoken to across those engagements?*
- *Have I spoken out of state, nationally, or internationally? Where?*
- *How many years have I been doing this work or been in my field?*
- *What are my certifications, degrees, and awards that relate to my work?*
- *What parts of my story help me to be a valuable guide and resource to my clients?*

Step back and give yourself five minutes to appreciate all that you have clearly accomplished. When complete, you've taken a valuable step in giving yourself more credit for what you have contributed to the world and done for yourself along the way.

Your answers to these questions would be an excellent start for your brand messaging, a step we talk about soon. For now, let us keep embracing our valuable story by defining it today, and continuing to do so.

The Guide, the Hero, and Reframing Self-Promotion

"Okay, but do I have to be in front of the camera?"

Over the years, I've directed more than a dozen branding photoshoots. In the course of planning, I almost always get asked this question. The business owners I work with don't often want to be "the star of the show." They'd much rather their clients take center stage. Many of my clients don't feel comfortable being the face of their businesses. They are motivated to help others and don't want to make anything about *them*.

But here's the thing: You can't help *them* if *they* don't get a chance to get to know, like, and trust *you*. That trust can't happen without you showing up—without *you* being featured within your business. But there are less-icky ways to do this than you may realize. Allow me to shed some hopefully liberating permission on this idea: You don't have to thrust a spotlight on yourself. It's a different mindset.

Showing up as a confident expert in your work with clients, in your sales calls, in your branding, and in your marketing efforts—that's not about *you*. It's actually about helping your clients. You have to show up as the confident expert *because* your clients need you to be their trusted guide on their journeys.

Many in marketing circles teach a version of Joseph Campbell's "The Hero's Journey" in a business context, taking the framework of classic storytelling and applying it to how you should market yourself.[9] Donald Miller has most popularized this concept by stating consistently in his marketing writing, courses, and interviews that you as the business owner/expert are only your client's "guide." He teaches that "the customer is the hero, not your brand" as the first principle of his StoryBrand framework in his book *Building a StoryBrand.*[10]

While I believe in this core concept, I want to take it further with you in the context of being a consultant, coach, or service business owner. I want you to see this overarching concept as permission to feel more comfortable showing up in your business, claiming your value, and coming off as someone who is confident about what they do.

As we explore together in this step of embracing your story, and throughout the book, your clients need you and expect you to be their confident guide. That's why they invest in you. When you have something that can truly help someone, you're not bothering them, you're helping them. You have value they need right now. This is even more important if you work with organizations. Not only do you have to convince your immediate client/connection, but you may also have to be front and center to gain the trust of multiple stakeholders, like directors, vice presidents, and even the founders or CEOs of the companies you may partner with.

In my deep work with Adele, I told her that I hated sales conversations because I was always worried about making people uncomfortable (about their current branding, their website, themselves, etc.). I personally hate fear-based, manipulative marketing tactics, and I was letting that keep me from acting like the expert on calls. I never want to come off *that* way.

What Adele adeptly pointed out to me has stuck with me for years. Adele countered, "Annie, people are already uncomfortable." She reminded me that when people came to my free consultation, they were already experiencing a problem—something that made them uncomfortable. I wasn't the source of the discomfort. Rather, I was the solution.

I'll say the same to you. When someone expresses interest in what you do, remember that when they're stuck, uncomfortable, or lost, *you aren't the source, you're the solution.*

So how can you show up like you're the solution? Worry less about being the "face" of your business and focus more on ways you can show up with confidence, driving awareness around the solutions you provide and the value you can give when someone is stuck, lost, or uncomfortable.

Famous investor, bestselling author, and business expert Neil Patel shares on his blog, "[R]eal value isn't about how often you self-promote. It's about problem-solving."[11]

So shift the story, become the guide, let them be the hero, and make sure they know you're there to help them on the journey ahead. That's what your job is. It's not to self-promote; it's to show up and add value where it's needed most. Be the guide they need. Confidently be their solution and provide what's most valuable to those who need it most.

BRANDING

Choose to Focus Where You're Most Valuable

When you're ready to own your story and expertise, a new level of success comes through choosing crucial clarity about what you do best and who you provide the most value to. Sometimes, that may mean a journey of letting go of services, clients, assumptions, limiting beliefs, and even shame. Whatever it involves, this will take you closer to realizing your greatest business.

Let Go of Trying to Be Everything

To focus where you can be your greatest and most valuable—to yourself and others—is a journey of change and letting go. It has been for me. Here's a story I used to be afraid to admit publicly: My company started as a much bigger business with four different specialties, and this approach was an important experiment that ultimately failed.

When I founded Greatest Story Creative in fall 2013, I had a big vision: to create a storytelling agency that told your story in every aspect of your life (weddings, events, business/career, and even everyday for custom gifts). I was in love with that idea, so I created it. In the years I ran it this way, the business looked and seemed successful on the outside. It sounded creative and always "got a reaction." But in the sales numbers and the day-to-day of running it, for me, it didn't truly work. It wasn't sustainable, it made barely any profit on my time and resources, and trying to do it all nearly burned me out completely.

To illustrate why this happened and why letting go has been so powerful to growth, let me break down what I was doing by having such a diverse brand and business. These used to be the lines of business that made up Greatest Story Creative:

1. Greatest Story Weddings
2. Greatest Story Events
3. Greatest Story for Business
4. Greatest Story Everyday

GREATEST STORY WEDDINGS

» *Services offered:* Custom wedding invitation and save the date writing and design, hand lettering for invitation envelopes, custom wedding art, table numbers, bridesmaid gifts, and more

» *Ideal clients:* Brides and couples needing help to get creative invitations that told their love story

Inspired by the writing I did for my own wedding in 2012, the heart of Greatest Story when it started was actually weddings, not business. At the time, no one to my knowledge was both designing and *writing* invitations, and I saw a big opportunity to provide what I called "wedding storytelling" but you may understand as "wedding branding." I created all the printed materials that cohesively looked great together and celebrated a couple's love story on their big day. I threw up my website, began talking and blogging about what I did, and I did get clients. Each project was basically custom.

I remember telling my dad once that weddings were my real passion and branding for business owners was "opportunistic" for me. How much can change in a few years!

GREATEST STORY EVENTS

- » *Services offered:* Custom invitations, event-related art, party favors, etc.
- » *Ideal clients:* Party organizers wanting to do something special and tell a story with their event

Similar to my wedding services, I extended my same skill set to events and helped brand several first-birthday parties, a retirement party, and other special occasions. Each project was basically custom.

GREATEST STORY BUSINESS

- » *Services offered:* Logo design, business cards, naming, websites, etc.
- » *Ideal clients:* Any business owner ages 20–60, in any type of business

I initially did business branding for a wide variety of clients: from writing the tagline and brand messaging of a new local restaurant to naming, branding, and creating the website of a baking business. I got clients here too, but every project was basically custom and required a lot of my time to do proposals, provide services, and deliver great results.

GREATEST STORY EVERYDAY

» *Services offered:* Custom gifts (from stationery to custom art), personal stationery and announcements, college and professional school application essay polishes, and resume and cover letter services
» *Ideal clients:* A freaking ton of different people, right? Oy! People who love stationery, high school/college students and their parents, oh, and any career professional needing help with their resume, cover letter, and LinkedIn profile

Definitely the most insane "department" of my business, I'd created a bucket to serve everything *to* everyone. And yes, every single project was custom here too. My clients ranged from strangers to close family friends.

—

Running four different businesses with a dozen "ideal clients" and infinite services was a recipe for emotional and financial burnout. I was in love with the creative notion behind Greatest Story Creative being a storytelling agency that people would work with throughout their lives. I thought I could help them brand their wedding, brand their baby announcement, brand their business, or brand their resume for their next career move! I was adamant that I didn't want to be just a graphic designer, or a copywriter, or anything too "simple."

However, I learned many lessons trying to run one business this way—the greatest being that I wasn't running *one* business,

I was running at least four! As a result, I wasn't running any of them particularly well. If I'd tracked my time back then, maybe I would have realized my epic mistakes here sooner.

But alas, it took me multiple years to see and face it. My coaching with Adele in 2016 was a turning point, as was working on a few weddings that emotionally burned me out because I didn't have a consistent process to deliver my services smoothly. I finally reckoned with this in 2017 when I could finally see a few things clearly:

- I can't sell four businesses as well as I can sell one.
- I can't market to a dozen different types of ideal clients as well as I can market to one.
- I can't deliver 20+ types of unrelated services as well as I can deliver a handful of related ones.
- I can't make as much money running for four businesses "just okay" as I can if I run one business extremely well.
- And if I want to be known for *something,* I have to give up wanting to be known for *everything.*

My last official wedding was in 2016, and I paused services behind the scenes for years until getting up the courage to remove everything but business branding.

The journey was still useful for me, as I'm sure your journey here has been, too. By muddling through running and marketing these businesses all at once, I learned a ton about myself, the types of clients I can help the most, and what I do best. I was incredibly lucky to help some amazingly wonderful people celebrate their weddings, retirements, birthdays, and even get their dream jobs or be offered acceptance to their dream schools. I also branded a lot of businesses and worked with a lot of business owners who aren't my ideal fits for my services now, but I still learned so much from that work and value being a part of those people's stories.

This said, I was emotionally very embarrassed to let these aspects of my business go officially in 2017. I was worried I may be losing the creativity that made me "stand out," but as I explain later, reactions don't equal revenue. I chose to quietly close the three other divisions of Greatest Story Creative in 2017, after spending about two years referring away any interest in those other services. I then continually narrowed down my ideal client for branding services from ages 20–60, any type of business—slowly—to coaches, consultants, and service business owners, typically ages 40–60 and usually women.

Once I did this and focused on implementing the best practices I share in this book (like creating systems to deliver my work smoothly), a miraculous thing happened: From 2016 (the last full year of offering all four services) to 2021, my revenue grew by more than 130%, I've consistently reached six figures multiple years running, *and* I've finally became known as a recognized expert at something (branding for service businesses).

So while I lost a very unique style of business that I loved and have felt shame over that failure, I'm also immensely grateful for what I gained in the tradeoff: the best possible version of my business today.

I share this to show you that I understand the temptations of wanting to serve a lot of different types of clients, having the ability to do that, and thinking you have to do everything you're capable of doing. As I break down in this section, giving in to those temptations created major learning moments that I hope to pass on to you and spare you from when possible.

Let's help you figure out what to let go and what to embrace, as you choose to focus on where you're most valuable and embrace your story.

Choose to Be Known for What You're Greatest At

I shared my "letting go" story because I know what you need to do next and it's hard. It requires crucial clarity. I want you to choose to define three deceptively hard-to-decide things:

1. What you want to be known for,
2. Who you can help the most (your primary ideal clients), and
3. The absolute best way you can help them (your most valuable solution to their biggest problem).

If you can focus and choose to clearly define these things, and then deploy them consistently, you will be light-years ahead of most entrepreneurs who still think the secret is some creative marketing tactic they learned from a Facebook ad. *Promise.*

To do this, you have to be willing to not only be clear, but focused and willing to decide and commit to things in ways that hinge on your survival. If you are constantly changing what you want to be known for, or you are trying to do it *all,* at best, you will stay stuck and at worst, your business will not survive.

I often teach, *"If you aim to be known for everything, you won't be known for anything."* But this is what so many of us do try to do—sometimes without even realizing it. It makes some psychological sense why so many people start businesses whose services are like a list of ingredients offered for you to make a recipe, rather than a gourmet meal.

Many of us come into the work we do without having run businesses before and we think, *Let's offer* all *the things we can do.* Here's the line of thought:

> *If I offer and showcase all the things I can do,*
> *I will appeal to as many people as possible,*
> *Which means I can book as many clients as possible,*
> *Which means I can make as much money as possible,*
> *And be successful as fast as possible.*

I often think of this as a "hedging my bets" strategy, and it's how many of us get started and get our first clients. We aren't super sure about any "one" thing we do, so instead we offer *everything* we can possibly do. Then we try to build a brand around it like a roll of duct tape, trying to make it all "make sense." We aren't super confident that we can help one particular person with a particular problem, so we say we can help just about *anyone.* We don't want to limit ourselves *(What if there's not enough business or interest if I'm too specific?*) so we cling to broader offerings and encourage people to consider us for every opportunity.

This makes a lot of sense—in your own head. It might have gotten you by and gotten you clients to this point. But is it working consistently? And do you really love trying to do *everything* for *everybody?*

Take a pause from how you've been doing it and consider another perspective. What's it like when *you* network with another business owner and they don't appear to have clearly focus on an ideal client, main service, or both? How do you perceive them? When you're asked to a virtual or in-person coffee date to network with a possible new referral partner, how do you react when that new person tells you about all of the very different services they offer and clients they serve? What do you actually remember about that type of person a month, or six months, or a year from that conversation?

When someone tells *you* that they are essentially "all things to all people" (for example, *I'm a leadership coach who helps college students, executive leaders, new managers, and nurses*), what do you mentally log about them on your end? My guess is not much. We each already know a ton of jacks-of-all-trades. Who sticks out in our minds are the clearly focused professionals we meet who can confidently tell us: This is what I do, this is who I help, and this is the problem I'm known to solve with my valuable solution of X, Y, or Z.

Imagine one of your clients was nervous about an upcoming company-wide presentation and asked you for a referral. Do you know anyone who can help? Would you know to recommend that leadership coach I described? *Maybe.* More likely, you'll waver and hesitate. You may think of the nine other leadership coaches you know but are nervous because nobody really stood out. So you might be wary to recommend anyone all, not sure if it'd be a waste of your client's valuable time.

Now, consider a different scenario. What if that initial leadership coach you'd networked with had been more laser focused on what they're best at? What if they had told you that they were an executive leadership coach who helps busy female CEOs and their teams present with more confidence? Through their signature "Speak Up for Success" program, they have short, self-paced trainings that could help a busy female CEO and their direct reports rock their next presentations without taking too much time away from their work. *You'd know to immediately and enthusiastically recommend them, right?* You wouldn't even give a thought to the bunch of other leadership coaches you know, because you saw a problem and easily remembered who exactly had a great-fit solution! A confident action step all around.

This is why it matters so much to your bottom line and future to define these things. As we explore more in "Be Clear (Not Creative)," this strategic thinking allows you to be the card in someone's deck, ready to be played as they encounter people who really need the value you offer. When you hedge your bets, you dilute your value and make yourself *less* memorable.

It's a hard instinct to fight against because you don't want to lose business and any interested client. But there's a reason why niching is so popular and phrases like *the riches are in the niches* exist. It first seems counterintuitive, but it isn't if you come at it strategically. In your initial line of thinking, you think that the more you offer, the more opportunity you will have to work with other people and organizations. But that's not really true when you realize how it works. You think, *Well, look at all these big companies I admire that have multiple divisions, offering all these services. Surely* **I** *can and should do the same thing, right? I mean . . . McDonald's doesn't niche! They serve everyone!*

While it's tempting to think that way, comparing yourself and your type of business to these big players isn't quite apples to apples. For one, you likely don't have the same level and depth resources these kinds of far bigger companies do. You probably don't have thousands (if not millions) of dollars to spend marketing each individual service well, nor do you have the time that you could leverage if you had a team working 40 hours or more a week to make that marketing effective. Instead, as a coach, consultant, or service business owner, give yourself the best shot possible with the resources you have. Your wasted time can be expensive to your emotional and financial well-being. When you stop to look at it, the reality is you'll never be able to brand, market, and serve eight different services as well and memorably as you could *one* truly great one, especially if marketing doesn't come naturally to you.

Secondly, don't forget that even the big companies target their services in operations, design, branding, sales, and marketing to *specific* types of clients. They have departments working on specific products, services, campaigns—people whose jobs it is to market something *specific* to someone *specific*. They often use the same strategies; they just have a ton more resources to be able to do it on an exponentially larger scale than the average solopreneur.

Some of the hardest work you'll ever do as an entrepreneur will be to stick to your guns and keep things simple. This means employing *continued* commitment to what you are able to do *best,* not just "able to do." It's about being excellent at what you're greatest at, then branding/marketing/selling/delivering it in its most valuable format to the type of client who needs it most. When you have successfully mastered this, then you can invite more complexity into your business (if you even want to by that point!).

If you're ready to stop hedging your bets, it's time to pick something very important.

Permission to Pick a Primary Ideal Client

Thus far, we've talked about embracing who you are and zeroing in on what you do as an expert, but there's an even bigger element we need to think about: your clients. These are the heroes of your business, *right?*

Let's make some decisions about who our heroes should be: those we can guide the *best.* Specifically, the best clients that are the ones you can help the *most.* These might be individuals or stakeholders at companies you partner with. They are what I'd refer to as your "primary ideal clients," or PIC.

I say *PIC* because really, to get to the next level, you will have to *pick.* If you've heard me that "hedging your bets" and trying to appeal to all people with all services keeps you stagnant, then hopefully you're willing to entertain the notion of being more specific with your ideal client.

There are lot of myths out there about focusing on a primary ideal client. Let's break down a couple of them.

Myth: Having one ideal client will limit the number of clients I can have and opportunities I get.

I used to worry that having just one type of client would limit or withhold opportunities from me. In what I've observed, it's actually quite the opposite. In fact, picking a primary ideal client can actually ensure that you can help those who need you the *most.* It can also help those people find you faster and more easily, which is exactly what we want them to do. There are individuals or organizations that desperately need the powerful services and transformation you can guide them or their people through, so it's only a good thing if we can connect you to them earlier.

How many times have you heard "I wish I'd known you existed sooner"? *That's* what we're trying to do by laser-focusing your branding, marketing, services, and overarching business: get on your ideal clients' radar faster, *not* limit how many clients you can have. To add to this, have you stopped to think how many clients you need in a year to be profitable/make the money you'd like to make in your business? My hunch is that you'll discover it's a lot fewer than you've been putting pressure on yourself to reach via "thousands of followers," for example. Many of us in service businesses think we need to be striving constantly to build an enormous network with a ton of social media followers. But if you only need 10–30 clients to make six figures or more in a year, why should you worry about reaching tens of thousands? *You don't have to.*

But if you niche, how do you get the attention of your best possible clients or companies? You become a lighthouse just for them—shining the light that specifically attracts them. That means defining who they are, putting them and their needs into your messaging, website, and business card. It means making sure that everyone in your network knows what you do and specifically *for whom!*

When you put that beacon out, you not only attract those clients who you can "hit it out of the park" for, you also gain the ability to be strategic with your time and resources. You can more easily get on podcasts that share an audience with yours. You get people on your email list who are actively interested in what you do and working with you. Simply put, your time, energy, and resources will go farther when you get more specific.

Myth: You need to create a client avatar, and an ideal client has to be super specific.

Generally speaking, we've all heard how powerful it is to niche, but we struggle with it. I hate the term *client avatar* and always found it unhelpful. Anytime I created a client persona or avatar, it ended up being annoyingly just like me. I was never even fully sure "they" *existed!*

I don't create client avatars, and I don't force my clients to do so. Instead, we focus on an overall category of client, such as a group of people that can be found in other groups (like associations, networking groups, or even Facebook groups). If you partner with individuals, this might look like millennial career professionals or owners of wellness practices. If you work with organizations, this could be something like female CEOs and founders of startups or HR directors at companies with 100+ employees. For Greatest Story, though I have a more detailed version, generally my primary ideal client is easily described as a coach, consultant, or service business owner. While not incredibly detailed, it does say clearly that I don't work on restaurants, or brick and mortar shops, or online product-based businesses. It gives you a good sense of the types of groups I'd want to speak to—organizations like International Coach Federation, where many of my clients are certified. It also helps me more easily create content that's valuable for this specific audience.

Your primary ideal clients could be as general as these or more specific, to your liking, to the extent it helps you provide a ton of value to that client and get more of them. If I were to get more specific, I'd likely say it's women business consultants who've been in business for five years and have been doing their branding piecemeal to this point. If I wanted to niche down to just business consultants or women business consultants, I'd probably do even better. But I like the business I have now, so I'm okay with my level of specificity. It serves me well. I want you to find what serves you well, not just who you "think" you need or "have to" offer your services to. While this is a good example of an individual client, the same specificity can be applied to help you with a primary ideal client at a company. This might be an executive or manager of a certain age range, gender identity, and department within a company (HR, talent acquisition, IT technology, etc.).

If you're not sure who your primary ideal client should be and hate the often-taught tactic of creating imaginary client avatars or personas, you can do the exercise I do often myself and teach my own consulting clients: go by your own data and then keep assessing it as you grow. I really don't like "inventing" who my ideal client is; I'd rather double-down on those who've been a pleasure to work with. In 2016, I worked with the data I already had to find my favorites among my past and current clients. Since then, I have used this insight to keep simplifying to my primary ideal client. That's something you can do right now.

EXERCISE

Uncover Your Ideal Client

This is a very simple process. In the *Establish Yourself Companion Workbook* or your own notebook, make a list of your past favorite clients in recent years.

Consider what they have in common—age-wise, industry-wise, problem-wise. Not sure? *Interview them!* Interviewing your clients can power your entire business, as I share with you in more detail and direction when we get to Fans & Feedback™ Process in "Reviews and Building Lifelong Client Relationships" (in Step Three: Translate Your Value).

For now, let me say that one of the things that really helped me unlock this was asking a very simple question: "Have you *already* helped a primary ideal client?"

For this exercise, jot down all of your most favorite clients to date. Then brainstorm the answers to each of these questions, with them in mind.

- *Do they share a type of occupation?*
- *Why did you love working with them?*
- *Did they say yes right on the spot?*
- *Did they really appreciate your solution?*
- *Did they really need you?*
- *How did they hear about you?*
- *Where do they hang out (online and offline)?*
- *Are they members of any associations, groups, etc.?*

As you will begin to see, there are many things that all primary ideal clients have in common. If you feel ready, take the brainstorm above and consider if you can summarize down to a short phrase or description who your ideal clients are (aka who your favorite clients—the ones you want to clone!— have been!).

If you're still on the fence, let's dive deeper into this notion of a primary ideal client.

3 Truths About Choosing Your Primary Ideal Client

1. They are ready and can invest in your profitable offer.

Whether you've already worked with this type of person/organization or not, a primary ideal client needs to be someone who can *afford* to work with you. They should have the ability to invest in your services.

If a client can't afford to work with you and pay the price your expertise and solution are worth, choosing to work with them anyway will ultimately burn you out—emotionally and financially. Marketing to them and trying to work with them will likely exhaust your marketing dollars and energy, both of which could someday close your business altogether.

To stay in business and really to reach the next level, you will find more joy and profit in your work if you are able to stop catering your limited marketing resources to those who don't have the budget for you. And as I explain in "Pricing and Profit," you can help them at lower rungs of your value ladder and a few other sustainable strategies.

2. You offer them the perfect, most valuable solution to their biggest, most crucial problem.

You can provide the most essential solution to the greatest problem your ideal clients are facing. When you have something highly valuable and you're the expert ready to deliver it, they'll be thrilled to invest in you.

3. You mesh well with them from a personality and a communication perspective.

Too often overlooked, it's important that you can communicate well and easily with your ideal clients. If you have attracted people who can afford you and who need your biggest solution, but who are not a joy to work with, you will ultimately burn you out.

I share more in "Navigating Boundaries, Bad-Fit Clients, and Brain Pickers" in Step Two: Shape Your Business about why bad clients aren't bad *people*. For now, let me say someone is not an ideal client for you if you have difficulty communicating well with them, they are not responsive, or they are otherwise challenging to work with successfully. I've called it out here because we all need to place a larger value on this. Bad-fit clients are expensive not just to your emotional well-being, but to your bottom-line numbers.

—

So if you can make sure you primary ideal client—the one you choose to market to—checks all three of these boxes, these major things can happen:

- You'll be able to build a fully passionate and profitable business,
- You'll finally become well known for something,
- And you'll keep permission to work with anyone you want, any time you want—no matter what!

Focus and ease come with not trying to market and serve everyone. You'll stay passionate about what you're doing because you work mostly with great-fit clients who don't risk burning you out. The secret to becoming well known is not trying to do everything, but in providing a high-value solution to a specific problem that your ideal clients have.

Finally, permission is something I'd wished I'd realized about niching so much sooner. You don't let go of flexibility by narrowing things down, you actually gain a lot of freedom. Even if you niche your marketing, branding, and services for one specific client, you can still absolutely choose to work with clients who don't fit that mold. You keep that permission. It becomes that much more intentional and sustainable.

For example, I work with coaches and consultants primarily. However, in 2020, I branded a physical therapy clinic because it came across my desk and I decided that I wanted to work on it. I loved the story behind the practice, and I felt that I could be the right partner for the project, while still using my same processes and systems to deliver great results for my clients. I wouldn't have taken it on if I had to reinvent what I do, because that could have put both my client experience and sanity at risk. These physical therapy clients didn't find me via my marketing; they knew me through a personal connection. And while I'm grateful for the experience, I'm also glad I don't spend a lot of time marketing to physical therapy clinics!

Keep in mind that you're always going to hear from prospective clients who have never seen your website and get referred. These may be people who never ever see your marketing. And that's just fine. What I'm advocating for with having a primary ideal client defined is that you relax and stop trying to reach everyone. Instead, use your powerful focus where it's most impactful, and trust you'll still get plenty of opportunities along the way that you keep the permission to say *yes* to.

If you're willing to say *yes* to embracing a narrowed-down primary ideal client, the next step is identifying the highest value problem you can solve for them.

Your Most Valuable Solution for Their Crucial Problem

When I worked at the movie studio Lionsgate, I'd often grab lunch from a well-loved Los Angeles establishment, Mrs. Winston's. It has perhaps the most impressive salad bar you've ever seen in your life. The bar itself stretches around the back of the shop with hundreds of options to top your greens. It's so legendary that they have a long-running promotion that if you can correctly guess the exact weight of your salad, it's free!

However, despite having a bazillion gourmet, delicious toppings, every time I'd make a salad at Mrs. Winston's, it'd turn out just okay. Why was that? Well, because I was the chef, for one! Second, I'd walk around the giant bar choosing ingredients that I liked on their own, without much consideration for how they'd go *together*. I'd inevitably check out with something like mixed greens, topped with bacon bits, mandarin oranges, and Caesar dressing. You know what doesn't belong in a Caesar salad? *Mandarin oranges!*

Every salad I'd make ended up pretty mediocre. But you know what I always enjoy for lunch? A gourmet salad at a restaurant—something the chef has created to be the *perfect* option for when I'm craving a refreshing salad. And it's never Caesar with mandarin oranges, surprisingly!

This illustrates why it's so valuable to focus and package what you do as a solution, rather than a menu of various services. You can be the salad bar of endless, overwhelming options *or* you can take your highest-quality ingredients and offer a gourmet salad for someone who craves the delicious flavors you've put together. Simply put, a chef is a professional, and I—the amateur salad maker—am not. The professional and his offer are worth paying for if I really want and need the *best* salad.

People pay experts more to solve their biggest problems, especially when they know it's something they can't solve on their own. Think of any time you've hired a professional in your life, even for a personal need like home decorating or caring for a loved one. In those instances, when it was really important to you and you weren't the expert, you wanted to *pay more for a solution, not just a service.*

That's what I encourage you to do: package your highest-ticket service into a valuable solution to your primary ideal client's most *crucial* problem. Not only because it's compelling, but also, because so many businesses like yours are out there being salad bars, yet your ideal client has no idea what salad they want!

As I've shared, part of what led me to my work with Adele was being ghosted by client proposals. I know now that much of the reason was that my proposals were essentially giant salad bars, and my prospective clients got overwhelmed when I asked them, "So, what do you want in your salad?" Since that time in 2016, I've continued to refine and simplify what I offer. I went from customizing every proposal to offering 12 packages and not customizing what was in them *(for example, every brand story guide comes with business cards)*. Then I narrowed it down to six. I kept seeing better results, but eventually growth maxed out when I didn't have the time on my schedule to take on more clients.

When I hit another plateau in 2020 and couldn't see how to financially grow more on my own, I sought fresh perspective from scaling and systems strategist Kate Rosenow of Work Well With Kate. My conversation with Kate helped me to see with clearer eyes that all the different iterations I was offering for my branding services could actually be simplified and presented as one, clean solution.

I realized that I could present my copywriting work (creation of your brand voice guide), my design work (creation of a consistent visual branding toolkit including your logo, known as the brand story guide), and a website that I write and design to bring those things together. I've simplified it today as a three-step, "Brand Story Solution." Here's an example of how it works:

As a general category, my primary ideal clients are:
Coaches, consultants, and service business owners

In a brief description, they:

- Have been in business for 5+ years, and have gotten clients and some degree of profit.
- Have been using pieced-together branding, but it's outdated and doesn't quite hang together visually or verbally.
- Feel uncomfortable marketing themselves because they struggle to communicate what they do clearly and consistently.
- Have grown as much as they can on their own.
- Know they are stuck and lacking confidence about their marketing abilities and ability to grow their business as a result.

Before we work together, they consider their most crucial problem to be: Struggling to grow because their marketing is unclear and inconsistent.

My most valuable solution for them is: Creating their clear, consistent marketing tools and materials *(aka their branding and website).*

I clearly explain this solution as:
A three-step Brand Story Solution in which I:

1. Write their clear marketing message,
2. Create their consistent visual brand, and
3. Use these elements to build their compelling website.

Now, there are a lot of things I do for clients, of course, even within these bullet points. That marketing message always includes your "about me" story and your tagline. The brand story guide covers your business cards, stationery, and even social media platform profile photos. And let it be known that not every client who works with me invests in the entire solution. Sometimes they need just the message, or just the message and visuals, because they have a website, and so forth. Sometimes they need help naming their business, and they elect to add that on. Other times, they need my Establish Yourself branding/business coaching/consulting on refining their brand on their own, setting up processes, or building in boundaries.

What I hope you can see here is that I'm not limiting myself by flying the main flag of the Brand Story Solution. I'm simply letting my network know about the *most* valuable thing I do. Because I really want people coming to me who one, know they have a very crucial problem, and two, are aware that I have a very valuable solution to it, ready to go.

Here's another example of how this can look, this time if you work more with companies and their employees.

You may remember Dawn Potter Sander, who I've shared with you is a talented leadership coach. Dawn's company is DPS Leadership, a consulting firm specializing in customized, strengths-based coaching, and team development for onboarding, transitioning, and energizing new leaders and their teams through seasons of change. She partners often with executives and HR managers at small to mid-size companies to impact their leadership and teams.

Before Dawn works with leaders and their teams, executives and HR managers consider their most crucial problem to be: Cost (lost productivity/money/time) of a failed integration between a newly promoted/newly hired leader and their team.

Dawn's most valuable solution for organization's with this problem is: Proactive, customized strengths-based coaching and team development to smoothly onboard, integrate, and energize a newly placed leader and their team to work well together.

Dawn clearly explains this solution as: The Energized Team Solution, *where she guides leaders and their teams through assessments and coaching that empowers:*

1. Game-Changing Insight (Discovering Team Strengths).
2. Action Planning (Navigating Team Dynamics).
3. Driving Forward Together (Maximizing Team Performance).

Dawn's solution uses her certification in CliftonStrengths and her rich expertise to bring teams together and help them navigate new—new seasons, new challenges, new hires, and integrations. While the specifics of the solution may change, it can be easily shared and narrowed down to these three steps to impact individuals and organizations overall.

Whether you work with just one or two stakeholders like I do, or partner with small and mid-size companies as Dawn does, everything I'd like to inspire you to build with this book comes down to what I've introduced in this section around branding: focus on what you're greatest at, choose who you can help the most, and put those things together profitably. Identify the most valuable solution you can provide for their most crucial problem.

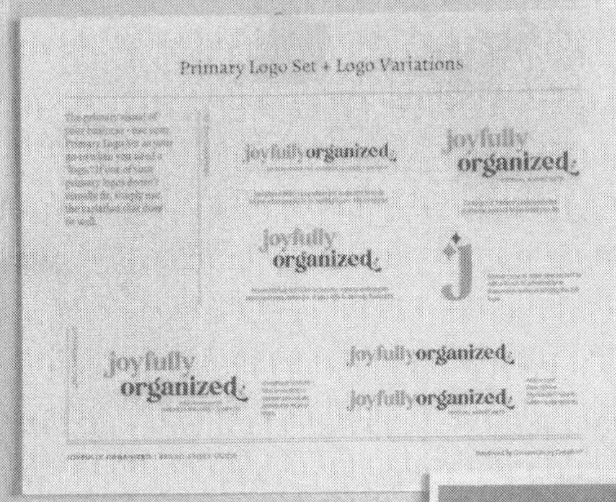

Brand Color Palette

Brand Voice Guide

Business Cards

BRANDING

Equip Yourself with a Branding Toolkit

When you know what you're doing and who it's really for, you're ready for the elevation that professional branding can give you. Let's identify what confident assets you'll need to grow to the next level and explore how having a branding toolkit could be a needle-mover in this next chapter of your business.

Branding and Marketing: A Love Story

"You don't have to be the greatest expert ever. You just have to be a couple of steps ahead of your ideal client."

A hand shot up. I was speaking to a group of women entrepreneurs, and I'd just said something that hit a nerve. I called on a woman named Caroline and she shared her frustration with me:

"I'm an expert with 39 years of experience in my field!! And there are these ridiculous consultants who have six months or a year of experience—and they're taking off! And I'm not. And that's not okay!"

I understood her point. Caroline's consulting business wasn't growing and that didn't feel fair. After all, she had decades of experience over her competitors, right? *How dare they call themselves experts!*

I get it. That can be a very frustrating thing, especially when your business isn't doing well. However, as I gently explained to Caroline that day, her "green" competitors were likely not her biggest obstacle to growing her consultancy. It was much more likely both a marketing and branding problem—and one that so many face.

Look at it from another angle: If you had the option to hire an incredible consultant to solve your problem and were choosing between someone with six months of experience and someone with 39 years, who would you choose? That's a no-brainer.

Let's play out that scenario again—this time in the context of working with a professional in the real world. If you needed to hire a consultant to solve a problem in your life or business, you'd first need to find them. You need to discover them actively marketing themselves in some way, then you need to read and connect to a message and visuals that clearly convey their level of experience. Then you need to have an easy way to contact them to discuss working together. *Want to bet who's got that all intentionally set up?* That's right: Caroline's way-less-experienced competitors have those systems in place because they understand branding, marketing, and how they work together.

My hunch was that Caroline was struggling because she wasn't doing both of those things (or doing them well). I don't believe she was losing business because some hotshots were claiming they're experts *(though certainly this is a "thing!")*. There are tons of thriving consultants with all levels of experience. Experience, while valuable, is not the *only* factor for gaining clients and credibility.

Rather, I believe that Caroline was losing opportunities because she wasn't one, marketing herself actively, and especially two, telling a clear brand story of how deeply experienced and valuable she is as a consultant. If she were doing those things, and then others compared her to those competitors, she'd clearly be a fantastic choice that her ideal clients would consistently opt to work with. Caroline wasn't leveraging the power of both branding and marketing, nor getting them to work together to grow her consultancy. If she had, she probably wouldn't have the time or energy to worry about the upstarts in the universe that are succeeding—because she'd be succeeding, too. Let's make sure you don't fall prey to the same trap.

Branding and marketing are two incredibly important aspects of your business that need your attention and investment. Though they aren't the same thing, they are interdependent. For a reminder, simply defined: Your **brand** is how people think and feel about your business. Your **brand identity** (your logo, your tagline, your website, etc.) refers to the foundational pieces you strategically use to confidently present your business to ideal clients. Branding is what makes your marketing relatable and helps your dream clients and partners connect to, engage with, and refer what you do. It's like having the most beautiful, most "you" perfect pair of shoes that make you feel like you're putting your best foot forward anywhere you go in them.

But the thing is, those shoes won't make an impression on anyone if you don't take them out on the town! The actual active presenting to others—getting eyes on these materials and ears to hear your brand message—*that's* **marketing.** Whether you speak to drive awareness about your business, start a networking group, have a great email newsletter, or host a podcast—all of these things are actions you're taking to get your business in front of your potential ideal clients for their consideration. To bring this to life, here's the real relationship:

If marketing is *action*, branding is *connection*.

It takes action to get your practice seen and considered by your dream clients (whether they visit your website, see a post of yours on social media, attend a virtual workshop, etc.). But the actions you take to market yourself won't matter unless those who see what you're presenting want to *connect* with it.

To become your client, they have to first feel interested in booking a discovery call, buying your training, or signing up for your newsletter because they like what they see and read from you. They won't connect unless they fall in love with your message, how your website makes them feel, or how valuable your emails are to them. It has to speak to them—and it can only do that if you've intentionally presented your brand visuals and message in a way that's been created just for *them.*

So, here's what you've got to keep in mind: Doing tons of marketing that doesn't use strategic brand visuals and messaging means that you're engaging in action *without* creating connection. Taking action without connection is a complete waste of your time. What good is it to post constantly about your business if no one understands what you do or connects to it to learn more? Similarly, strategic branding like a logo, colors, or a tagline can't do anything for you if you never get them in front of people. Connection *without* action just isn't possible.

Whether you're six months or 39 years into the incredible work you do, the lesson is the same: If you have no brand strategy to speak of, stop marketing yourself and fix that before you waste more time and energy. If you're hiding behind your computer, continuing to tweak a website that you haven't told anyone about, stop doing that and start getting eyeballs on it through marketing action.

So why cover branding now, but marketing later in the Establish Yourself Framework? Well, branding is truly foundational. It impacts all elements of your business's success—not just how you market it. We dive into marketing (the action you will take to get it front of new prospective clients) in the Step Three: Translate Your Value later in this book.

For now, I'm teaching you a first step of embracing your story and that has to mean creating foundational branding tools to help you tell the story across the board. Because the reality is that you won't just tell the story in your marketing. It can and will impact everything from here forward—from what you choose to name your most valuable solution to the professional letterhead you use while working with clients.

Clear, consistent branding in the words you use, the tone you strike, the colors and fonts, and everything in between will either elevate or distract from the greatest business you're working to realize. So let's close this section by giving you insight into what you need to develop to have that branding toolkit ready to help you grow—from operations to marketing.

Is it Time to Rebrand, Rename, or Both?

When you're considering creating or updating your branding toolkit, a big question has to be answered first: Should you rebrand, rename, or both? When's the right time to do these things?

The answer is simply when you've outgrown them. For example, sometimes you may have outgrown your branding because you never quite had a professional "brand identity" in the first place. Maybe you have a DIY logo, or just three brand colors, and nothing really quite hangs together visually because it wasn't professionally done. You could have outgrown your branding because your business has grown, your ideal clients have changed a lot, and you now do something far more valuable for them than your current branding communicates. It's also possible that it's time to rebrand, rename, or both because you're ready to grow, communicate more value, and have a confident branding toolkit that visually and verbally tells the most valuable story it can about what you do.

If you're considering renaming, that decision would be best before you create a branding toolkit. Every coach, consultant, and service business owner (myself included) has wrestled with this question at one point in time or another: Should my practice be my name or should it be something else? And if so, *what?*

As you are working to establish yourself and write the next chapter of your business, this could be a time to make a shift, perhaps to rename your practice under your own name or create a name beyond your personal one—especially if you've outgrown or are ready to grow beyond your current name. Maybe you even want to switch from one creative name to another, to better reflect how your services or clients have changed over time.

As a professional who helps clients rename their businesses, if you're split between using your personal name versus a business name, here are some key considerations.

What Are Your Plans for the Future of Your Practice?

As you think ahead a few years or even to the next decade, do you envision bringing on employees and having those people do what you do? Or will the business mostly stay you, perhaps with a virtual or full-time assistant? Might you want to sell the business at some point, perhaps part of your retirement?

If you're thinking you'd want the business to grow beyond just you and have the best shot at selling it, it would be wise to consider naming (or renaming) your practice a business name. If you're Jenna Carlson Consulting, what happens when you, Jenna, want to have an associate drive a project? Will your client *only* want to work with you, since your name is front and center? And with equity tied into your personal name, how likely would it be that someone would want to buy it?

Of course, there are some strategies here to keep your personal name, but still build in flexibility. Jenna Carlson Consulting might become something like Carlson Company to become broader and more flexible for the future.

Do You Have A Lot of Equity Built into Your Personal Name?

When clients have a business name but are debating whether it's effective, I often ask, "Well, how many people say they want to work with *Tracy* versus Change Makers Coaching?" Most answer, "Tracy. Every time."

If you've been around for years and you're a solopreneur, even if you have a business name, most people will know you by your name—not by the name of your business. That's not necessarily a bad thing. In these cases, though, I sometimes recommend rebranding as your name to capture *your* equity. If your business name isn't adding value, it may be obscuring you and your value. Get it out of the way if no one remembers it.

Is Your Name Hard to Spell and/or Pronounce? Or Super Common, Like Sarah Smith?

If your first and/or last name is hard for a majority of people in your audience to pronounce, spell, or both, consider keeping a business name or creating a business name that uses a portion of your name. One example comes from my signature workshop that lives under my business brand. My last name is hard to spell and pronounce for a general audience *(fran-chess-key, if you're curious!)* so my workshop is called "Branding with Annie." You can adopt a similar strategy to keep equity of your personal name and sidestep possible confusion.

You can also do this if you want to lean into your equity but your first and last names are very common in your area or the general population.

Do You Have a Unique Approach to Business?

Back in 2012 when I was toying with the idea of starting the business that would become Greatest Story Creative, I was debating whether to use my personal name as *the* name.

What swayed me to create a business name (Greatest Story Creative) was having a deep desire to highlight how my approach to branding was unique. I wanted the name to help me market the business and drive awareness of what made me valuable (my emphasis on story). It had the added benefit of playing into a well-known reference to the Bible as "the greatest story ever told" so it'd be easy to spell, pronounce, and remember.

I was also able to trademark it, which is another consideration if you're debating between your personal name and a business name. The former most likely can't be trademarked (with some exceptions) while the latter possibly can. A trademarked asset is valuable to you when you run your business and later, if you opt to sell it.

I have no current plans to sell my business, nor do I envision bringing on client-facing team members. Yet, having a business name that helps me tell a bit more of the story and the value upfront functions as marketing and drives memorability across my network.

Lastly, Can Your Current Business Name or Intended New Name Pass the "Easy Test"?

Many years ago, I developed a simple assessment to gauge the viability of any possible name for your business (assuming it's available). Whether you're reconsidering your current name or toying with a new idea, make sure it can pass the "easy test."

Your business name should be:

- Easy to *spell,*
- Easy to *pronounce,* and
- Easy to *remember.*

You want it to be easy to spell so people can easily type your business name into Google and find you! It needs to be easily pronounced by most people so prospective clients and referral partners will feel confident talking about you (and don't avoid doing so for fear of mispronunciation). Lastly, you should aim for it to be easy to remember—something that relates back to you and the work you do so the connection is inherently memorable (and therefore easier to refer).

How are you feeling about your current practice name? Does it reflect your goals and work for the new chapter ahead? Keep this in mind as we journey forward into the seven pivotal types of branding assets that'll give you confidence to grow and present your business from here on.

The 7 Types of Branding for Your Toolkit

If the right time to rebrand is when you've outgrown yours, the right time to invest in professional branding is as soon as you can. It might feel like a significant business expense right now. Yet, as you think about what can take you to the next level, I encourage you to reconsider branding less as an expense and more as a momentum-building *investment* in your confidence and growth.

As consumers ourselves, we already intrinsically know the value of branding and make our big purchasing decisions because of it. Nearly every time we go to invest in solving a big problem in our lives or businesses, we are more powerfully drawn to those professionals who are well-branded. They tell a clear story. They immediately look like the experts they are. They are consistent everywhere you see them marketing, and their websites pull us in, conveying that they really understand our problems and have the right solution for us. We feel good about working with them. By the same token, when we go to invest with a partner who doesn't have these confident assets in place, we pause and worry. *Am I making the right decision?*

This is why the best time to get that massive edge for yourself and your business is *as soon as you can.* For many, branding is a bottleneck—to confidently selling yourself, raising your rates, getting better clients, and letting go of poorer fits. But when you do get a professional branding guide with the story and tools to tell it, you gain the ability to clearly and consistently communicate your value to clients.

What might that be worth? With what you could charge for your well-branded version of your high-ticket solution, how many clients would you need to get for that branding investment to quickly and easily pay for itself? How many clients would you be excited to share your website with and get on board *if* you felt clearer about how you were presenting your business? What incredible things would you feel more empowered to do to grow your business *if* you felt more confident in how it looks and sounds? *That's* what a truly professional branding toolkit can do for you and how it pays off: It gives you the momentum to get going and growing again.

But if you've never done branding with an agency or consultant before, how do you know what you'll need in terms of tools? And what might you be able to keep from your existing brand materials, if you have any? Let's explore this together.

I'm going to break down seven pivotal types of branding to consider investing in and their value to your business going forward. As a branding consultant, I know the power that comes with having as confident and complete a branding toolkit as possible; for that reason, I provide nearly everything I've listed via my Brand Story Solution (all but the actual brand photography and videography services, which I refer out to incredible professionals in those fields).

Walk through the following and consider what you may need to go to the next level. At the end of this section is a special gut-check exercise to help you identify those elements you're most in need of to reach your ideal clients.

The seven pivotal types of branding for service business owners are:

1. Strategy,
2. Messaging,
3. Visuals,
4. Marketing Materials,
5. Website,
6. Photography, and
7. Videography.

STRATEGY

Your logo *isn't* your brand. So much of a great business begins with the often-overlooked yet sexiest S: strategy. *What does your brand stand for? Where do you want your business to go? Who is it really for?*

Here are the key elements of defining the strategic vision for how you brand your business. These are what I help clients identify before we design a logo, build a website, or write a tagline. Setting down these elements ensures a strong foundation for embracing your story, shaping your business, and translating your value through branding and beyond. A branding consultant like me can lead you through defining these so every bit of branding that follows is "on strategy" and will consistently tie into your goals and vision. I also teach how you can do this work on your own in my signature brand strategy self-paced training, "Streamline Your Story."

Essential strategy elements:

- Category *(the field you work in)*
- Hook *(what you're most known for)*
- Ideal clients
- Problem *(the crucial problem you solve)*
- Solution *(the most valuable solution to that problem)*
- Your 5–7 key brand and marketing stories *(the overall themes as to why your ideal clients choose you over all other options)*
- Analysis of key competitors *(so you understand their key stories, too)*
- Tone *(how your business should feel to your clients)*

Who could help you with brand strategy: branding consultants, branding coaches, business coaches, marketing and branding agencies

MESSAGING

Your logo isn't your message, either! When you've set down a brand strategy, you want to ensure that you're creating client-facing language to communicate that value. That isn't easy and can take someone who can provide an objective perspective and marketing writing skill set to accomplish.

To do this work for my clients, I write their brand voice guide, a dynamic document defining their 10 most-essential foundational pieces of client-facing writing. These are the pieces that they will use countless times while marketing and running their business. Sometimes, they'll simply cut and paste; other times, they'll use this document as a valuable memory jogger to inspire everything from new social media posts to names of new services or presentations. Having a foundational messaging guide like this can also give you a lot of peace of mind that you're being clear and consistent every time you write or talk about your business, even if you're not a writer.

Here's what I include in every brand voice guide to ensure it's as useful a tool as possible.

Essential messaging pieces:

- Primary tagline *(the main, short memorable phrase you use to communicate what you do)*
- Secondary taglines *(other key phrases for marketing; perfect for program names, tops of ads, headers for slides, and more)*
- Brand word bank *(a guiding list of keywords to use consistently when you talk about your business)*
- Business positioning statement *(what you do, written to your ideal client)*
- 2-sentence and 1-sentence statements *(for when you need to quickly describe what you do)*
- A "topper" *(my invented phrase for quick, inviting language to use at the "top" of your website or marketing materials, like a brochure)*
- About story *(the "why" behind what you do)*
- Biography *(perfect for when you're a featured speaker or guest on a podcast/show)*
- 30-second elevator pitch *(ready to go for referral meetings)*

Who could help you with brand messaging: branding consultants, copywriters, branding coaches, marketing and branding agencies

VISUALS

Yes, you need a logo! But not just *any* logo. You need a full toolkit of consistent visual assets. This means having a primary logo set that includes your tagline. This means logo variations—that is, having alternate versions of your wide logo ready so it can fit in a tall space, or a square space, or a circular space. This also means know what exact fonts and colors to use so people can begin to recognize your brand as you use them regularly.

If you've been getting by for a long time with just one logo file, you probably have felt the pain of trying to make that little guy work for everything you do. Or how tough it is when you're not even sure what your brand colors are. Fix that by having brand visuals professionally developed.

Here's what I include for every client who gets a consistent visual brand toolkit from me. This comes as part of a more robust version of a traditional brand style guide. It's something I call a "brand story guide" because it also includes your messaging (brand voice guide).

Essential visuals:

- Primary logo set *(your main logo, a version with your primary tagline, and a small version)*
- Logo variations *(alternate versions of your main logo that fit other-sized spaces and can be one color for printing needs)*

- Brand color palette *(5–10 colors including primary, accent, and neutrals, listing their HEX and other codes so you can use them consistently)*
- Brand fonts *(2–3 fonts that look good together, and directions on how to size them and organize them for printed materials)*
- Secondary graphics *(from signature icons to patterns, graphics to add brand personality to documents, slides, and more without having to repeat the main image in your logo)*

Who could help you with brand visuals: branding consultants, graphic designers who understand logo design, marketing and branding agencies

MARKETING MATERIALS

So many business owners skip this step, but it's such a simple and effective opportunity to elevate your client experience. Branding the initial pieces that you're going to use often with clients, with referral partners, and in marketing settings will provide a complete, inviting picture of what you do and the type of established expert you are.

For these reasons, here are the pieces I always include (along with messaging and visuals) in my clients' brand story guides.

Essential marketing materials:

- Business cards *(they communicate your commitment to your business and make an impression—even if they are sometimes thrown away later)*

- Stationery notecard and return address *(so you look like a caring pro every time you mail a real thank-you note or client welcome gift)*
- Digital letterhead *(so you can easily brand all of your client-facing documents, providing a memorable and professional client experience)*
- Email signature *(along with a branded email, with every note you send, you can remind people of your value and include a link to a next step like a free consultation)*
- Social media profile graphics and writing *(from your cover photo to your main description, ensure that when possible clients and current clients look you up on social, you are telling a clear, consistent story across platforms)*

Who could help you with core marketing materials: branding consultants, graphic designers, marketing and branding agencies

WEBSITE

Most people know they need a website but never realize that what they need first is a clear, consistent brand. Trying to build a website without that brand story is like trying to build a house on sand. The foundation that makes it all work isn't there—and is near impossible to put together while you try to build a website at the same time.

Of course, websites are incredibly important to growing your business. However, they are one tool for doing that. Websites are one vehicle to communicate your clear, consistent brand story. They are a marketing and business tool that should make it easy for clients to work with you, get on a free sales call, and get to know your business before they decide to invest. If you're a coach, consultant, or service business owner, a website really exists more to connect you to ideal clients than to directly sell or function on its own.

I often tell my website clients that the biggest job of their site is not to sell their services, but to sell a free consultation—to get someone to know, like, and trust you and what you do enough to talk to you. Your website doesn't have to be 30 pages long, and it doesn't have to sell a million coffee cups. Instead, if you can get someone to speak with you directly about their problem, and you have the most valuable solution they need, it's a match.

If you're nearly all service-based, 10 pages is more than enough for your website to be a fantastic tool for you. I recommend making sure that your site is hosted on a platform that you know how to update (or you have a virtual assistant [VA] who can do it). And lastly, more than anything, you want to ensure that it tells a clear, consistent, and compelling story that makes your client the hero and presents *you* as their best guide. For these reasons, a core part of my Brand Story Solution is both writing *and* designing my clients' websites. We take the foundational work of the strategy and the brand story guide (the messaging, visuals, and core marketing materials) and build them into an easy-to-update website that shares their value with clients.

If you have a website, or are thinking of getting one, and you need help to brand it, my best advice is to always work with a partner (or partners) who covers both the web design and writing. The copywriting piece can be challenging (even when a pro helps) and is often the reason website projects can take six months to a year to complete with some providers. In my experience, a website project can take a few weeks if you've done the foundational brand building (visuals and writing) beforehand with your website partner—or have a branding toolkit to share with them.

> *Who could help you with a well-branded website:* branding consultants who offer web design, website design agencies who offer copywriting, marketing and branding agencies

PHOTOGRAPHY

At a minimum, you want to have a professional headshot that presents you as warm, inviting, and approachable—the way you'd likely want to be seen if someone were to spot you in person. You want someone who sees your headshot to think they could easily come up to talk with you, and ask more about your services and how you can help them. That means your photo needs to have you making eye contact, so it really feels like the beginning of a relationship with meeting you.

Beyond that main headshot lies so much opportunity for branding your business the way top coaches and consultants do: brand photography. While you can get away with high-quality stock photography, especially if you have help selecting the right images, nothing takes the place of custom brand photography.

I don't personally do photography, but I do consult on streamlining the process for many. I've directed dozens of brand photography shoots for clients using my insider strategy to get hundreds of photos done in just one day—maximizing your photography investment and giving you a branded photo library for years to come. I've bottled the secrets, templates, and process for getting those incredible images of you working with clients, new headshots, and branded stock photos into my self-paced training "Brand Photo Plan."

What I've learned in helping oversee thousands of custom brand images and working them into dozens of client websites is that brand photography that tells your story really *does* sell and share your story in an unbelievably dynamic way.

Essential brand photography:

- A professional headshot *(at a minimum)*
- A set of high-quality stock photography that fits your brand *(at least 3–5 images that you can use consistently)*
- Custom brand photography *(especially images that show your client experience and transformation; do this when you can to look as high quality an option as possible)*

Who could help you with a well-branded websites: brand or commercial photographers, branding consultants, marketing and branding agencies

VIDEOGRAPHY

If you're needing to really update your branding, website, and photography, adding the investment of videography may not be feasible all at once. However, if you do have flexibility with investment or you already have a lot of these pieces in place, adding video content centered on your brand and business can be an incredibly effective way to tell your story and show your value to your ideal clients.

If your business is unique, has an interesting story, or often needs explanation, a short video can be pivotal to helping your value be better understood and converting more clients. If you're new to video, I recommend a 90-second to three-minute "trailer" that tells the story of your business and the value you provide to your ideal clients. Don't invest in this until you've at least nailed down your essential strategy and messaging pieces. With those in hand, you can ensure that anything you share in a video aligns with the vision and promise of your greatest business.

Who could help you with brand videography: videographers who work with business owners and commercial clients, marketing and branding agencies

What Do You Need Now?

As you've read, a lot goes into a professional and authentic brand for your business. Because "as soon as you can" differs for everyone, you may be in a season where you can invest in a full rebranding, or you might need to pick a handful of things that will be difference-makers for right now. No matter what you're ready to do, it can get overwhelming if you've tried to do it yourself or work with a bunch of freelancers to do different pieces of it.

No matter how you move forward with any rebranding or branding you may need or want to do, having the right partner or company to make it as seamless, simple, and *fun (!)* a process as possible can be really valuable and make a huge difference to getting those confident tools ready in your toolkit. First, know you don't have to do it alone if you want to look, feel, and sound the part of being the expert you are. Second, it can help to clarify what area needs the *most* attention, especially if you're only able to tackle one area or two areas for now. Is it messaging? Or the visuals? Maybe your website.

To do this exploration for yourself, I've created a free, self-guided branding assessment called the "Brand & Marketing Gut Check."

EXERCISE

Do a Brand and Marketing Gut Check

FREE RESOURCE

Access my **Brand & Marketing Gut Check free online tool** at greateststorycreative.com/gutcheck or click the link in your *Establish Yourself Companion Workbook.*

Using your current or future primary ideal client as the barometer, you can easily determine what parts of branding you should focus on first.

Professional Branding Is Like Producing Your Hit Song

As you've been working on embracing your story through branding, we've looked at giving yourself permission to be the expert you are. We've set down some crucial focus of who you can help most and what you can offer that's most valuable to them. And we've even considered what professional branding could do to set you apart in every aspect of how you do business and present that powerful story. Of the Four Key Cs, in many ways we've hit on areas that really highlight courageous confidence including giving yourself credit, reframing yourself as the guide, and letting go of trying to be everything. We've explored a lot of crucial clarity when it comes to choosing to be an expert at what you're greatest at, deciding on your most valuable solution, and narrowing down what you need in your branding toolkit.

With these in mind, it's time to for the other two Cs: coordinated consistency and continued commitment to shine. In embracing your story, you're choosing to make some big decisions about yourself and your business:

- *I am the expert who is greatest at X.*
- *This is who I'm going to help the most.*
- *This is the most valuable thing I'm going to do for them.*
- *I'm going to embrace how I got here, where I am now, and how I'm going to brand myself for this next chapter.*

For those choices to have an impact, they will require you to be conscious about consistently using them and continually committed to doing so. Because what good would your courageous confidence and crucial clarity be if you don't use them in everything from your networking to your email signature to your sales conversations? And how much benefit will you see if you're consistent for a few months but give up before people have had a chance to really learn what you do and engage with it? What good will getting a branding toolkit be if you let it rust?

In this way, we can learn a lot from the stories of every scrappy band who made it big by focusing on getting their first hit song. Think about your all-time favorite song—the one you can't help but sing along to when it comes on the radio. Do you ever stop to think how that song came to be? How did it become your favorite song? How did it become a hit song at all?

Generally speaking, for that song to have become *your all-time favorite* and for you to have even heard it in the first place, that band had to make a lot of things happen. First, the band wrote the lyrics and melody for that incredible song. But that alone didn't get you hearing it. They needed some help to do that.

To make sure that you could hear that song, they went to professionals. Like asking for the help of branding experts or marketing agencies, they sought experts like music producers and mixers to help them record that song to polish it and make it sound great. They probably have a record label who professionally designed their cover art for the single and packaged it into something polished, professional, and ready to be played over the radio (and online!).

But just having a song polished and packaged isn't enough for a song to become a hit. For a song to become a hit, a band has to perform that song—and not just once, but hundreds of times. In dusty clubs, at state fairs, at local arenas—everywhere and anywhere they can perform. They play it on the radio, on television, on YouTube, getting that one song heard as much as humanly possible. Maybe the band even has to travel across the country in a stinky tour bus, making it essentially their full-time job to play that hit song.

Only by doing that consistently for months, if not years, does the song actually become a hit—a song that you and I know and can happily sing the lyrics to when it comes on the radio. The hit often leads the band to fame, fortune, and most especially lifelong fans: people who love the song so much that they buy the album, buy all the future albums, buy the t-shirt and the merchandise, and most definitely tell all their friends about them—singing the lyrics and their praises to anyone who could be a potential new fan.

The big-picture branding strategy I recommend for creating your greatest business is a lot like this journey. Whether we're talking the foundations of your work, the behind-the-scenes of your business, or branding and marketing it, everything comes down to the long, hard, but extremely rewarding work of consistency and commitment. If you want to do great work, have the best clients (lifelong fans), and be known, it takes commitment to your choices about your business and holding fast to the clarity you've defined. If you are constantly changing your job title, or your category, or who your ideal clients are, no one has enough time to learn your hit song.

One of the oldest adages of marketing is something called "The Rule of 7." Australian marketing agency Assemblo shares that studies have shown that people need to encounter a message "at least seven times before it sinks in."[12] Seven times. I used to think if I said something more than once, or shared something more than once, I'd be "bothering people." Nope, we're all too busy these days. Take this to heart.

I used to resist the wisdom in this. I once thought being a business owner was all about reinventing myself and staying fresh/creative. Being unique constantly was how I thought I should get attention. Yet, producing my hit song and committing to singing it has paid off. For example, I've run my "Branding with Annie" workshop for more than four years—but it took a solid 18 months of speaking nearly every single month to sold-out rooms before I was "known" locally for it. That's about when someone came up to me at a networking event and declared, "I know you: *You're Brand Annie!*" That was the song that got sung back to me, and it's what's built a community of fans over time.

I dive deeper into the value of playing your hit song and why you should stick to the lyrics when we get to "Simplified Systems for Magic Marketing" (where it becomes incredibly essential to relationships, sales, and marketing). For now, when it comes to all the ways you brand yourself, think about how you structure, present, and sell the work of your business to your current clients and to those you're meeting for the first time.

While it's not easy to be consistent and hold tight to your choices (especially when everyone's trying to tell you to host a magical social media challenge), hang in there. Your job is to confidently embrace your story and play your hit song long enough to create the lifelong fans that will sustain your business for years, if not decades, to come. So get ready to rock on.

YOUR BRANDING "KEY C" CHECK

This book is built to help you identify your next best action step to establish yourself and grow your greatest business possible the moment you finish reading it. To help you figure out that number one thing to do, at the end of each of the six essential areas of business, I'm inviting you do this "Key C" Check exercise.

In this gut check, you'll take some intentional time to think back on the area of business you just finished reading about (in this case, branding) and brainstorm where you and your business may be stuck when it comes to each of the Four Key Cs *(courageous confidence, crucial clarity, conscious consistency, and continued commitment).*

Designed to help you consider the best practices and insights you've gained in that specific area, note what you'd like to work on *most* to get you to the next level. At the end of each exercise, you have an opportunity to choose the most urgent and important item in that specific area of business. Then at the very end of the book, we look at all six "Key C" Checks and do a clarifying exercise to help you see exactly *which* big action step to take after finishing the book.

Sound awesome? Here goes!

As you worked on embracing your story through branding, we took a closer look at:

- Permission to own your expertise,
- The power of giving yourself credit,
- Presenting yourself as the guide, not the hero,
- Deciding what you most want to be known for,
- Focusing your practice on an ideal client,
- Centering your services on providing a valuable solution to an ideal client's crucial problem,

- Figuring out whether to rebrand, rename, or both,
- Determining what you need to have in your professional branding toolkit, and
- Why you need to keep to your choices, branding, and focus on playing your hit song with consistency and commitment.

With these aspects in mind, take 10–15 minutes to reflect on and answer the following questions here in this book, in the *Establish Yourself Companion Workbook*, or in your own notebook. Though these questions are intended to help you find clarity about what feels uncertain, the very first question will allow you to give yourself much-deserved credit! You're on your way.

WHAT'S WORKING

What's *one* thing you're really proud of in terms of your branding and how you're embracing your story?

COURAGEOUS CONFIDENCE

What's *one* thing you wish you hade more courage and confidence about with how you're branding yourself?

CRUCIAL CLARITY

What's *one* thing you need more focus and clarity on?

CONSCIOUS CONSISTENCY

What's *one* thing you need more consistency with?

CONTINUED COMMITMENT

What's *one* thing you want to commit more to with regard to branding and owning your expertise?

Now, which *one* of these things feels most urgent to you?
List that one in the form of an action step here.

For example, feeling unclear about your business name might become- "Brainstorm new practice names," or desiring more consistency in your branding might inspire you to write an action step of- "Do the Brand & Marketing Gut Check exercise."

MY MOST VALUABLE ACTION STEP FOR **BRANDING:**

For this step, **are there any professionals and/or tools you may need to make that top action step happen?** *List your thoughts on this here.*

STEP TWO
Shape Your Business

Would you rather talk about the behind the scenes of your business or market it? Which feels more important? More urgent? *Maybe you'd rather avoid both—am I right!?*

I'm betting that most people would say that marketing is king *and* it's the thing they stress the most about. In my first outline for this book, the second step was about marketing. (That is now Step Three: Translate Your Value.) Originally, marketing came next because it felt like many readers would expect it to appear earlier in a business book. I've since learned the value of working backward from the client's journey, finding reverse revenue, and thinking about things differently. I realized that moving onto marketing as a second step in establishing yourself is bad strategy. Why? Because doing so is "fixating on frosting."

Imagine your business is a cake. It seems like all anyone recommends you worry about is the frosting—*the marketing!* After all, it's the buttercream and sprinkles that gets everyone interested and excited to eat the cake, right? But here's the problem with that: When *all* you focus on is frosting, you don't even bake the cake. And while you can definitely have a cake with no frosting, frosting on its own . . . well, that's *not* cake. It's likely not even *food.*

I've found the same is true in a profitable business. You can have a successful business without fancy marketing, but you won't have a business if all you spend your time and worry on is marketing. I've seen way too many business owners spend weeks, months, and years worrying about their marketing, but never take the time to define something profitable to sell and set up a business model that can deliver those services. That's a waste.

Many forget that the *cake* is what you're actually serving up to your clients, not just the frosting. Your business—and how it operates—is the substance. It's what provides the most valuable transformation and solution to your client's most crucial problem. The exciting marketing that got them in the door doesn't and can't do that work.

So, the cake itself needs to be *good.* It needs to be made with high-quality ingredients and baked well. You've got to have a fine-tuned recipe, a plan, the right tools, and the team, time, or both to bake it. Because who wants to eat a beautifully iced cupcake that tastes like sawdust? The word's going to spread that, no matter how good the frosting looked, that cupcake's a big waste of money bound to leave a bad taste in your mouth.

Great food metaphors aside, there are many reasons why it's so tempting to fixate on the frosting because you feel like you need to do that to grow. For one, running a smart, profitable business can be hard to do and establish. It takes strategy. In my experience, it takes time, systems, boundaries, and specific goals. Working on our pricing, saying *no* to bad-fit clients, saying *yes* to consultants who can help us grow—these can be scary, boring, or both in some ways.

The most incredible marketing can't fix a broken business. Actually, it risks putting you out of business *faster.* So there's no way out but through when it comes to setting up your business for success. It takes the behind-the-scenes work to be baked in *before* you can advertise it well. In order to do that, you've got to get down to the foundations and choose to shape your business (even if you don't generally love "the business stuff").

Oxford Languages defines the verb form of *shape* to mean "[d]etermine the nature of; have a great influence on."[13] I want to point your attention to the word ***great.*** "Have a great influence on." Shaping your business is your opportunity to go to the next level—one where you love what you do even more and get paid well for doing it.

While I know things like boundaries, goal-setting, and systems can feel vanilla, they have the incredible, often-too-overlooked ability to transform your life and your work. I used to resist this myself, but once I started working intentionally on developing the operations of my business, I became hooked. I fell in love with the type of transformations shaping your business makes possible—things like:

- Making more money while working *less!*
- Attracting awesome fit clients.
- Smoother client experiences.
- More consistent client results and bigger transformations.
- Less stress in my work.
- More joy for what I do and whom I help.

The benefits are strong, but it can be a tough path to navigate when you get super intentional about *how* you're doing business. You may already worry about losing flexibility, facing doubts and insecurities around raising your prices/charging for your value, and reckoning with fears of being seen as "unreasonable" if you set boundaries. It can get overwhelming fast.

But let's look at this from another angle. Might we reframe these haunting concerns as valuable opportunities? If you've shied away from streamlining your business in the past, now is your opportunity to consider what it could do for you and your life. In "Shape Your Business," I share stories and tips with you along these lines (including the time I got screamed at and how it ended up being a totally great thing!). Together, we break down these best practices of operations, reinforcing a strong, behind-the-scenes foundation of what you're doing and why.

My hope is that you'll end this second step clearer about what you want to do to shape *your* greatest business going forward. You'll be glad this section came before marketing because you won't give as much of a damn about the frosting anymore. Instead, you'll be ready and excited to bake the very best cake you can. Onward. *Here's hoping it's a piece of cake!*

Operations

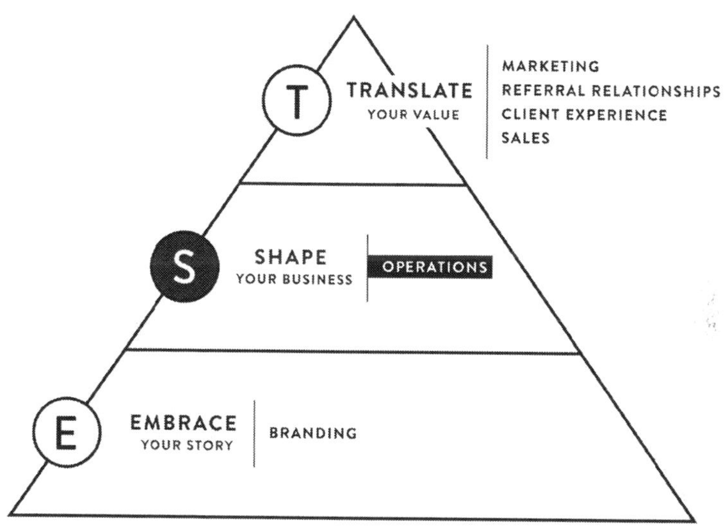

When it's time to focus on baking the cake, there's no better way to shape your business than optimizing your operations: the back end of the work that you do. This is the unsexy, underlying foundation of your practice that encompasses everything from pricing to bookkeeping to every process you use across your business.

I used to think it was a real snooze festival, until I got really busy in the second half of 2016. Fueled by my coaching experience with Adele and inundated by the busiest influx of new clients I'd ever experienced, I got so overwhelmed by new business that I stopped all client work entirely and had my first Batch December to fix it and refocus, as I shared earlier.

Though it didn't seem fun at the time, an enormous part of that first Batch December experiment was getting the back end of my operations organized. I took the time to do what I never really ever had time to do when I had client work: document every process, streamline my systems, create templates for emails I'd send over and over again. To do that well, I needed to make a lot of decisions and set a lot of goals for any of these systems to matter. I had to really stop and think through the type of business I wanted to have (and the type I really didn't). This intentional project did something I never expected: It kicked off my love affair with operations.

Through making tough choices, defining boundaries, and setting up smart systems in alignment with those goals, the proof was in the pudding. Nearly from the first day I embraced prioritizing the operations of my business, I enjoyed the benefits that came with them. I was more profitable. I was happier. My clients were happier. I got better at saying *no* to the wrong fits and opportunities and was freer to say *yes* to the right ones when they came along.

It was and has been eye-opening over these past five years since I began spending intentional time to improve the back end of my business. I've since coached and consulted many of my other clients to see how powerful this area can be, and from here I share with you what I've learned. It's time for more business bravery.

OPERATIONS

Simple Goals, Clear Data, and Courageous Decisions

Courage in how you choose to run your business is just as important as the bravery it takes to brand yourself as an expert. From six-figure worshipping to tracking your time, we explore the big considerations, important goal-setting, data-collecting, and soul-searching you may need to do to confidently shape your business for greater success from here.

Being a Business Owner Means Having 2 Jobs

Having worked with so many amazing coaches, consultants, and service professionals, I've picked up on something very common: Many people who are great at what they do as coach, consultant, or service-business owner often absolutely hate and/or avoid the "business side" of their business. There are a lot of valid reasons for feeling like this. However, there are also a lot of ways to reframe so you don't hate it or feel like you have to avoid it.

But if you do hate or avoid it, I'm going to lower the boom on you now. Assuming you're the owner and there are no other business partners, no matter how much you outsource the running of your business, there's no getting around this reality:

Being a business owner means having *two* jobs:

- The work you do for clients—*your expertise/zone of genius*
- The work you do as a business owner—*the strategic mind that drives your business*

A lot of things can be outsourced, from your social media marketing, to creating your brand toolkit, to doing your bookkeeping, and even help executing administrative tasks with a virtual assistant. However, you can never outsource being the decision-maker of your business. **No one can drive your business forward but *you.***

I've had many consulting sessions with clients who were so deferential to me and to other partners that they were ceding one of their biggest responsibilities (and opportunities) for success: *their* role as the strategic mind that decides and drives the business. But it's not your VA's responsibility or ability to grow your business, nor your marketing company's, nor your tax accountant's. It's always going to be yours.

While it's okay not to be your happiest while doing the "business" side of the work, it's important to remember that, by being a business owner, you're choosing to take on that job, too. There's no version in which you can just be an expert without a boss being involved. Either you're the boss of your own business, or it may be a moment to consider going back to a traditional career job—a path that comes with someone else being the boss.

Over the years, I've met many people who get so overwhelmed by branding, marketing, and general business decisions that I wonder why they stay entrepreneurs. They seem genuinely exhausted by anything business-related, and they resist taking action and implementing advice, even when they've paid for it. They want me or whomever they're working with to take on the responsibility of the success of the business so they can get back to what they really enjoy doing: their core expertise (coaching their favorite clients, for example). And hey, I really get it! It's a completely rational thing to want to spend all of your time working in your zone of genius/providing the value you have to give others. But if that's the only place you can imagine spending your time, business ownership may not be the best fit for you.

I'm grateful to have done both types of roles in my career and have the wisdom to know that entrepreneurship (and its two jobs) is the best fit for *me*.

So that's the permission I want to give you as we dive into shaping your business: If you truly detest the idea of shaping your business and wish you could just do "the work you love," you absolutely can. You just need to do that as a job for *someone else's* company. That person might be a new business partner who loves the operations side, or it could be a boss of some kind who hires you—even if it's for a long-term, full-time contract. You could even join a collective of other coaches, run by another business owner who handles all of this back-end work.

Whatever it is, I encourage you to choose your best-fit path—eyes wide open. Because your business can't grow until you're willing to fully step into the job it is to run it and be the CEO of it. If you're up for it, I truly think you can do it, especially when you see what embracing your story, shaping your business, and translating your value can do for you—and how none of it has to mean becoming some unbelievable marketing or business expert.

On Being a 6-Figure Business Owner

Shortly, I'm going to lead you through how to set simple, powerful goals for your business. Before that, I want to get you ready by demystifying a very common goal that so many coaches and consultants have: **six figures.**

Reaching six figures in revenue can feel like the holy grail of business ownership, especially if it's just you in your practice! We're constantly taught that this level is synonymous with success, yet so few business owners get there—especially if you're a woman. On average just 12% of women entrepreneurs reach this milestone, according to a study by American Express.[14]

Yet, is it really worth worshipping?
Is it worth feeling inferior unless you have it?
And what *is* it worth giving up to get there?

I went full-time in my business in early 2014. After my experience with Adele and doubling-down on smart strategy, consistency, and systems, I could have become a six-figure business in fewer than three years, by 2017. That year, I came within $9,000 reaching it. The following year (2018), I came within just a few thousand (about one project or so). It wasn't until five full years later, in 2019, that I officially crossed over that six-figure annual revenue threshold.

For context, as you know, I began doing a Batch December in 2016. It was a sabbatical of taking the entire month of December to work on business development and keep myself from burning out from client work. This meant I worked on average 11 months or fewer of the year (typically 10 or fewer, including holidays/vacations). Had I kept myself open for client work in December 2017, I *could* have made it to $100K or more sooner. Had I been open for work in December 2018, I could have made it then, too.

Though getting to that mythic six figures was a big goal of mine, it wasn't the *only* goal in my business or my life that mattered. Having that Batch December sabbatical was crucial to my growth and also to the enjoyment of my business. Sure, I could have given it up and taken on the business to make myself a six-figure-business on paper—but to what end? What would I have been sacrificing?

Yes, I've always wanted to become a six-figure founder, and I'm very proud of the fact that I am one now. But I'm also very proud that I didn't sacrifice other really valuable and important things to me to do it. I prioritized things like Batch December and taking off every break my husband had from PT school so we could spend time together. I'm glad that I said *no* to bad-fit clients, rather than take them on in support of my big financial goal. I'm happy that I got there without huge expenses and keeping 60% or more of what I earn as profit/salary. It feels right that I've gone at the pace I needed to invest in and hire help so I could learn how to make more and work less. I'm grateful that what I earned each year—even though it wasn't a perfect six-figure salary for years—was enough to cover my family's living expenses and self-pay for fertility treatments, the birth of our son, and my husband's physical therapy school tuition (which has kept us out of debt).

So, the thing is, when I finally got to that magical number six years into my business instead of the three that were in reach, it felt that much greater, important, and satisfying to me, because I knew I'd reached it without sacrificing what mattered and without taking risks I wasn't ready to take.

Now that I can claim that six-figure status, I definitely have more confidence in what I'm doing. It's helped me grow my business, increase my authority, and gain more credibility. But so did that time I spent on the journey to it including all that I've learned (and continue to learn) along the way—the insights and perspective I share with my clients in our work together today.

Psychologist and author Shawn Achor of *The Happiness Advantage* shares a gem in his viral TED Talk "The Happy Secret to Better Work."[15] He reminds us that once we reach one goal, we forget to celebrate and immediately turn our attention to the next goal. Shawn refers to this as us "pushing happiness over the cognitive horizon." Generally explained, this means we don't sit in the "now" and intentionally feel and enjoy happiness.

In business, I've found to be this to be the case with making six figures. You finally get there! You're thrilled! Then, suddenly, it's not good enough. You're thinking and seeing gurus posting, *Well, how about multiple six figures? Wait—how about seven!? You should really be making eight!*

There's really no perfect moment of success in business that you ever arrive at—in a business, in your career, or even in your life. With your practice, there's your first client, your first $1K or $5K or $10K month, six figures, multiple six figures, seven . . . lord, eight figures! I could go on. And while some business owners share loudly that they make six, or seven, or eight figures and have hundreds of thousands of followers, keep in mind that you have zero idea what their expenses and profit margins truly are. They don't share their behind-the-scenes numbers. They may employ large teams. They may have big business debt and maxed-out credit cards. They may only take home 5% of their gross revenue, because followers don't equal figures, applause doesn't mean action, and revenue doesn't equal profit.

For these reasons and others, there's no need to idolize it, sacrifice everything to it, or feel less than if you haven't reach it. Six figures is but one of many outward signs of success that lend you credibility and give you confidence to do great work that changes lives including your own. But no one sees your numbers except your CPA. No one knows what goals you value most, and what needs matter to you beyond purely financial dreams.

So no matter what your revenue or profit is right now, always stay true to the definition of success that matters most—*yours.* And rather than chase numbers on paper, celebrate the journey of what you earn and how you earn it, because whatever comes of it, you're doing it on your own terms, in ways that are the most meaningful for you and your life. Now, on to simple goal-setting.

Simplify Your Goals to Reach Them

"Success isn't about how your life looks to others.
It's about how it feels to you."
—Michelle Obama

What does success look like in *your* greatest business? You already started this work at the beginning of this book by writing your greatest business vision. Now is the time to set goals to make it a reality. Having goals to shape your business is so critically important because of a simple truth: If you don't dictate what your business is, others will. Your clients, your audience, your competitors—even your friends and family—will shape *your* life's work and happiness. Yet that should be wholly up to you.

In my experience, setting good goals doesn't mean having to spend countless hours on it or update a formal "business plan."

I've never found such plans to be all that helpful to my own process. *(Heck, I have a Google Calendar reminder that comes up weekly reminding me to work on my business plan. It's been doing that since 2013, and I've been too lazy to delete it!)*

What you really need is an action plan—one guided by your most important goals. What are the biggest things you care about for yourself and your business? Knowing your current goals, even if they are simplified, as I like to do them, can help you make really strong *yes* and *no* decisions—the kind of decisiveness and strategy it takes to be an established business owner.

So how do you do that without getting bogged down in the existential crises that can come with traditional, uber-specific goal-setting? Keep it *super* simple. Focus on what you want to do more (and less) of in the next three months. In 2019, I set down my goals as four simple directions that were easy to remember and possible to achieve:

1. Speak more
2. Make more
3. Work less
4. Have fun

Though they were just two words each, they were my gut check for every business decision I made that year. By having them top of mind I was able to do exactly what they stated. In 2019, I spoke more, made more, worked less, and had a lot of fun! This was what I came back to when I was tempted to take on too much client work or needed to prioritize time spent on growing my speaking career.

Having these goals also took off a lot of pressure. Notice none of those goals were "make more than $100,000 in revenue" or "work only ten months of the year." I wasn't locked into those numbers, but I was able to achieve both of those goals.

Here's how I arrived at this simple goal-setting strategy, and how you can put it into action right now using your *Establish Yourself Companion Workbook* or your own notebook. This is a five-step process and exercise easily remembered as "G.O.A.L.S."

G | Gather
O | Outline
A | Abbreviate
L | Locate
S | Stick

EXERCISE

Swipe My Simplified Goal-Setting Strategy

In your *Establish Yourself Companion Workbook* or your own notebook, work through the following five steps of G.O.A.L.S. to create your simple goals for the next three months (or more).

GATHER

Gather your thoughts about what did *and* didn't work well for you over the past 12 months. First, create two lists. Title one "What Worked Well" and the other "What Didn't Work Well."

Then, like an annual review of sorts, spend five to 10 minutes brainstorming on each one. List the things you've really enjoyed about your business, clients you had, projects you did, marketing you tried, and so forth. Conversely, spell out those things that didn't go smoothly, that didn't work out, that weren't profitable, and even those "sandpaper" client experiences. We all have them.

You can do this in a notebook, but I even did this the first time on a flight using the notes app on my phone. Easy!

OUTLINE

Outline what you'd like to do more of and less of over the next three months (or more). Using your recently brainstormed lists about what did and didn't work well, create two new lists. Spend five to 10 minutes making two new lists, titled "What I Want to Do More Of" and "What I Want to Do Less Of" in the year ahead.

ABBREVIATE

Abbreviate your "more of" and "less of" lists down to two-to three-word versions of those goals. Summarize each entry on the "More of" and "Less of" lists as a two-word version: "More X, Less Y."

LOCATE

Locate your most important three to five goals from the two- or three-word versions of your "more of" and "less of" lists. Select three to five goals overall to prioritize for the next three months (or more). Pick those that feel the most urgent.

STICK

Stick those three to five simple, two-or-three-word goals up somewhere you can see them every day (and ***share*** them with others!). When you keep your main goals front and center, and easy to remember, and you share with others, you'll have a gut check to keep your decisions grounded—*and* more people will be aware of what you're working on.

That's how more opportunities will come your way: People will actually know what your goals are!

—

I encourage you to try this out if you have a few minutes. Setting simple goals and the brainstorming process of thinking through what really matters most to you will help you shape your business in incredible ways as we continue to work through best practices together.

Track What Matters to Work Less and Make More

Now that you have simplified goals, I want you to have the clear data to back them up and make them happen. A lot of the work of having strong operations will come with sticking to boundaries, strategically increasing pricing, and other things that can feel icky, challenging, or just all around hard. Having data—key information from the history of your business—can be your guide to more confidently navigate those aspects of operations. Keeping the data front and center can also be one of your most valuable tools for working less, making more, and continuing to love what you do.

If you've never paid much attention to your sales, clients, or time spent in the business, doing so will blow your mind! Over the years, I've become a big champion of tracking three critical elements of my business in real time. This is data that I consistently update, review, learn from on a near-daily basis, and make big and small changes to all aspects of my business as a result. The three categories I religiously track are:

- Sales and expenses,
- Clients, and
- Time.

TRACKING SALES AND EXPENSES

I've always tracked receipts and business expenses. I mean, you have to for taxes. What I haven't always done is tracked my ongoing sales in real time. Since 2017, I've kept a spreadsheet that I call my "Realtime Revenue Tracker." In this document, I track every free consultation call I have. I track whether I offered the client consulting, a project, or both, and what the value of that offer was worth.

I track every line of revenue within my business and keep a master look at the financial year in one tab that totals my financial goals against my real-time results. It even lists my historical year-to-date revenue since I started my business in 2013.

Why do this? In one word: momentum. I update this spreadsheet every few days, every week, every month, and every year in my business. I can see at any given moment how sales are doing and where I am in gross revenue for the year, and I can even compare it to last year to get a sense of how this year is going. It's one of the best things I do to drive myself forward in my business every day, knowing I'm building something bigger and I have a great grasp of where the business is headed at any point in any given year.

It also gives me excellent historical information to see what services are selling best (or not selling), what marketing activities are the most effective at bringing me the highest-value projects, and what opportunities I may have to grow other areas of the business. Tracking this information helped me to see that my consulting services—once a small side offer I did for two clients in 2017—had the potential to become a five-figure business. It did officially in 2020, and by 2021 it had grown to be about 25% of my annual revenue. I share more about how my consulting services grew out of solving a problem in the upcoming section, "Navigating Boundaries, Bad-Fit Clients, and Brain Pickers."

TRACKING CLIENTS

As I shared about primary ideal clients, I prefer to study my past favorite clients rather than "create" a client avatar. My Realtime Revenue Tracker allows me to keep that data easily accessible all year long. I use it to track the outcome of discovery calls and whether clients say *yes* or *no* to proposals (what's my conversion rate?). I track when a client inquired versus when they booked (how long did the sales cycle take?). I track where the client found me in the first place (what marketing activities are working best?). If they were a referral, *who referred them* (who are my best referral partners?)? If they came to a workshop, *which one* (are there topics I teach that convert more than others?)?

With this type of simple yet value-packed information, I can go back once or twice a year and sort all of my clients into lists that can inform changes I should make to my operations, branding, marketing, and beyond. I ask myself questions like:

- *Of everyone, who were the best fits?*
- *Who spent the most?*
- *Who had the smoothest client experience?*
- *Of those people, where did they come from marketing-wise?*
- *Should I do more of those activities?*

- *What do these best-fit clients have in common?*
- *Should I tweak who my ideal clients are based on this information?*
- *Do past best-fit clients need ongoing support or a solution I don't have yet, but should build for them?*

By tracking where clients come from, how much they spend, and how long it takes them to invest, I continually learn so much about my business and how to grow it. Clients for you might be individuals or stakeholders at companies, but the same types of questions can apply, as can the utility of tracking what you know about the people who hire you to work for their organizations.

The other thing that really helps me gain insight in this area is using my Fans & Feedback process, something I share with you in detail when we get to "Reviews and Building Lifelong Client Relationships" in Step Three: Translate Your Value.

TRACKING TIME

I resisted tracking my time for years. I thought being "on the clock" was an inflexibility that I didn't have to subscribe to once I was out of the corporate world. Boy, was I wrong.

Tracking my time is the #1 most valuable thing I do to ensure I stay passionate and profitable.

It's my greatest singular success tip *ever.* If you do nothing else, track your time. When you're a service business owner, your time is literally money. So much depends on how you spend your time, but many business owners have no clue where their time is going. Financial guru Dave Ramsey often teaches the value of making a budget because if you don't tell your money where to go, you'll wonder where it went. The same, I've found, is true about your time. Once you start tracking, you won't be able to look away, and that'll change your business and life for the better.

I encouraged a fellow six-figure business owner to track her time recently. She was reluctant, just like I had once been. Two weeks later, she came back to me and shared, "Oh my gosh, Annie! I had no idea! I've been doing all this work for free! Literally 25% of my work last week was free for a business I'm not even working for." Seeing where her time was going became the firepower that finally got her to push back and set healthy boundaries with a referral partner. Backed by the data of her time, she put an end to the partnership arrangement, and going forward she'll get paid for that exact type of work. She just couldn't see the game-changing insight of time-tracking until she saw where her time was actually going.

I started tracking my time in 2017 using the free app Toggl. Since then, just about every day for years, I've tracked my time on everything I do in the business—both for clients and for myself on the operations side. It can be as easy as pressing "play" and clicking a few labels for each task I do in a day.

Within just a few weeks of starting to time track, I discovered exactly where my time was going—and it was eye-opening! For example, I was spending hours on projects that I thought were taking me just minutes. I realized I was wasting an hour a week writing a newsletter with zero direct results. I saw what bad-fit clients were financially costing me. I could see how profitable smooth client experiences were because I made double or *triple* per hour on them. I saw what a black hole social media was for me time-wise and that I should spend my time on better, more "me" strategies to build my visibility. I could finally see what time I was spending on things that I should delegate to my virtual assistant, who could handle them at a more efficient rate than what I charge my clients for my time.

Tracking my time has become one of my superpowers. It's taught me exactly how much time it takes me to do things, so I don't misquote projects or procrastinate to disaster. It's helped me effectively work less and make more, and even hire help. Because I have the real-time data, I can tell you, for example, that in the big pandemic year of 2020, I only worked seven months because of my maternity leave. I worked 17% less than I did in 2019, but made 26% *more* money. So that means, I made 26% more money in 2020 than I did in 2019, even though I worked five *months* fewer than I had the year before. I could confidently say that not only did I thrive in business through a maternity leave, I was actually able to work less and make more—by a lot.

How do I know this? Because I track my time, I can track and improve my profitability. The genius thing is, you can, too. It's literally free to do. And all you need are a time-tracking app and a spreadsheet in Excel or Google Sheets. Done.

—

Between your sales/expenses, your clients, and your time, you can and should have the data to back you up and shape your greatest business from here forward.

EXERCISE

Start Tracking What Matters!

If you'd love to be tracking sales and clients, make your own spreadsheet now, or if you want it all set up for you, you can invest in my **Realtime Revenue Tracker template** as part of the Establish Yourself Vault (which you can read more about at howtoestablishyourself.com or in "Ready to Establish Yourself?" in this book).

To begin tracking your time, set up a free Toggl.com account, scope out other options like Harvest, create a spreadsheet, or simply journal and jot down where your time spent in your business is going.

OPERATIONS

Navigating Boundaries, Bad-Fit Clients, and Brain Pickers

Now that you've defined a clear vision for your business and are tracking what matters to make it happen, you need to protect that vision, your happiness, and your bottom line. You can do this by bravely setting boundaries that support your goals, sticking to your non-negotiable values (even if it means turning down work), and inviting "brain pickers" to invest in you—even if that feels awkward at first. Get ready. Boundaries are about to transform you and your business for the better.

Yes, No, and What Confident Boundaries Buy Us

The two most profitable words in business are ***yes*** and ***no.*** What you say *yes* to and what you say *no* to represent your boundaries. What will you let into your business and your life, and what won't you? I've found that boundaries are essential to the growth and happiness you get from your business *(and your life, but that's another book).* They are hard to set, sometimes challenging to enforce, but always rewarding to practice.

I'm often a people-pleaser and hopefully healthy enneagram 3 (the Achiever). I definitely like to make people happy and I want them to like me, so I sometimes find it difficult to hold to good boundaries. However, like me, what you say *yes* and *no* to in business are the most impactful decisions you will make. Make them with your goals in mind and hold true to your non-negotiable values when opportunities and issues come your way.

Keep in mind that a confident *yes!* can mean:

- Taking on a project that stretches your skills.
- Investing in a coach or consultant to get you unstuck.
- Joining a mastermind to gain a supportive community.
- Bravely sharing your website and work online.
- Public speaking to market your business, even though that feels scary.
- Blocking your calendar to take vacations and growth time for yourself.
- Setting office hours so you have clearer definition between work life and home life.

Yes can take a lot of bravery. It sometimes involves stretching your abilities, your resources, and even your faith in yourself. It's called a leap of faith for a reason, right?

While many of us get the value of the yes—even the scary ones—equally important but often overlooked is saying *no.*

It can be valuable to say an intentional *no* to:

- Lowering your price.
- Bad-fit clients/companies that are hard to communicate with.

- Working on the weekends.
- Answering emails in the middle of the night.
- Doing extra work without charging for it.
- Spending hours on marketing yourself on social media (if you hate it).
- Taking discouraging advice from others who don't share your vision.
- Playing the comparison game and giving into imposter syndrome.
- Feeling like you have to be internet famous to be successful.
- Chasing six figures (or seven, or eight!).

A lot of shaping your business comes down to fighting for those *nos. No* can be a very expensive word. As we explore shortly, if you don't say *no* to that bad-fit client, you can lose money, time, and even your reputation if things don't go well. *No* can also be super profitable word for you. "No, I won't work all the time" can mean that you save space for your own self-care, giving you the time and mental headspace to grow and create a vision for the business without burning out.

I know firsthand it takes so much courage sometimes to say *no* to the draining things and to say *yes* to the energizing ones. That's why in this section, I share some best practices I've developed to do just that. Along the way, we look at systems, boundaries, and other strategies you can use to practice both of these profitable words, and say *yes* to your greatest business and *no* to anyone else's expectations of what that has to look like.

For New Work, Check Wendy's "Will of Rights"

One of the toughest *nos* to say is no to booking new work or a new client. I've been there so many times, and it's one of the hardest things I have to practice in my business. There are several valid reasons why you might want to say *no* to any particular project. Sometimes, it's even in our best interest to say *no* to what sound like amazing opportunities in order to protect our bigger-picture goals and needs.

How many times have you said *yes,* then weeks later wanted to kick yourself for doing that when you were up late on a Saturday night, trying to stay awake and just knock it out? Or how about when you got a million changes or questions back from your client? Or when you're buried in back-to-back coaching sessions, pushing you to the edge of burnout? Sometimes there's no greater regret than a *yes* that should have definitely been a *no,* if only you'd listened to your gut that day.

I have a "New Work Check" that helps me and can help you with this very same dilemma. It came to life when I was discussing this very common problem with my dear friend and client, presentation consultant Wendy Gates Corbett. She was debating taking on an incredibly exciting project, even though she knew deep down that the timing was tough and might ultimately stress her out. I advised Wendy to listen to those instincts and that sometimes—even when the opportunity is awesome—if you don't think you can really deliver, it's so important to say *no,* not only to protect your time, but also your reputation if you can't deliver later.

This conversation inspired Wendy to devise four big considerations for evaluating whether taking on this project was a good decision. I thought her approach was brilliant and asked if I could brand it in her honor as Wendy's "Will of Rights"—as in "I will *only* do this project if these four things are right!"

According to Wendy, and with my 100% backing, *Wendy's Will of Rights* are:

1. The Right Client.
2. The Right Project.
3. The Right Time.
4. The Right Reasons.

THE RIGHT CLIENT

I've learned the hard way many times that only saying *yes* to clients who really "get you" is important. Even if the project, the timing, and the reasons are great, if you can't communicate well with the client or stakeholders at the company you want to work with, they don't pay you on time, and so on, then it's not the right thing for you. I've also observed that how people and organizations act in the sales process is *exactly* how they'll be when you work together—so things won't normally get better once you sign a contract. So saying *yes* without confidently checking this box can become hugely expensive, emotionally and financially, as we explore shortly.

THE RIGHT PROJECT

Sometimes you adore the friend, connection, or past client who wants to work with you, *but* what they're asking you to do isn't a fit for your business or isn't something you do well. While you could do it, it could take a lot of time to figure out how to do it well. That might be time you don't have, expertise, or both. Ultimately, it's not the right project. If you take it on, you risk delivering a less-than-stellar client experience, service/product, or all of the above—and that could risk your incredible relationship with that person or former client. Again, it could be costly to your brand and business.

THE RIGHT TIME

It seems all but inevitable that I have a dream project and client come my way in November every single year! But of course, I always have to say, "You can book services for next year, but no, I'm not available for a December start date" if I want to protect my annual sabbatical of Batch December. No matter the client, the money, the project, the reasons . . . if I waver here, I lose one of my most essential breaks of the year—the one that drives both my financial profit and emotional satisfaction in my business. So while something amazing can be tempting, sometimes it's just not the right time. Your time is valuable, as you know, so only sell it when it's truly available.

Moreover, if you take on a project because you love the client, or have wonderful reasons for doing it, but you honestly don't have time to deliver, you're taking some big risks with your client relationship, your larger reputation, and your own daily sanity. If you're overworked, it's simply not the right time.

THE RIGHT REASONS

If everything else looks good, but your heart's not in the work, don't say *yes.* I've learned too many times that doing things because they sound good strategically but don't align with my values or needs at the time can be a big mistake. Work is hard: that's why it's called work. If you're not agreeing to do it for the right reasons (i.e., it makes emotional and sustainable sense to you as a business owner), don't take it on. Too often, it'll backfire on you personally and possibly professionally.

—

In my experiences and in guiding other entrepreneurs, I've discovered that we do our best, most profitable work when we can check all four of these boxes and confidently say *yes!* And we can *also* do our best, most profitable work when we confidently say *no* at moments when we can't check them all.

So let Wendy and her "Will of Rights" inspire you the next time you're evaluating a new project or client. Go through the boxes and, if you can check all but one of the four, see if there's any way to talk with your client to come up with a fresh option to make things "right," like changing the timing, the scope, or something else.

Whatever you do, let this best practice remind you of the great emotional and financial value to your success and health as a business owner to say both *yes* and *no* wholeheartedly.

Bad-Fit Clients Are Expensive

Legendary acting teacher Constantin Stanislavski famously wrote, *"There are no small parts, there are only small actors."*[16] What I'll tell you is *"There are no bad clients, only bad client experiences."*

Generally speaking, "bad" clients are not bad *people.* Many of them are lovely people, in fact. However, at times, they may have been *bad* for your business/the way you work/what you do and probably you shouldn't have worked with them in the first place. Unfortunately, the state of your branding, marketing, sales, and client experience processes (or lack thereof) may have contributed to attracting and booking them. This could be especially true if you didn't communicate boundaries and or exercise the ability to say *no* when red flags went up. In short, in more cases than you probably realize, *those bad clients?* They may have been *your* fault!

Hey, my "bad" clients (or as I sometimes call them, "learning opportunities"—*ha!)* have been my fault, too. It took me a few years to realize that for my branding, marketing, and client experience to be their best, they should attract my best-fit clients *and* repel the bad-fit ones. The repelling can be as valuable as the attracting. It's essential, but being essential doesn't make it easy. That's why we're talking about it.

For a long time, I felt it especially hard to say *no* to clients even when I saw red flags coming or a project suddenly became bumpy. I'd agonize on my end: writing long emails about process, obsessing over every word, and wasting hours of time to smooth out the client experience—because frankly, I hate to disappoint anyone. I fear criticism and failure, and I never want to let anyone down, in my professional life and in my personal life. However, continuing to say *yes* and bending over backward for bad-fit clients threatened my business many more times than I'd like to admit. That's because, if you stop to think about it, ***bad-fit clients are very expensive.***

You may think that when you take on someone who's a potential bad fit it's okay because you're getting paid (possibly even paid well!) and you might even be establishing or continuing a relationship with an entire company of opportunities. But think through what typically happens next.

You say *yes* to someone, yet you know in your gut it's not right and it would never pass Wendy's "Will of Rights." You start working together and inevitably there's discontent, confusion, challenges with communication, perceived quality of work, or all of the above. But now you're in a sticky situation because money's been exchanged, like a deposit. The person or company stakeholders you're working with may be dissatisfied or even angry with your arrangement.

So you waste additional time carefully wording emails, or setting emergency Zooms to sort through issues to try to work together. You debate giving back a deposit. You possibly cancel the project and/or deliver what you've done thus far. They leave your business not only disappointed, but also possibly motivated to discuss their experience publicly and tell other people not to work with you.

It's an awful scenario that just about every business owner has been through at some point. If you've been there, consider this: The expensive part hits you more than you realize, even if you keep the person's initial deposit or retainer fee. When you end up with an unhappy client who wants to cancel:

- You've lost the value of the rest of the project's or engagement's income.

- You've lost the value of an ideal client who you could have worked with instead of the bad-fit one (if you'd had the time available).
- You've lost the value of all the additional time you spent carefully writing emails or hosting emergency calls to communicate process needs.
- You've lost potential business and hurt your overall reputation by having a less-than-stellar client experience (even if you did absolutely everything you could to do a good job).
- If you're working with a company, you've possibly lost future business across the entire organization.

Did you know that "Americans tell an average of 15 people about a poor service experience, versus the 11 people they'll tell about a good experience?"[17] All of this could add up to thousands of dollars of value in revenue and reputation. So is saying *no* to money when you suspect someone's going to be a bad fit really worth it? I'd say *yes,* 10 times over!

I know firsthand it can take a lot of moral support to hold to this type of boundary, so let me introduce you to one of the most impactful processes you can put into in your practice: a 15-minute meeting with a new client that'll save your business—and your sanity—just about *every* time.

The 15-Minute Meeting That'll Save Your Business

"Annie, don't be so *sensitive!!!*" the voice on the other line barked at me.

My eyes grew wide. I grasped the arms of my office chair, trying to keep my composure and stay professional. *What can I say back that's calm, but firm?* I wondered.

At the time of this phone call, I'd been in business for five years and had never quite been yelled at that way—not in my business, nor in my career in Hollywood, a place notorious for screaming bosses. Would you believe that this happened during a meeting with a *prospective* client? It was in a contract review call and, needless to say, it wasn't going *well.*

Since 2017, I've mandated that any prospective client who wants to move forward do a 15-minute contract review meeting with me before we officially work together. In this brief Zoom call, I walk my prospective client through our project contract to go over general terms and policies for working together (how to submit feedback, etc.) and the critical importance of the project timeline to ensure our mutual success. *Everyone* has to do a contract review to book my services, even if they are my dad—actually, *especially* if they are my dad.

I began to require this meeting after learning how necessary it was. I'd spent years navigating bumpy, bad-fit client experiences that flabbergasted me. Almost all of the bumps related to things that I'd spelled out clearly in their contracts well in advance. Too often, I was putting out fires, debating whether to enforce policies, and fielding questions I'd already answered in the agreement up-front. *No, we can't do your business cards first; they come after the logo! Yes, I can do another revision, but that's subject to a revision rate.*

Every time an issue came up, I felt frustrated and like I had to be a cop if I were to say, "Per our contract" or "Per our agreement" in an email or a phone call. I swallowed moments when I was "right" and subsequently did a lot of unpaid work that my clients didn't even value, because they didn't think it was "extra" or "above and beyond." In the stress, I often wondered, wringing my hands and debating how to handle the latest bumpy road, *Did these people even* **read** *my contract!?*

No. The answer is no—no, they did not. How many contracts do *you* actually read? Read, not *skim*. See? There, exactly. Point proven. Most of us don't actually read the fine print of contracts.

So, I had a thought: If I were to have a brief contract review (say 15 minutes?), I could provide an opportunity in my process to improve communication with my soon-to-be official client. In these meetings, I go over general policies at a time when none of them are in play. This allows me to be more of a client's *partner,* rather than a policeman later.

That's exactly who I want to be: a partner. Contracts aren't perfect, but part of the reason why you should always have one is to communicate expectations and ensure as smooth a client experience as possible. Because now, rather than relying *(hoping! praying!)* that my clients read my thoughtful policies, the contract review meeting allows me to proactively communicate healthy boundaries about our work together. In effect, reviewing it ahead of time can stop problems for someone's client experience far before they start.

Having a contract review provides an important dialogue for both me and a prospective client. Even when I work with someone who knows me extremely well personally or someone who's a past client, always, without fail, a key question comes up during the contract review meeting. And that provides me a wonderful, necessary opportunity to clarify, respond, and generally ensure that my client knows exactly what they're getting, how they're getting it, and how we can most successfully work together.

While I was nervous to first implement this process *(who wants to add another meeting to their sales process, right?),* it's proven itself insanely valuable dozens of times through the years. This little meeting has helped me nearly always get paid on time. It has ensured that clients understand and are happy to pay for additional revisions if they'd like them. It keeps clients turning things around to me on time. And ultimately, it helps turn my clients into raving fans of our work together because I deliver what I say I will *when* I say I will.

Anytime a request for out-of-scope work comes up, I don't have to be a policeman. Instead I can be a partner because my clients already know my policies about how we can work together to their benefit. Any hiccup along the way becomes a conversation (rather than an *accusation*) because we started playing the game together by reading the rule book together *first* as part of the same team.

But don't people hate having to take time to review the contract? What about that person who screamed at you? Well, I've found that some of my best-fit, most ideal clients were those who have *loved* the contract meeting! They will often compliment me on my smooth working policies and say things like, "Ooo, I need that clause in *my* contract!" Moreover, of the clients I've wanted to work with, not a single one has objected to this meeting or not signed with me afterward.

With that in mind, let us return to the guy who screamed at me. He is a perfect example of why this 15-minute meeting is so very valuable! Our call together gave us one last chance to address any red flags on *both* sides before a deposit was exchanged. It's designed to help both me and my prospective client to do a gut check: "Yes, this is the right solution and partner for me" or "No, it's not." Sometimes the feeling is mutual; other times, like with the screaming dude, it's *not.*

You don't have to work with absolutely every client. In fact, if you want to protect your business, your brand, and your sanity, only work with those who know that you can "hit a home run" for. That guy who yelled at me? He was almost immediately annoyed by the formality of my contract and having to review it with me. He took issue with every single policy. He accused me of being very inflexible about my process.

And you know what? *He was right!* My process and policies definitely weren't a fit for him or what he wanted to accomplish in our work together. That's what I told him (repeatedly) in our 45-minute version of the intended 15-minute meeting: "It sounds like I may not be the ideal partner for your project, and I absolutely think you should work with a partner who fits your needs best." I meant it. Yet, with an emotionally abusive tone, this person wouldn't agree because he "really wanted to work with" me! So after being berated and having to keep my cool for the entire call, I hopped off without saying a direct *no.* I couldn't muster it then. However, I did say *no* firmly and kindly in an email the next day, in a format that felt safer and easier to communicate.

In this instance, the contract review call did exactly what I count on it to do each time: either solidify an amazing working relationship with a future client *or* repel a potential client who'd be a bad fit for my business. Both are valuable outcomes for me and that prospective client. Both are profitable outcomes.

Duke business school professor and author Dorie Clark wrote in her book *Entrepreneurial You,* "*Sometimes, to preserve your happiness, you have to say no to the money.*"[18] I'd add that sometimes to preserve *everyone's* happiness, you have to say no to the money. That *no* "cost" me several thousand dollars in new business. But it was the right *no* because it kept me happy, left my calendar free to work with better-fit clients, and ensured that I didn't spend four months working with a client who inevitably would've been disappointed, or worse.

Sometimes people aren't willing to admit that you're not the right fit for them and they will force you to be the one to say *no.* But being the one to say *no* isn't being inflexible, it's actually being wise. It's also being kind and genuinely having another person's best interests at heart. If you don't think you can hit it out of the park for someone, be transparent and straightforward about that. Though not a great feeling, it's way easier to disappoint someone before you've worked together than later, when money's been exchanged, work has been done, and everyone's upset.

So, opt for the latter, have thoughtful, smooth working policies in your contracts, and add a live Zoom or phone contract review if you don't have already do one. I know you'll love having fewer bad-fit clients and hearing how much your best-fit clients value this new, helpful step in your process.

Turn Brain Pickers into Clients

As tough as bad-fit clients are, I've also struggled with the "brain pickers." I bet you know exactly who I'm talking about.

I remember one day in 2016 when I'd just had it! I'd gotten home from yet another coffee that had turned into an unexpected, free "Let me pick your brain" session. A new financial advisor had invited me to meet for coffee. He didn't offer to pay, so I paid for us both to be generous. We sat down and I learned that he hadn't done any research on me. In my nature of wanting to be helpful, I proceeded to spend nearly an hour giving free advice (consulting!) on his new practice—including a great idea for an entire marketing system, informed by my years of profitable experience with a similar style. After we parted ways, I emailed him a "great to meet you" note, and—wouldn't you know it?—I never heard from him again.

Have you been there too? Do you dread getting that email with someone you know asking if they can "pick your brain?" Can they "take you to lunch" or "treat you to coffee" or "run something by you"?

Let's be real: Your time, experience, and expertise combined—they are worth far more than what coffee costs. But how can you say that *without* coming off like an entitled jerk to somebody? Is it *okay* to charge for your time like this? Are you really *that* much of an expert at this point? These are the questions that loomed over me for years, when, as a people-pleaser, I went to coffee after coffee, giving one-sided value and feeling unappreciated—all because I felt really uncomfortable and unable to say *no.*

But here's the irony: Everything changed when I started saying the other most profitable word in business: *yes!* A few years ago, I started to say, "Yes! I'd love to help you and give you the advice you need. In fact, I offer consulting sessions to do just that. Here's how to book yours!" That simple change, plus the advice I'm about to share with you here, helped me create and enforce a good boundary that's directly led to a five-figure revenue stream and 60+ happy coaching/consulting clients since 2017. Here's how you can also turn brain pickers into clients—and let go of the guilt along the way!

EXERCISE

Convert Brain Pickers into Clients in 2 Simple Steps

1. Create a one-hour, advice-oriented "Brain Picker Conversion Offer."
2. Confidently offer this service to your brain pickers (and prospective clients!) as desired.

That's it! To help you make it happen, here are a few of my best practices for steps 1 and 2, which I've honed over the years. Use these insights to craft your Brain Picker Conversion Offer and finally say goodbye to wasted time at coffees with people who don't value your awesomeness.

TIPS FOR STEP 1 (CREATING THE OFFER)

Choose to provide a service that's essentially an hour (or X minutes) of your time to "pick your brain." Here are four ways to optimize that service so it's not just "hiring you for an hour" but something that's very valuable to both you and your client.

- **Structure it:** Determine the exact length (if not 60 minutes), format (Zoom, phone call, in-person, etc.), terms, overall/common topics, price, and easy booking steps.
- **Brand it:** Rather than refer to your offer as a consulting, mentoring, or Q&A session, give it a branded name. For example, I've taken the same offer but renamed it and marketed it based on a popular topic. My "Rock Your 1st Book" session spoke to an overarching theme of writing, marketing, and publishing as an entrepreneur.
- **Add time-free value:** Brainstorm what you can add to your offer so it isn't just one hour with you—like providing a video recording, an action plan recap, or something else that doesn't take you a lot of time but elevates your client's experience.

- **Bundle it:** Consider clever ways to incentivize bigger investment in your offer, such as offering it ala carte or as a bundle at a savings. (I began offering three-packs of consulting sessions at a $150 savings, and doing so *doubled* my consulting income from the previous year!)

TIPS FOR STEP 2 (SELLING THE OFFER)

Once you've created this offer, you need to actually tell people about it—especially those who pop into your inbox or LinkedIn messages hoping to get your free advice. Keep the following best practices in mind when you get up the nerve to share your new service.

- **Believe in it:** Trust that an hour of *your* time is valuable; that's exactly why a person is asking for it in the first place!
- **Give them the opportunity:** Before you worry about offending someone, realize they might be happy to know the opportunity exists. That'll only happen *if* you tell them about it.
- **Practice "Yes, and . . . ":** When a person asks you for free advice, reply with *"Yes, and I'd love to help through one of my (sessions). It can help you do X, Y, and Z. Here's the link to book!"*
- **Respond to *nos* with alternate value:** If someone can't invest in your offer for whatever reason, offer another form of value that doesn't tax your time or devalue your expertise. This might look like sending links to blog posts you've written, providing a scholarship to one of your digital products, or offering to answer one key question via email.

—

Keep in mind that these are wonderful strategies to consider if advice-giving/guidance is *not* your primary source of revenue and you're looking for a streamlined way to pick up more opportunistic income from a variety of people hopping in your inbox. If advice-giving/guidance is typically your primary deliverable as a business (for example: you're a coach), you'll want to package that as a high-ticket (non-hourly) service priced at the top of your value ladder, a concept I share with you shortly. If you have some people asking you how to develop a business like yours, this brain picker conversion offer could be a great way to provide value without giving yours away.

Personally, after developing my Establish Yourself Framework and experiencing more demand, I've been offering my coaching/consulting advice as a high-ticket service in my business since 2021. Because of this, I have graduated from providing the more hourly focused offers that I once had.

What I've shared with you are excellent, proven practices to follow if you are in the boat of wanting to add an income-generating opportunity, especially if you don't currently sell any way for others to "pick your brain." Start now with two steps: designing your service and having the guts to offer it. With just this, you can protect your sanity and time, and possibly make more money and create more happy clients in the process. That's a win all around—both for you and the brain pickers.

THE STORY OF YOUR SUCCESS

OPERATIONS

Pricing and Profit

Being clear on what you want and establishing boundaries that serve you and your clients can continue to get you to new levels of your practice. Being similarly strategic about pricing and profit can take you sky high *if* you approach these tough areas with fresh eyes. From here, let's worry less about specific dollar signs and focus more on business money mindset, setting our work up to be profitable, and seeing ourselves and our services as needing to be valuable, not *reasonable.*

You're Not Unreasonable, You're Valuable

"Looking for someone to design my logo who is reasonably priced!"

"Recommendations for someone reasonably priced who does business coaching?"

"Hi everyone, I'm looking for a reasonably priced CPA for a startup in the area."

"Can anyone recommend a reasonably priced photographer to take a few headshots? Thanks!"

In every single Facebook networking group, you're bound to be bombarded daily with this term: ***reasonably priced.*** You may have even used it yourself from time to time. We all do. When we use it, we mean "I don't want to overpay for something. I'm on a budget."

However, I'd like to recommend that we outright retire this term, because it's toxic for growing your business and considering investment in other businesses. The phrase *reasonably priced* inherently implies that there are business owners out there who are *unreasonably* priced. It implies there are truly business owners who are unreasonable, and you may be one of them *if* you don't charge the lowest price possible.

Oxford Languages defines *unreasonable* as:

- "Not guided by or based on good sense"
- "Beyond the limits of acceptability or fairness."[19]

Now, the issue I have with this is that "beyond the limits of acceptability or fairness" is completely subjective. It's likely different for every person. If I were to ask 10 people what they think would be a reasonable price to pay for professional headshots, I'd likely get 10 different answers. Being reasonably priced is subjective. Too often, especially when people ask for recommendations online, it starts to mean "as cheap as possible." *That expectation* is what's really unreasonable and beyond the limits of acceptability or fairness to any of us.

I'm sure you've been there and felt what a gut-wrencher this can be. Perhaps you or your business is tagged in a post online, and before you can respond, the comments are 50+ deep with people vying for that one client or project! I call this the "race to the bottom." The comment thread on posts like these quickly gets so desperate and saturated sometimes that I often joke that I start to see graphic designers offer "Hey, not only will I do your logo for free, I'll pay *you* to do your logo!!"

Now, unfortunately it's easy to feel defeated by these exchanges. *Another* opportunity lost to the lowest bidder! But if you are the high-value coach or consultant I know you are, I want you to see clearly that these types of ponds are not your primary place to go fishing. They are an excellent place for people just starting out—working to get opportunities to test programs, build case studies, or add to their portfolio.

But these types of projects and clients aren't *your* best fits. Your ideal clients aren't looking for a "reasonable" recommendation. Rather, they are looking for a valuable solution to a big problem, and they will value *you* for solving it. It won't only be about the price tag. While we all get the occasional client from places like social media platforms, you are less likely to find these people searching for "reasonable" recommendations in a Facebook group.

It's helpful to consider why anyone chooses to use the term *reasonably priced*. Think about why you might use it. We choose it for reasons typically related to our own fears and insecurities. When we're looking to hire for something we can't do ourselves or are uncomfortable doing, we often begin that process feeling inherently vulnerable. We are unsure what we're going to pay for will ultimately pay off, so we're nervous about spending money and think the safest thing to do would be to spend as little as possible. We figure if we start where the price is "right," "less," or "affordable," we are exposing ourselves and our businesses to less risk. That can be true in some situations. So it feels like a good idea to go with or ask for what's or who is "reasonably priced."

But I'll tell you, I don't know many high-value, high-touch experts who pipe up personally in those 50+ comment chains on Facebook. The reason? They're often too busy running successful, profitable businesses to hang out and pitch themselves, constantly bidding for new business.

I don't have the time to nominate myself in a post shared by someone who is looking for a "reasonably priced" logo designer, website builder, or copywriter—though I do offer all of these branding services. Generally I'm too booked with client work and opportunities to be fishing in that pond. I don't have a lot of time for searching at all (nor do I like doing that) because my inbox and calendar are typically populated by prospective ideal-fit clients who've emailed or set consultations, seeking *me* out as a solution to their problem.

From time to time, past clients tag me on these types of Facebook posts, and I leave a brief, friendly link to my calendar to book a free consult—and then I don't worry about it anymore. I don't dwell on a lost opportunity the way I would have in the early days of my business. That's because I'm not focused on the feeding frenzy or trying to serve people who are nervous to take a risk on a bigger business investment. I recognize that some of them may not be the right fit for me—and if they are, they'll have a chat with me, and we can go from there.

I've found in growing my business, elevating my client experience, and attracting more and more of my ideal clients that not only is being "reasonable" subjective, but for the right people, pricing is much more married to value than you might realize.

Consider this: Four years ago, I had a free consultation once with someone who was interested in a brand voice guide. She asked me what the price was. When I quoted it, she laughed loudly—shocked. "Well, that's great that you can get clients to pay that!"

The price for a brand voice guide has increased more than 100% since that conversation. Of course, I've elevated the service, expanded it, and brought more experience to it. But with the new price tag it carries, I still easily book clients for the service who are ready and excited about it. In fact, I often have a several-week (sometimes months-long) waitlist for branding services in general, even though the investment has grown since someone literally laughed in my face about it.

Recently, I had a consult with a new client who barely registered the price when I told her about it, even though it was a lot more than it was four years ago. This new client came to me ready—thrilled to do a brand voice guide as her ideal solution. When I quoted the investment, she instantly raved to me, "See, *that's* affordable! If I went to the X Agency, it'd be $20,000 or $30,000! You're really freakin' affordable!"

From laughter to validation, value is in the eye of the wallet holder. If you steadily do the work of being clear, consistent, committed, and confident, you can raise your prices and your ideal clients will come to you—loving your work and ready to pay for the value you can give them.

In that first call I shared, that person wasn't my ideal client because she didn't value the service or me to provide it. She was struggling to grow her business and saw what I offered as a big expense. But what if she'd seen working with me as an investment, rather than an expense? What if she'd invested in learning from someone like me who had learned how to charge more than the bare minimum for their services, rather than being immediately skeptical? In any case, it's okay. I wished her well in her season of business. I know that she just wasn't my fish.

As you work to price yourself for value, you should know what a dear client of mine, Tim Barnes of Gazelle business management software, once taught me about a theory of pricing and selling. He shared that one-third of people always buy on price alone. Another third of people always buy based on quality and value. The last third? They buy on price for most things, except those things they most *value.*

As a coach or consultant with high-ticket services, it can be helpful to focus more on the latter two-thirds of *all* people. In the context of your primary ideal clients, people that fit this bill are *your* people. They are the ones who are ready and interested in valuing you and your solution, and there are more than enough of them out there to fill your practice. They aren't seeking reasonable solutions, but *valuable* ones. Where they are is where you should be fishing with your marketing, because those fish *are* your fish. Don't worry about the Facebook pond; that's a feeding frenzy and likely always will be. Feel free to stay busy and out of those waters.

Create a Value Ladder to Reach Your Goals

Striving to be valuable versus "reasonably priced" isn't just a mindset shift that can majorly benefit you, it's one that can benefit your clients, too. Keep in mind that you can be valuable at every level, and some of those levels can be more affordable than others. When you're a high-ticket, high-value expert, you can serve clients in various ways that connect to each other. You can do this through free content, less-expensive/less-time-intensive content like books and digital products, and your highest-touch/most-time-intensive services, each at different price points.

This approach can allow you to raise your prices for your services as you grow in experience, while still allowing for many ways to provide enormous value to those at *all* levels of emotional and financial readiness to invest in elements of your expert solution.

My favorite way to do this is by streamlining, simplifying, and structuring your services using a special type of "value ladder." In 1924, General Motors Chairman Alfred P. Sloan popularized the concept of a value ladder or "pricing ladder" when he introduced the idea of a "Ladder of Success," a model that gave the company a way to distinguish between its value cars and more luxury models. The concept empowered GM to develop five distinct car brands, offered at five different price points, marketed to five unique types of consumers across increasing levels of social status.[20] You know these brands today as Chevrolet, Pontiac, Oldsmobile, Buick, and Cadillac. As noted by *Harvard Business Review,* Sloan's "Ladder of Success" was described as a way to create "a car for every purse and purpose."[21]

Whether you call it a value ladder or a price ladder, the overall notion is that this tool can represent a curve of a customer's "willingness to pay" or "ability to invest" in relation to what your business offers. It showcases what's termed "good–better–best" pricing. You see this type of pricing every time you visit the gas pump and select regular, super, or premium. Similarly, as a client moves up a value ladder, both the value to them *and* the investment they make in it increase.

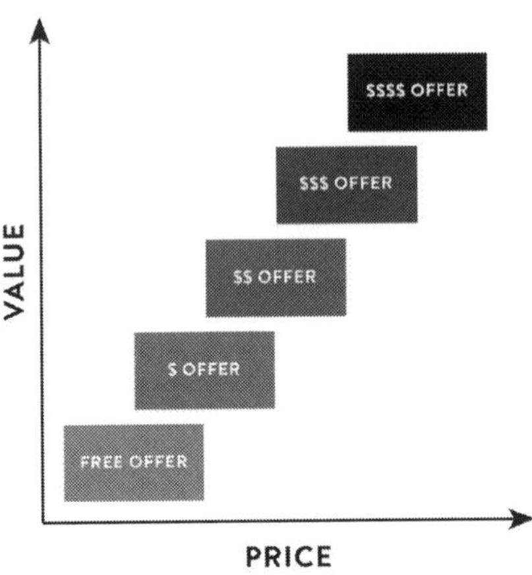

A basic value ladder illustration

As General Motors "every purse and purpose" suggests, many value ladder models today seem to be geared (pun intended) toward serving a wide variety of customers—each at a different price point. This makes a lot of sense if you're General Motors, and you have the money to fund whole teams and departments dedicated to branding, marketing, and selling to each kind of customer and each differentiated product.

But what if you're a coach who doesn't have an entire department at your disposal? What if the very thought of five or six different levels of clients and offers sends your head spinning, when you already feel overwhelmed by the business and marketing of it all?

You can't do all that, and I really don't want you to try. It's how many people with businesses like yours and mine burn out. Keep the crucial clarity you're finding about whom you serve and what you do for them. To make this concept way easier and simpler, let me introduce you to how I do this with my spin: the **Streamlined Service Value Ladder™.**

If you're a one-person-run (or -driven) business, you might love the notion of a Streamlined Service Value Ladder to organize your services.

The idea of a Streamlined Service Value Ladder is that each level, from *free* to your most expensive offer (maybe $5K, $10K, $15K or more), is:

- For the same ideal client (or company), *not* for several totally different ones.
- For a slimmed-down version of your highest offer, *not* wildly different offers.

So rather than for every purse and purpose, your Streamlined Service Value Ladder is for solely your *primary ideal client,* broken into offers to meet them at *every stage of their emotional and financial readiness to work with you!*

Each offer, whether it be $10, $100, or $1,000, should provide some valuable steps toward your most valuable (highest) solution. If you do this, you can take your highest solution and distill it down simply. Maybe the highest level is your most hands-on: the most time with you, the most resources, and so forth. Perhaps the middle level is 50% of the time with you, less resources, or a tighter area of focus. Maybe the lowest level is a one-time consulting session with you or even an e-book with strategies.

This is still "Good—Better—Best" pricing, but as I'm proposing it, it's not about a bunch of different consumers: It's more about meeting the *same* consumer, with the *same* problem, at different points of their emotional and/or financial readiness.

Several of Greatest Story Creative's offers/services shown in a Streamlined Service Value Ladder model (crafted for one ideal client at different levels of emotional and financial readiness)

As you see here, on a simplified version of my ladder that doesn't include my newly added Establish Yourself coaching/consulting programs or all of my free offers, the very top tier is the Brand Story Solution (my most hands-on, high-value service, in which I create your messaging, branding, and website). However, if you go further down, you can opt to just do the first and/or second steps (the brand story guide or the brand voice guide), for example. Further from there, I have an on-demand training on what I do for my clients (their brand strategy) so you can teach yourself. Still farther down is this very book to help you improve your brand, business, and marketing and start to solve part of the problem for yourself. *(I personally use a more detailed version of a ladder like this to provide big picture visibility to everything I offer and how it all fits together. It acts as an amazing business planning template.)*

Investing at any level doesn't preclude a client's opportunity to solve more of their crucial problem at a higher level later. The more urgent their problem and the more resources they can put on something essential to their business's or life's success, the higher they may opt to go. Making all of your services at every level solely for your primary ideal client—focused on the crucial problem overall—will allow you to wave a flag of awareness to them more clearly! *Hey, I'm here! I can solve your biggest problem.*

When you constantly drive awareness of providing a valuable solution to a crucial problem, you won't have to pitch yourself anymore or feel pressure to do fear-based marketing. Instead, interested clients will come to you already knowing they have a problem and looking to you for the solution. We want to focus on getting that flag in front of the people who have the biggest problem and can invest in the most valuable solution, or get on the road to doing that at some point. We expand more on this idea as we work on Step Three: Translate Your Value.

What's nice about using a Streamlined Service Value Ladder is the simplification and power you gain by not having to split your or your audience's attention. This way, you're most likely to capture those with the biggest problem and ability to invest in the valuable solution. And, if you meet people who fit your mold but are not fully ready to face their problem and/or can't yet afford the powerful solution you provide, you've thoughtfully crafted your value ladder to be ready for them—whenever and wherever they may be.

A Streamlined Service Value Ladder lets you focus on:

- Providing one valuable solution simplified and offered in five to eight ways *(varying in price point, relative to increasing value for investment).*

- One specific type of client *(your primary ideal client).*
- Highlighting awareness of the most crucial problem your ideal clients face *(the one they want to* **pay** *someone to help them solve).*

EXERCISE

Create Your Own Streamlined Service Value Ladder

Invest in my plug-and-play template and training in the Establish Yourself Vault at howtoestablishyourself.com, or build your own version.

No matter how you create it, here are a few of my best practices for a Streamline Service Value Ladder:

- Leave space for five to eight levels, including a free level *(for example, free, less than $100, less than $500, less than $1,000, etc.).*
- If you have ongoing clients and not projects, feel free to place solutions based on a yearly value *(for example, a virtual assistant whose clients pay $500/month would list that service at the level of $6,000, representing total yearly investment on their value ladder).*
- Your highest level should be your most expensive *and* highest-value service/solution to your client's most crucial problem.
- To create the other offers, simplify your operations, marketing, and life by taking that highest level offer and stripping it down to the other value levels. *What can you remove to make a $5,000 service cost $1,000—without compromising your value? Can you spend less time? Offer just the first step of three? Provide the same framework in a group setting versus a private one?*

- Until you're a well-oiled machine of a business that's growing as much as you'd like it to be, keep this simple:
    - Resist the urge to offer something at *every* single level.
    - Try to strive for just one or two things in a level. The point is to simplify and better utilize your time for both operations and marketing, *not to add a million programs or products that would split your focus.*
- Include your "Brain Picker Conversion Offer" (if you add one) at a middle or lower level.
- Offer sustainable value at your lower levels by offering a self-paced digital training, course, or product instead of live time with you.
- Include and plan for valuable introductory content that's free, like your newsletter, a podcast, or complimentary workshop series.
- Lastly, increase your pricing over time, as the value you provide grows. *You are more valuable to your clients than you were a year ago, and a year before that, especially if you've been investing in yourself (coaching, courses, etc.), gaining more experience, and making your solutions better as you go!*

—

When you develop a value ladder for your primary ideal client, it will empower you to brand, market, and sell yourself and your work, and give you a robust collection of tiered solutions. It allows you to market yourself without a team, tons of marketing dollars, and a lot of time wasted on social media. It also keeps you focused on offering only what you are *best* at doing and only the services/solution you most believe in.

When you truly believe in what you sell to people and/or organizations, selling becomes less icky and more about adding value. Moreover, the less you complicate your services and the more you envision them as the same thing, offered in varying degrees of value for investment, the easier it will be for you to deliver excellent client experiences and spend less time not just marketing your business, but also working in it.

As we dive deeper into client experience and referral relationships, your job can simply become to show up, be valuable, and consistently communicate who you help, what their crucial problem is, and what insanely valuable solution you offer to solve it. That's what it would mean to have your own ladder of success. You get to set up your business back end to be simplified, organized, and profitable—ready to help your primary ideal client, meet them where they are, and give them value, without sacrificing yours.

How to Serve Others Who Can't Afford You

Creating a Streamlined Service Value Ladder just for your primary ideal client can be an empowering business tool. It's another level of continued commitment you can make to serving those who need you most. As you may remember, a primary ideal client—one who you work incredibly hard to market yourself to and design your services for—can afford and wants to invest in your highest-value solution.

This said, I promised you that if you narrow your focus to a primary ideal client, you keep a lot of permission, too. You keep permission to help those who don't fit that paradigm and/or can't afford the price of your solution. If you opt to help such clients, to best protect your value and your time, let's look at ways to do that sustainably.

If you meet people you'd really love to help—those for whom your services are essential but who can't afford to work with you due to personal circumstances—that's okay. There are so many ways to still provide value *without* sacrificing your sustainability as a business and burning out.

To graciously help clients who can't afford your services, you might try:

- Offering sliding-scale pricing *(based on someone's income level or ability to pay).*
- Serving a specific number or percentage of clients a year on sliding-scale pricing or complimentary *(for example, providing complimentary coaching to three entrepreneurs a year or doing 20% of your annual projects at a non-profit organization rate).*
- Providing less-time-intensive options such as on-demand digital trainings or courses complimentary or at a discount (items that are lower on your ladder) *(protecting a valuable resource of yours [your time] while still helping someone).*

You could get specific and creative in the ways you'd like to help communities of people, too. For example, in 2020, in a commitment to provide value to the black entrepreneurial community, I mentored five black entrepreneurs in complimentary consulting sessions. The only requirement to apply for the opportunity was to be someone who needed business advice but felt they had barriers to getting it and/or affording it due to systemic racism and other factors. I didn't know this would happen, but this small program then inspired a local branding photographer to provide each of those business owners with complimentary brand photography shoots, which was kind of amazing! I've also done complimentary consulting for a woman business owner who, like me, has struggled with infertility. I've also given scholarships to my group workshops to ensure someone who didn't have the resources could get the help they needed.

Remember: Your value ladder and choice of ideal clients are ways you can deliberately choose to grow simply and strongly. You continue to stay in the driver's seat always. Any or all of the options I've suggested can allow you to still serve people you have a heart to help, without sacrificing your ability to grow and profit from the hard work you do in your business.

No matter what you decide here, don't invest your time, money, and resources in creating services for and marketing to clients who can't afford to work with you. While you can still serve them compassionately in these and other ways, you can't afford to keep your own doors open and keep offering value if you try to build your revenue from those who aren't able to sustain you right now. Choose to help them in ways that will keep you both going.

OPERATIONS

Systems, Strategy, and Support

Goals, boundaries, pricing—these are all intentional decisions that you can make to strengthen your practice. But what do you do when your business has grown as much as it can under you?

To get going or growing again, could more time, better processes, more perspective, or administrative support move that needle? Would streamlining your systems with apps or assistants help? As we round out our journey through operations, I invite you to consider the tools you could invest in to grow beyond what you can see today: the systems, strategy, and support you may need most to move forward.

The Freedom and Power of Smart Systems

For the first several years of my business, I hated the idea of having a process for pretty much anything. As a lifelong creative person, I've always valued flexibility. I love the opportunity to use my time however I'd like to create whatever I imagine and not feel "boxed in." For a long time, I attributed much of my success in school and my career to that kind of creative freedom.

When I became a business owner in 2013, to protect this value, I shied away from any specific ways of doing things because to do so felt antithetical to that principle. *If I set office hours,* I thought, *I have to work those hours. If I commit to doing it one way, I can't innovate and do it another way. Forget that!*

But I was 100% dead wrong. 100%. In fact, today I'd tell you that developing smart, strategic business systems for myself and others may be my favorite, most creatively satisfying work I do. Sometimes I imagine that I'd like to spend every workday doing this because I love systems so much. So how did that flip happen? What convinced me and won me over?

During my first Batch December sabbatical, I finally added some systems to my business. I recorded, revised, and realized every process I had—behind the scenes and client-facing. I asked myself, *What could be better? What could be simpler? What could be automated, delegated, or even removed?* Then I put those new processes into action!

I emerged from that month-long experiment and watched that intentional work pay off quickly and in spades. Not only did it help me grow my profitability exponentially, it even brought me *more* freedom and flexibility. It made every project easier to do because I knew what steps to follow to achieve the best results. That alone cleared my mind for other ideas and possibilities. My new office hours in my email signature sent a clear, friendly signal to all I connected with that I wasn't available at midnight for emails, so I stopped worrying about responding on the weekends. I was free. There was more room to breathe—and, ironically, to create! I was floored and hooked.

I've since systematized just about everything I can for Greatest Story Creative: from creating my newsletter content, to social media posts, to my sales process, referral process, client experience process, and beyond. Creating systems has allowed me to work less, make more, and hand off more things to support partners like my virtual assistant and design assistant. It's allowed me to provide smoother, more consistent, and better client experiences, outcomes, and results. And it's freed me—mind and body—to not work all the time and have regular days off, weeks off, and even that December month off to freely and flexibly work on whatever I'd like to!

I get the benefit of all of that from employing a simple concept: take what you do already, give it a smart shape with steps, and then just follow the steps. I've learned that's all a system or process in your business needs to be. Sometimes, it'll have nothing to do with an app, a consultant, or a VA. Sometimes it will. But you have the power right now to free yourself up for more growth and all it might take is paper and a pencil.

If you'd like to take me up on this, let's do it. Try out my process for creating smart systems in your business.

EXERCISE

Follow My 3-Step Process to Smarter Systems, Record/Revise/Realize

In my three-step record/revise/realize process for smarter systems, you first discover that you likely already have a process or "way" of doing things within your business, even if you're not very aware of it.

The secret and power lie in getting it out of your head and onto paper so you can see how you typically do things and where opportunities lie to make your existing process 10x or 100x better!

1. RECORD

Take five to 10 minutes in your *Establish Yourself Companion Workbook* or your notebook to brainstorm a list of all the things you "do" in your business.

Here are a few examples of what might be on this list:

- How I typically work with a client
- How a client books my services
- How I create estimates for clients
- How I set up a new offer or service
- How I answer email/manage my inbox
- How I network for my business
- How I handle business taxes
- How I create my social media marketing
- How I create or write content for my email list
- How I get people to join my email list

Now, select *one* of these things you do in your business.

With another five to 10 minutes, write out and ***record***, step-by-step, how that process in your business works today. Though maybe it's been different each time, try to think of the *best* time you've done it—the best client project, the best result—and then document each step you can remember that you took to make that thing in your business happen. Don't overthink for now—just document. You could even draw it out like a flowchart if you're a visual person. *(When I did this the very first time, I made a flowchart in Keynote for every type of client project I offered with arrows and everything! I'm a nerd.)*

2. REVISE

With this step-by-step list, take about 10 minutes to ***revise*** this one process!

Here are some questions you might consider to help you revise, tighten, strengthen, and streamline your process. Look for ways to save time for you and anyone else involved (like a client), make things easier on you and others, get better results, and automate.

- Do all the steps make sense?
- Are the steps in the right order?
- Can any steps be combined to save time and get better results?
- Should that meeting be an email? *(Probably!)*
- Are any steps unnecessary?
- Are any steps missing?
- Do *I* need to do all of these steps?
- Are there any steps that an assistant could do?
- Are there any steps that an app or tool could do automatically if it was set up?
- Are there any steps I could do ahead of time and/or once, then just repeat *(like email templates)?*

As you answer these questions, create a new version of the same process—this time, revamped and ready for the final step.

3. REALIZE

With just a paper and pen, you now have a way better process (or system!) for this common thing you do in your business. This last step is to ***realize*** that system—to put it into use!

With the changes you made, what do you need to do to be able to follow this process every single time? Do you need to write some email templates and save them? Do you need to hand over parts of this to someone like an assistant (or get one to help?)? In your last task in the process, make a list of what you need to do next to realize the power of your new system! *Repeat as you'd like, and here's hoping as you see the wonderful results of processes, you'll become a nerd about it like me!*

Scrappy to Strategic: Invest in You by Investing in Others

Another limiting belief I carried into my life as a business owner was that I had to do everything on my own. I come by it honestly as an only child and creative spirit who sought to win every writing award, scholarship, *trophy (!)*, and opportunity with my talent and persistence all on my own. This mindset was rewarded through high school, into college, and into my corporate career in Hollywood. Depending on just yourself can feel like a good plan. If it's all on your shoulders, it feels like you're not risking as much disappointment, right?

After becoming an entrepreneur in 2013, for many years I resisted any sort of professional help unless it was absolutely necessary. I thought, *I'm creative, I'm capable, and I can and should do as much on my own, as cheaply as possible. Scrappiness is valued by society, and I can make just about anything happen.*

Looking back now, I think there was a lot of fear underscoring this mindset, too. If you identify with some of the reasons why I resisted investing in consultants and other help, maybe you also feel these.

When I was trying to do it all and grow with just my own wits about me, I was afraid of many things and masking it as "confidence in my skill sets." I worried about wasting money and not having enough to contribute to our savings. I was concerned about trusting others and being let down. I was worried about not being "perfect" in my own eyes and especially in the eyes of clients. I felt doubt about my abilities and felt concerned about hiring someone who did what I did, as that might admit that I was, in fact, not perfect.

But here's the kicker: Much like I experienced with the freedom revolution systems brought me, so too I've become an advocate and avid practitioner of hiring professionals to help me grow my business. Why? I finally got up the guts to start doing it, saw results, and have since completely shifted my perspective about it.

As you already know, I'm big on profitability and tracking your time, expenses, and income. I want to make money for my time and work as little as possible, and I want that for you. Old "business me" thought that hiring a scaling coach or having a branded video created were expenses that would threaten those goals.

I've found the opposite to be true. Now, when I have had crucial clarity about what I wanted or needed in my business, and recognized that I can't do that thing well, don't have time to do that thing, or have already done as much as I could on my own, I hire the best person or company to help. I invest in a valuable solution (just like the solution I want you to offer to others!). It is a risk. It does take thoughtfulness and strategy to identify what you need and who the right person or project is—but when you do, it can really pay off. Even with pros that haven't worked out perfectly, I've still grown both financially and emotionally from the experience. Having jumped in and hired at least one expert a year since 2015, I have grown in my passion for investing in professional perspective and have seen my bottom-line growth increase as I do more and more of it.

Does this mean that every expert or expert solution has had a direct X% financial return on investment? No. Not everything does or will. It means I've grown as a business owner and the business has grown overall the more that I've asked for the right professional help or invested in professional solutions—versus cobbling together all that fabulous, free advice on the internet.

It has paid off. Investing in experts has helped me more than triple my annual revenue. To date, my business has grown year over year the *more* that I've hired professionals, and in total, has grown more than 350% from 2014 (the last year I did everything on my own).

To bring this to life, here's an example. In 2020, I invested in a scaling coach to take a fresh-eyed look at my business. After three hours with her, I was able to implement changes later that year that easily brought in tens of thousands of dollars into the business *without* a ton of work that would have normally been associated with that income. The result? In that year, I had my *best* year financially to that point despite me personally working less than ever before (and doing so in a year when the world was in crisis). When I celebrated that achievement, I knew it definitely couldn't have happened without this kind of insight.

I continue to find that making such investments keeps me accountable and helps me to see strategies that I'm not able to see on my own. They allow me to gain more "time" and provide valuable community to keep me going through all the peaks and valleys.

Here's a window into my business investment timeline and the types of professionals and valuable solutions that have moved the needle for me personally—even as someone who can and does do her own branding and marketing.

YEAR	INVESTMENT IN EXPERTS/EXPERT SOLUTIONS
2013	No experts or expert solutions
2014	No experts or expert solutions
2015	Professional headshots/one-day brand photoshoot Design business online course Website design online course
2016	Sales coaching (with Adele Michal) Brand videography
2017	Sales coaching Marketing consulting Virtual assistant (1-2 hours/month)
2018	(My first book, *Permission to Try*, was released in October 2018) Book editor and proofreader Book publishing consultant Audiobook production Trademark lawyer Virtual assistant (4-5 hours/month)
2019	Business and maternity leave mentoring Virtual assistant (4-5 hours/month)
2020	*Post-maternity leave* Productivity consulting Scaling coaching Trademark lawyer Virtual assistant and operations consulting (20 hours/month) Design assistant (10-12 hours/month)
2021	CliftonStrengths coaching Scaling coaching Business growth mastermind Book editor and proofreader *(for this book)* Virtual assistant and operations consulting (20 hours/month) Design assistant (10-12 hours/month) Brand and book photoshoot Brand and book videoshoot

Notice that while I don't have a team, I have hired and still use both a virtual assistant and a design assistant. Shortly, I dive into delegating and how I finally figured out *my* way of doing it.

From her experience working with more than 150 business owners, pricing expert Natalie Coombe has observed that the average running costs for a solopreneur service businesses range between $20,000 and 80,000 per year (excluding taxes). She's seen many coaches and consultants struggle not because they're spending *too* much on business investment/expenses, but not *enough!*[22] For example, if you're on the lower end of that range or below that $20,000 threshold, you could be under-investing—not getting the important resources you'd need to grow or scale what you're doing into a healthy, profitable business. In that scenario, ironically, under-investing may be part of what's keeping you where you are.

As you consider this, I invite you to think about and write notes on *who* or *what* you may need this year. Who or what can help you break past where you are? What would that help be worth to you? Your return on investment might be confidence, clarity, income, profit, joy, balance, professionalism, or some combination of all of these wonderful things. Like your definition of your greatest business, you get to decide what would be game-changing for you.

Of course, there are very valid life and business reasons to wait on investing in a person or a project you need. For me, from 2015 to 2019, my husband and I weathered an unbelievably expensive season in our lives while we navigated infertility and he was a full-time graduate student. Infertility treatment, as you may know, can feel like you're constantly signing blank checks in hopes that they'll change your future. Every investment I made in that time, including writing my first book and the several thousand dollars it cost to self-publish, had to be made carefully and strategically.

There's so much to consider about investing in others to grow your business and yourself. However, always pay attention to what's stopping you. Is it other life priorities or needs? Is it fear? Is it worry that you have to do it all yourself? Is it coming from inexperience with taking leaps? If you're getting stuck around some emotional or limiting beliefs, trust yourself to take manageable risks. I spent too much time worried about such risks but didn't spend much time at all thinking about the worthwhile rewards of them.

If you need to walk before you can run on anything, take just a first step. Set that free consultation with the person or project you're thinking about. If they have a high-value, high-investment solution but you're not sure or not ready, ask if you can hire them for an hour or if they do consulting. Think of them as investment and a valuable partner, and they'll propose ways to help you if they're awesome. Maybe trying this out can help you manage that risk a little better, get started, and get some momentum going. Here's hoping to you find the right people and projects that'll help you grow whoever you want to go from here.

Assistants: How I Learned to Love to Delegate

While hiring consultants and investing in expert solutions was something I resisted for many years, an enormous block for me within that was handing off the administrative details: all the things I *could* do myself. I started my business wearing absolutely every hat, from bookkeeper to CEO. While being a business owner undoubtedly will always require many hats, just two years ago I finally learned the hats that would be better worn by others as investments.

Much like my mindset around investing in experts, I had a lot of fear around delegating and giving over control of even the smallest tasks to someone like a virtual assistant or a design assistant. I worried about the cost and saw it as an expense—rather than an investment—and I worried about what might happen if things changed, or people left or made mistakes. *Would it cost me clients? Would my job turn into managing people rather than being creative? I have no interest in managing people—and how would I even do that if I wanted to? Won't it take too much time to delegate it? I should just do it myself!* These worries had me holding a lot close to my chest.

In fact, up until June 2020, I did the large majority of administrative work in my business on my own, even though I'd had a virtual assistant doing a couple things a month for years. Even while I started regularly investing in things like brand photography, videography, and business coaches and consultants in areas where I needed to grow, I avoided delegating. I was hesitant to hand anything significant over for the first six years of my business.

It ultimately took something more powerful than my hesitancy to move past it: the life-changing arrival of my first child, Leo. This joyful lion cub arrived in January 2020. A few months later, the pandemic gripped the United States and a lockdown began in March 2020. I was planning to return from mat leave on April 1st, but then, suddenly, like for all of us, my plans dramatically changed.

Our plan to put Leo in daycare was completely thrown out the window! My husband, Gus, and I began splitting our days into two-hour chunks and passed that beautiful baby between us all day long. Time—the thing I always had such great control over through tracking and time management—was suddenly my most valuable commodity, and it was *tight.*

With my time shrinking, the financial pressure was on. This all came at the height of a very expensive personal season in June 2020: Leo's birth medical expenses were due, Gus's grad school tuition bill came, and I was still earning the only household income—two months into reopening my business during a global crisis after having been closed for a four-month leave.

For me, it took these two factors to see the light: I needed help if I was going to be able to work less and make more. Little did I know, this challenge would yield a profitable growth lesson for me—not only how to delegate, but how to love what delegating can do for my life and business.

During summer 2020, I finally faced down the worries I had about delegating and learned the reality of it. I went from using my virtual assistant, Sarah, for just a few hours each month to using her between 20 and 40 hours a month. I hired my design assistant, Amanda, for flat-rate help with things that were time-consuming, like exporting files. She began helping me about 10–12 hours a month. After reviewing the numbers a month later, not only did I have my best month in business ever, I realized that by trusting others to help me, I gained incredible partners *and* I got my valuable time back.

Here are the worries I was able to put to rest about delegating:

***Worry:* How could I delegate anything? I don't know how to really train anybody in what I do, and I definitely don't have time to do it!**

Getting past this sort of happened by accident, at a moment when I just couldn't be the polished pro I wanted to be. With the pressure on, I decided to start meeting with my virtual assistant once a week instead of just emailing her perfectly organized projects. In that first meeting that summer, I was so overwhelmed. I showed up not knowing what I'd even discuss. That was really uncomfortable for me. In the past, I'd spend time carefully organizing a process for Sarah to do or follow, putting together a thoughtful email, and so on. It took time but helped me to feel that I was "delegating well."

But I hadn't done that this time. I showed up a mess. I told Sarah I had no idea what we should look at, and then something magical happened. This gave Sarah an opportunity to do what she does best: organize. I spent that hour together updating Sarah on everything going on—giving myself permission to not have it "perfectly tied in a bow" and realizing she was interested and able to take on a lot of it. The next week, we did it again, and again. We got into a monthly rhythm, I got things off my plate, projects moved forward, and I got my time back. *Was this really delegating?*

Soon after, when Sarah invested in branding her virtual assistant practice, we nicknamed these sessions "Sort it Out with Sarah" ("SOS"). They continue to this day. Now, I show up (sometimes still a mess, unclear on what to do next) and Sarah helps me sort it out. And more than sort it out, by asking for her perspective, I've also gained an incredible expert who doubles as my ideal client! Sarah is an operations genius with a great mind for process. My "SOS" sessions are often half taking tasks off my plate and half getting her feedback and advice on things. *(Side note: If you want more feedback from your ideal clients, hire them as consultants to review your stuff! It's gold!)*

Now, I've worked with Sarah since 2017—but I only tapped into Sarah's incredible value in 2020, and that's thanks to allowing myself to be less polished and prepared. It's thanks to acknowledging that I can't do it all, asking for help, and giving myself permission to ask for help in the ways that feel natural and easy for my time. For me, a Zoom call is far easier than writing an email, for example.

I'll also say that beyond trusting Sarah to *help* me delegate, something else that really helped was a tip I learned from health and productivity expert Marcey Rader of Rader Co. During a speakers' networking meeting, Marcey once shared that when she needs to hand something off to her assistant, she shoots a quick screenshare video walking through her need or the process by which she needs something done. This totally blew my mind. It never occurred to me that I could train someone using video! I'm so much faster on video than writing. It has been a total game-changer.

Making regular dates with my VA and giving myself permission not to be so polished when asking for help really opened up delegating to me as a huge opportunity. To recap how I've overcome this worry, here are some of my favorite ways to get stuff of my plate! Feel free to swipe whatever inspires you.

My favorite ways to delegate:

- Holding regular one-hour meetings with my VA (1 time per week)
- Keeping a shared agenda document between my VA and me to track ongoing projects
- Emailing my VA something I'm thinking about in the subject line with "add to the agenda" (she then adds it

to the shared document and we discuss it at our next touch-base meeting)

- Recording screenshare videos to show how I need something done, updated, or corrected
- Creating a system or process once with templates, recording a video to talk through it, then passing it on to be repeated by my VA or someone else
- Embracing a mindset that I don't have to have all the answers
- Treating my VA and other support professionals as the valuable experts they are and as thinking partners: asking for their professional perspective, including on how to do things and how best to prioritize them

Worry: I'm not ready to hire a team! That would be too much commitment.

For a long time, I didn't realize that I didn't have to think of hiring support as everything or nothing proposition. And when I began thinking about what I needed, contractor help made more sense than an employee. With contractors like my VA and design assistant, I've been able to try things out.

Sarah and I did a first project together to see if it was a fit. My design assistant, Amanda, and I did an initial project or two to feel it out, and have since added more services as we've gotten to know each other. In both cases, I needed to test things out to feel comfortable, but both have turned into wonderful relationships, both personally and professionally.

The creativity that you have when you work with contractors in particular is that they're also business owners and may not want or need a long commitment. They want to have a great working relationship as much as you do, and that takes time to establish.

To practice this, you can always start with an initial project or a certain number of days you want to treat as a trial period before committing to a longer-term relationship.

Worry: But how would I even go about hiring someone? Do I need to post a job? Interview people? Sounds like a ton of work.

As much as I resisted having any help, I really felt nervous about handing over any piece of my design work. To me, that's such an intrinsic part of what I do for a client's branding and I worried about trusting anyone to be involved in that, even behind the scenes.

But in 2020, I was pushed to do it and am glad I was. To hire a design assistant, rather than stress about job listings and searching, I felt it out simply by asking a handful of women business owners who I really admired. *Hey, do you know anyone who does graphic design whom you really trust?*

This led me to Amanda and her awesomeness. A Zoom call later, we signed a subcontracting agreement. A month or two later, she was handling *all* of my design exporting. A month after that she was helping me start logo projects, develop icons, and more. Now that I have a design assistant, I can't really remember (nor do I want to) how I was doing it all myself before! Pretty amazing for a simple step of asking my trusted network, *"Hey, who do you know who's fantastic?"*

Worry: But I have zero interest in managing a team! I don't want to be somebody's boss.

Well, this has really been an eye-opener for me. For years, the largest piece that's had me thinking I don't want to have help—not even a VA or design assistant—is because I didn't want to be anybody's boss. I was afraid that, if I delegated, my job would need to become about managing those people rather than the creative, energizing work I love to do.

I was wrong about this. In fact, ironically, delegating has given me more time to do that creative, energizing work. It's also made that work *better.* The business I have now is unbelievably better with Sarah's eyes on it and support behind it. My branding work is better with another designer's perspective, efficiency, and turnaround time. I sleep better knowing I'm not the only person making Greatest Story great, and I'm relieved I don't have to do it all (even though I once thought I could and should).

In 2020, I got my biggest monthly invoice from Sarah ever. It was 40 hours in one month. I took one look at it and felt only gratitude. That was 40 hours of work that needed to be done in my business that *I* didn't have to do. It was 40 hours of value that was provided while I rested, while I pushed other things forward, while I used my genius more, and while I reveled in baby laughter and walks as a family. It was 40 hours well spent in so many ways.

—

If I have one regret about delegating and using it to grow it's that I didn't know its promise sooner. Had I known the freedom, joy, friendship, partnership, and business bottom-line growth it would give me earlier, I would have been doing it many years ago.

As they often say, better late than never. If you have been on the fence to ask for supportive help, do it. If you have pros on your team but you're wondering if you could hand more to them or get more perspective from them, ask. Do what I ultimately had to do: give yourself permission to not be perfect or have all the answers. Raise your hand and invest in yourself by investing in others—especially those who can handle those important, life-giving, business-growing details. You can sort it out. If I can finally hand things over, you can too.

The Business-Changing Magic of Tools and Apps

In shaping your business, we've talked a lot about the value of systems. They are processes that can make your business easier to run and can come to life through your work, the help of professionals, and even the ever-growing world of online tools and apps. For a long time, I didn't realize that these tools *aren't* systems themselves. No, they are literally just tools. They are only as useful or good as the strategic process you've thought through and put into place to use them. When you start with the strategy, as we did in this section, you can confidently not waste money on a million different tools *(there are so many out there!)* and, instead, invest in the ones that really will save you time and headache, delight clients, and keep your business running 24/7/365. Remember that you can also do free trials (or just one month's subscription) and you can also try tools/apps one at a time to see what works best for you.

Since streamlining my own processes and systematizing so much of my business, I've figured out the top tools that have become essential to growing my business. I invest in them and don't think of them as expenses. Rather, the tools I use are investments that save me money and help me grow my revenue, while improving the quality of my client experiences.

I don't have every tool, but what I do have, have become essential and well-worth paying for to ensure and grow *my* greatest business. In this section, I break down the types of tools that are most useful to me currently. As you review them, feel free to circle the types of tools that intrigue you and may offer value (if you don't have them yet). Please note that I've skipped over obvious things like business email and have shared some unexpected things that you may not have imagined can be needle movers.

SCHEDULING

When I moved from scheduling meetings manually to using a link provided by a paid scheduling tool, I got six hours or more of time back every single week. *Every* week. A scheduling tool allows me to set availability for different types of meetings, charge for hourly consulting, and schedule and reschedule meetings with a click; and it cuts the back and forth of scheduling emails with clients, prospective clients, and partners down to next to nothing. While I could have handed this off to my VA, instead, for less than $20 a month, I have a powerhouse ability to save myself time, get paid for my expertise, and keep my time efficiently organized. It's absolutely brilliant.

Currently using a paid tool: Acuity Scheduling

INVOICING, PAYMENTS, BOOKKEEPING, AND ONLINE CONTRACT SIGNING

Knowing your numbers and getting paid are essential to profitability. Having the ability to quickly and easily invoice clients or charge for simple templates, trainings, and more is empowering. I feel confident and professional when I can invoice and trust that the numbers are adding up with my bookkeeping. Same goes for having a contract-signing software—being able to set good boundaries and set up projects with confidence through secure, easy online signing is essential to my growth.

Currently using a free tool: Wave Apps (for invoicing, payments, and bookkeeping), HelloSign (contracts)

TIME TRACKING

As you spotted, I've dedicated an entire story in this book to how much I learn from and value time tracking! Having a software that's available on my desktop computer at virtually all times helps me easily track times, assign them to client projects or my own projects, and run reports. It's epic—and it's free!

Currently using a free tool: Toggl

TO-DO LIST

Over the years, I've kept a paper and pen to-do list for daily things and used my Google calendar to schedule overall work. In late 2020, I discovered an incredible tool that lets me do both:

have a daily to do list *and* schedule tasks for lots of ongoing work. I leave my to-do list tool up on my computer all day, along with my time-tracker app. I also use it to track session use for consulting clients, house notes for various projects, and make templates for work I repeat (so I can easily duplicate it into my daily to-do list). It's a huge time-saver that's also cleaned up my calendar so it's not constantly covered in time blocks for projects.

Currently using a free tool: ClickUp

WEBSITE/PROJECT MANAGEMENT HOME BASE

My website isn't just an amazing 24/7 marketing tool for me, it's also a business tool for providing high-quality, seamless client experiences. I create a private page for each of my clients as a "client home base" or portal. My VA can set this up and update it with links to their contracts, invoices, files, and more. It functions as client communication as well, so everybody knows that clear next step.

Currently using a paid tool: Squarespace

VIRTUAL MEETING PLATFORM

During the pandemic, nearly everyone began meeting online and discovered an app called Zoom. I was lucky for meeting Adele in 2016: She first introduced me to that now-household name! Yep, I was—and still am—on Zoom before it was cool. Having a robust, reliable virtual meeting tool has been critically important to growing my business, especially with building relationships without in-person meetings and sharing visual deliverables like logos and branding. It's also wonderful to be able to record meetings or workshops and then provide that recording as additional value with very little additional time involved on my end. That allows my consulting and trainings to become that much more profitable. I'm consistently amazed that I've had two of my best years ever in business without ever having a single in-person client meeting. Technology really is amazing!

Currently using a paid tool: Zoom

TEXT SHORTCUTS AND EMAIL TEMPLATES

I'll be forever thankful to speaker and podcast host Hank Hoffmeier, who first introduced me to the dazzling kind of software that is TextExpander. A type of productivity app, TextExpander and tools like it can allow you to create a database of shortcut keystrokes for *all* of those things you're constantly typing out. So instead of writing my whole welcome email to a client, I can literally write #welcome, and the entire thing magically fills my screen. Instead of typing out my website address every time, I can just enter .web and—poof—the whole string appears in my browser!

I use TextExpander multiple times a day to bring a huge amount of consistency to my practice, with nearly every type of project email and process email saved as a shortcut. I can drop my speaker's biography into any presentation proposal in fewer than five seconds. I can send scheduling links quickly for any type of meeting without having to open that tool and copy that specific link.

I can even use it to enter long technical confirmation codes to try to get concert tickets quickly! What a bonus. Perhaps even more than my scheduling tool does, my text shortcut software saves me countless hours a year, frees up my brain, *and* creates smooth, consistent experiences for clients and partners without a thought from me beyond that first time I set up a shortcut. It's automatic magic at its best, and if you don't have something like this, scope it out! #Awesome

Currently using a paid tool: TextExpander

SOCIAL MEDIA POSTING AND SCHEDULING

Last but not least, the tool that allows me to barely touch or work on my social media posts every year, yet still have consistently weekly content, is a total hero. After years of agonizing about what to post daily, I stopped being so scrappy, spent an afternoon or two batch designing and developing some on-brand content, and paid to put it into a social media posting and scheduling tool.

My tool is so smart, I can drop graphic or text posts into categories, create a weekly posting plan for those categories on different platforms like Facebook and LinkedIn, then allow the tool to do the posting *for me!* It'll even run the posts three times, in order, before they expire. So 52 quote posts? Those could run 1–52 and not repeat for a year! And they'd run for three full years if I never touched them.

Even better, I can create templates, delegate the content to my VA, and have *her* put them into the tool for me. For just about $20/a month, I get to enjoy social media consistency and engagement and only have to create new content every year to 18 months—not every day. And really, I get to stop worrying about it.

As I share more about this consistency container Step Tree: Translate Your Value, often social media is so not worth worrying about. Spending time on it, as I used to, was expensive given all the other things I could be doing with that time instead, like consulting for clients! I'm so glad a smart app and some pre-planning can take it off my plate. I love to help other entrepreneurs realize they can do the same for social, depending on their business model.

Currently using a paid tool: SmarterQueue

—

While I use many other apps and tools to streamline or automate parts of my business, these are the biggest, most needle-moving categories for me. And I'd love for you to have visibility to *everything* I'm currently using.

Since this is a book and technology is rapidly evolving as I type, I've intentionally generalized the type of tool first. From here, you are invited to download a free PDF listing *all* of the tools I currently use in my business today when you're reading this (assuming the internet is still a thing, of course!).

FREE RESOURCE

See All My Current Tools

Get your copy of **My Current Tools** at greateststorycreative.com/tools, or see the link in your *Establish Yourself Companion Workbook.*

Your Business, Not Theirs: Hold Tight to Your Goals

She leaned across the table and challenged me, "Don't you want to make a million dollars?!"

Well, yeah, sure. Who doesn't?

I was at a networking lunch with a well-connected, fast-paced business owner. This woman had built (and sold!) multi-million-dollar companies, had a great reputation, and was passionate about her work. I'd just shared with her my goals for growing my business—specifically how (at the time) I wanted to have the business just be me and wasn't looking to hire or scale, at least in the traditional or startup sense.

Her reply to me was "Don't you want to make a million dollars?" Well, I did—and I do, to be clear!—because again, *who doesn't?* However, it's *my* business and *my* vision for it. The impression she gave was that my vision wasn't good enough or big enough to her. But hey, that's okay. It's big enough for *me.*

Following are snippets of other conversations that I've had over the years in which others have pushed back on my goals, choices, and business vision.

> With a brand-new connection during a 1:1 phone call: *"The problem with your business is the constant churn of clients."*
>
> I'm sorry—did I tell you there was a problem with my business?

With friends when I decided to go full-time in my business: *"Are you sure you couldn't just do both a job and the business at the same time?"*

Yep, that wasn't for me either.

Here's the thing. Currently, I'm not trying to become the next Sara Blakely, the CEO of SPANX, a multi-million-dollar company she sold after growing it from nothing and a little red backpack, though she's incredible. In business, I'm trying to be the best *me*. I don't want a ton of employees. I don't want to be a "CEO" and have my job be about growing a business rather than working directly with clients. I have no interest in raising and/or risking thousands if not millions of dollars in capital to grow a multi-million-dollar enterprise. And no, Aunt So-and-So, I'm not trying to get on *Shark Tank.*

What I *am* doing is shaping and scaling my business in *my* way—figuring out what it means for me to be able to work less, make more, and continue to love what I do right now. Whether you want your business to make a million dollars or ten thousand dollars, both are valid. Your goals are your choice, as is what you do, what you don't do, who you serve in terms of ideal clients—and who you don't. It may even be the number of clients. You don't *need* millions of followers to work with you when you can only take 15 clients a year, right?

When you've spent the time to clearly define these things like your boundaries and goals, then making them reality with systems, strategy, and support comes down to practicing *courageous* confidence. Because as long as you're in business, others will be in the business of telling you what's *what*: why you should make more money, or offer such service, or change your model . . . but it's not their business, it's yours. It's your name on the marquee, on the invoice, and on the expenses you pay to keep it running.

That's the beauty of it. Hold firm. Hold tight to your boundaries and what you believe in, especially as we turn next to the more front-and-center work of sales and client experience. With Step Two: Shape Your Business in mind, keep to the goals you're setting for yourself, the processes you're creating, the professionals you're asking for help, and the things you value most. You're in business to make it *yours,* and that vision doesn't belong to anyone but you!

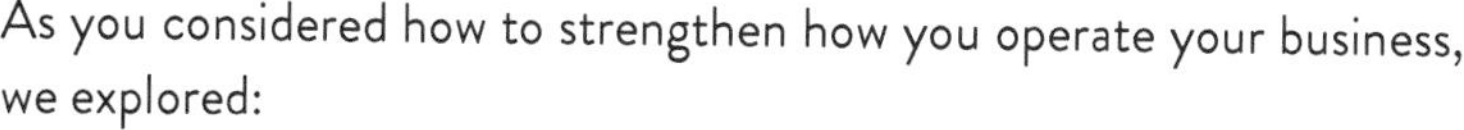

YOUR OPERATIONS "KEY C" CHECK

As you considered how to strengthen how you operate your business, we explored:

- Setting clear, confident goals, and making decisions.
- Tracking your time, sales, and clients to work less and make more.
- The profitable words of *yes* and *no.*
- Wendy's Will of Rights.
- Navigating bad-fit clients, boundaries, and contract reviews.
- How to turn brain pickers into clients.
- Adopting a valuable, not "reasonable," perspective on pricing.
- Developing your Simplified Service Value Ladder.
- The record/revise/realize process to create smarter systems.
- When to invest in professionals, support, and tools.
- Holding tight to your boundaries, goals, and business vision.

With these aspects in mind, take 10–15 minutes to reflect on and answer the questions here in the book, in your *Establish Yourself Companion Workbook*, or in your own notebook. Though these questions are intended to help you find clarity about what feels uncertain, the very first question will allow you to give yourself much-deserved credit! You're on your way.

WHAT'S WORKING

What's *one* thing you're really proud of in terms of how you run your business behind the scenes?

COURAGEOUS CONFIDENCE

What's *one* thing you wish you had more courage and confidence about?

CRUCIAL CLARITY

What's *one* thing you need more focus and clarity on?

CONSCIOUS CONSISTENCY

What's *one* thing you need more consistency with?

CONTINUED COMMITMENT

What's *one* thing you want to commit more to in terms of how you're running your business?

Now, which *one* of the these things feels most urgent to you?
List that one in the form of an action step here.

MY MOST VALUABLE ACTION STEP FOR **OPERATIONS:**

For this step, **are there any professionals and/or tools you may need to make that top action step happen?** *List your thoughts on this here.*

STEP THREE

Translate Your Value

In my own sales process, when I do a branding proposal for a client I always explain the first step of their project (the "getting your story" phase) as being an important moment. It begins with a famous questionnaire I've honed over the years that clients have called their "favorite, not-so-favorite" part of the process because it requires so much deep thought and reflection, and yields powerful insights that inform their branding and businesses.

I'm always careful to explain why I do this and why I ask so many questions. The reason is that, unlike a lot of marketing agencies, I'm not here to "invent" anything about you. Rather, I'm here to listen and ***translate***—to shine a light on what makes *you* great, so your ideal clients don't miss those things. I do that work for my clients by writing their clear marketing messaging and creating consistent visual branding (translating their value into confident brand tools).

To translate comes from the Latin word *translat,* which means "carried across."[23] To translate is to communicate—to bridge divides and bring people together who literally don't speak the same language. With branding or marketing, the right words, visuals, positioning—these things can translate what's incredible about you and your business into "language" that your ideal clients can take notice of, understand, and connect with.

That's why the third step in the Establish Yourself Framework is to translate your value. This is the value you provide to your clients that has the ability to change their businesses, their lives, or both. In the first step of the framework (embrace your story), you work to *define* your amazing value about you through self-confidence and branding. In the second step (shape your business), as you just discovered, you learn how to *protect* that value through smart systems, boundaries, and support. Now, you are ready to turn your attention to the magical step that brings your value to others: *communication* (translate your value.)

In this third and final step, I share my best practices with you across the four remaining essential areas of business: sales, client experience, referral relationships, and marketing. We move specifically in that order of reverse revenue, as we work from the people you're already working with, or are about to work with, to smartly strengthening business relationships that drive referrals, and finally to high-quality marketing practices to attract both new people and those already living in your world of influence.

Some books that cover marketing might only tell you to focus on your email list or start a podcast. While those things have their place, there can be so much more to effectively marketing your business—especially if you want to do it in authentic, more natural ways that center on value.

For these reasons, along the way, I show you how to sell with confidence, create more raving fans and repeat clients, refine your messaging, clearly communicate what you do to referral partners, and consistently market yourself well without wasting your time.

Ultimately, your greatest business will come down to translating your value every chance you get. Because if you've done the work to define your value and protect it, then communicating it well becomes your opportunity to close more sales, gain better clients, stop worrying about social media, make more profit with less effort, and love what you do more than ever before! With that, let's translate your value.

ESTABLISH
YOURSELF

Sales and Client Experience

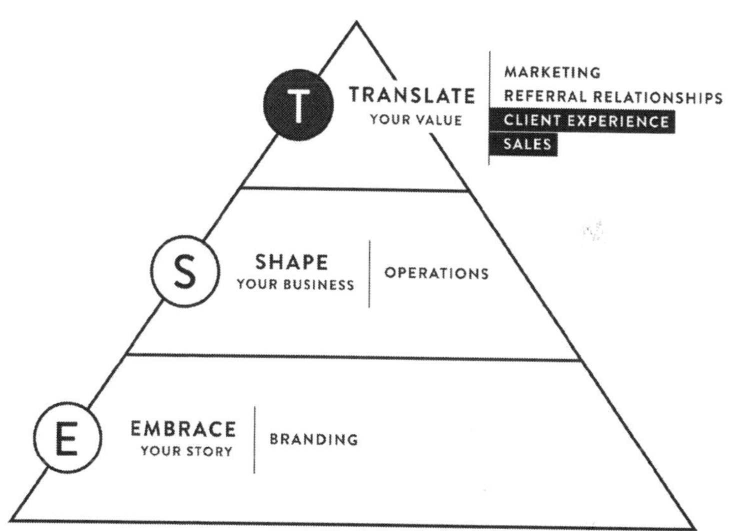

As you remember from the beginning of this book, hating selling nearly killed my business and almost sent me running back to Corporate America. When I was panicking in 2016 and afraid to sell with confidence, I didn't realize how much sales—when done authentically—can be about providing much needed and desired value. I didn't know then that selling is basically about clearly offering a valuable solution to a potential client's critical problem.

If you hate sales, too, or it's not your favorite, you'll enjoy and glean some rocket fuel from these best practices about sales and client experience. Sales, and specifically your sales process, are really the beginning of your client experience: the transformational journey that you take your clients through when they work with you. Because they flow from one to another, and are both about service, I've paired these two areas together. Truly, sales is the first step in your client experience. It kicks off solving an important problem, providing a much-wanted transformation, and becoming a valuable guide to someone who needs you.

With this mindset, sales can become a more natural, joyful, and effective experience—and working with your clients can not only create raving fans, but also repeat business. And if you put the same amount of energy into optimizing your sales and client experience processes as you have been worrying about social media marketing, in my experience, you'll be amazed at the results.

Since refining my sales and client experience processes years ago, I've come to love both—weirdly, and especially, sales. I currently host an average of 85 free, 20-minute zoom consultations every year, with 93% or more of those people I speak with being a good fit for one or more of the services I offer on my Streamlined Service Value Ladder (meaning that nearly *all* of those meetings are worth my time!). I close an average of 84% of proposals for branding projects. In 2021, 62% of past clients returned for another project or clarity consulting, and nearly 70% of all my business came from referrals. *How do I know all this?* Well, I track it as part of shaping my business!

As you may soon see, there's often so much potential to grow your business hiding in how you sell your value and how you deliver that value to your clients. Let's unpack that and start with the part that gets a lot of us stuck: sales.

SALES

Confidently Sell Your Value

As consumers ourselves, we all hate being "pitched." We shop and buy when we're ready to and have a problem we want to solve or a desire we want to fulfill.

That's why confidently selling your value isn't really about pitching yourself. When done well, smartly, simply, and in inviting ways, your sales process can come down to connecting potential clients with crucial problems to your very valuable solutions. If you can reframe sales to remove the sleaze, you streamline a process that instills confidence in your prospective clients. With that inviting process, you can clearly communicate your expert value to them. When you do that, you can watch your sales, satisfaction, and great-fit clients soar.

Permission to Be In Demand, Not Demanding

Despite what a lot of sales-people will sell you on, you do not have to cold-call or cold-message people to have a thriving, profitable business. I haven't cold-pitched my services to anyone in a direct message since 2015. I do remember awkwardly Facebook messaging people I knew who'd recently gotten engaged to see if they needed wedding invitations (for the Greatest Story Weddings brand). It felt icky then, it wasn't effective at all, but it felt like something I *had* to do. It seemed like something everyone taught (and many still teach). Pitch! Prospect! Offer your services! Ugh, even today if I get one more LinkedIn message like this, I'm gonna lose it.

When I intentionally revamped my processes in 2016, including my sales process, I committed to doing things differently. It felt there had to be a better way, and there has been—at least for me. I systematized everything I did, including both sales and marketing. I stopped obsessing about social media and stopped prospecting. I haven't sent one of these uncomfortable, out-of-the-blue pitch messages to anyone since 2015. The funny thing is, I haven't had to.

Rather than sending those awkward messages and making super cold calls, I chose to build up my reputation through good, high-quality work and driving awareness of what I do and whom I help. I doubled down on doing excellent work that delights clients, creating referral relationships, and doing simplified but effective marketing online and offline. I started to have a waitlist for all branding projects. Year after year, referrals continue to flow in consistently via consistent marketing and strong relationships with partners and past/current clients. As a result, I never, ever have to pitch myself or cold-call. The good news is that you don't have to directly pitch yourself *either!*

I call this approach working to be in demand, not demanding. Though I share more in detail about this strategy when we get to "Be Clear (Not Creative)" later in Step Three, being "in demand" gives you permission to sell with confidence and offer solutions without pressuring people. Because if selling doesn't mean have to mean "prospecting" (and the uncomfortable energy that surrounds that), a lot of possibilities open up for you. Selling can become what it really is: serving others and offering the right people (not *all* people) the value and transformation they need to get from where they are to where they want to be.

For me, shifting my sales from being demanding to an in-demand mindset began with the choice to embrace one clear action step that kicks off my sales process: a free, 20-minute Zoom consultation. No matter how you might meet me—via an email introduction, via attending my free workshop series, via my newsletter, or even via reading this book—if you want to talk about investing in branding services or clarity consulting, you're invited to set a complimentary consultation with me. That will always happen first: before getting a proposal, having me design your logo, or beginning a coaching program. Even if I've known you for years, a consultation is the singular step that has to happen for us to work together if we're doing so for the first time. It's a smart, consistent way to establish a working relationship and connect people with problems to the solutions they need to resolve them.

Having one clear action step has allowed me to streamline my entire sales process. It saves me from 15 back-and-forth emails about "estimates" and what I offer—conversation threads that take hours to write and weeks to wrap up. It protects me from spending my in-demand time with people who aren't ready to invest, and it makes it easy for those who are to invest!

Moreover, having a free consultation allows me to have one very specific, clear call to action that I can market and advertise. It can go in my email signature with a link to my calendar. It can be in the emails I send to my marketing list. It can be featured in social media posts. I can make this valuable time with me highly visible, easily available, and consistently offered so it becomes clear and memorable to others.

Because I focus on this, a beautiful thing happens: I don't ever have to prospect for or chase down new clients. Simply, if you have a problem that I can solve and we share any degree of a network, you've likely already seen throughout my marketing that I offer a way to spend 20 minutes with me in a free consultation. There's literally a big red button on my website to take action on it *(check it out!)*. You're invited to press that button whenever *you're* ready, not when I show up in your messages telling you that you should do so.

I like this way because it respects my ideal clients more than I feel so many other businesses do. Nobody likes to be told they have a problem, but they do like to talk to people who offer ways to solve a problem when they have identified that they have one. By offering a free consult and highlighting it as a problem-solver in all my marketing, I shine a light toward help for those who are struggling. The instant result is that anyone I meet doesn't have to be convinced they have a problem—they just need to be shown the right solution. Suddenly sales isn't fear-mongering, it's adding value.

Now, there are probably a lot of salespeople who would tell me they hate this advice and I'm leaving money on the table, but I love it. It's more me. Because I never really have to sell myself. I just make it my job for people to know what I do and what that first step is to get my help. I'm never pushy and, thankfully, I don't have to be.

Could I make more sales if I was out there prospecting and being demanding? Maybe, but honestly I don't feel like I have time for that. I also hate what it'd do to my brand reputation. These days, I'm too busy profitably growing my business, working with ideal clients, and providing value to be out there cold-calling or cold-pitching. That focus feels good to me.

If this feels like a good direction for you, let's take it to the next level. If you have a free consultation or similar clear step, how can you show up with confidence in that sales conversation? How can you find the right balance between being supportive and welcoming, and selling something that requires a financial investment? Well, you sell as their doctor, not their friend.

Sell as the Doctor, Not the Friend

Before I was a business owner, I spent five years working in the film industry, many of them at The Walt Disney Studios. Though I left Corporate America behind eight years ago, not a day goes by that I don't draw from my experiences there. When I think about sales, one story in particular always comes to mind.

A moment came as I was doing a project check-in with the vice president of our department, Roger. I had been tasked with creating a keynote presentation of strategic ideas to grow a TV animation franchise. It felt like a big, creative opportunity and one I didn't want to blow.

When it came time to share it with him, I sat down in Roger's office. I quickly opened my laptop and began to explain some caveats, "Okay, here are a few things I need to tell you first—"

"Don't do that," he immediately interrupted me. "Don't apologize up-front. Just present. I'm sure it's great."

Whew—so I presented. He confirmed it *was* great. Then he reminded me never to apologize up-front like that.

I think about this moment from my career at Disney often when I think about the importance of owning my expertise and holding onto my confidence. I was nervous to present to Roger. I wanted to impress him. What he taught me that day was not to cede my credibility when it was my turn to shine or share my expertise. There are always caveats, context, and things to explain when you present, when you sell, when you speak—but don't start there. That's what answering questions at the end is for, right?

My moment with Roger always helps me remember to show unapologetically and that my work will be all the better if I do. This is true at every stage of my client journey, from an initial email or consultation, to that very last "end of project" meeting. But the first few years of my business, I didn't show up that way in my sales conversations with prospective clients. As I've shared with you about my experience with Adele, I didn't show up as the expert.

What happened most often was I'd come off like a "buddy" or friend—in wanting to cheer on the person, I didn't come off like I was a confident professional ready to solve their problem. I lost more business than I care to think of doing that, but I get how. As a woman in business especially, I struggled with showing up confidently, without caveats, ready to help someone solve a problem. I didn't want to overpromise and underdeliver, and I wasn't showing up like even *I* believed that I was valuable.

You know who's typically perceived as a confident professional in every conversation? *A doctor.* When you don't feel well and you want a solution, you go to the doctor (even if you hate the doctor!). You trust what they say and take the medicine (solution) they prescribe because *they're* the doctor—the pro with the degree on the wall who knows what they are talking about.

Would you trust a doctor who said, "You could do this,

this, or this. I'm just hoping you get better!" *Um, no.* You trust a doctor who confidently diagnoses your problem and literally hands you the best solution. You respect that person more, and you're likely to refer them—especially if that solution helps you feel better.

I've found that selling with authenticity is no different from that. If you're willing to embrace that doctor mindset—being ready to listen well and provide a valuable prescription—then it's really more about caring for your clients *(your patients!)* than it is about forcing anything on anybody.

Your clients come to you because they have an urgent problem they want to solve. They don't need a buddy in that moment, and you don't need to worry about making them uncomfortable by talking about or offering your service/offer or other right solution. The reality that Adele helped me see is that they're *already* uncomfortable and they're literally coming to you to seek a remedy.

Be the doctor, not the buddy—and never apologize for showing up as the expert. The expert is literally *who* people have come to see. Show them you're here and embrace your story.

While this covers how to show up in a consultation or sales conversation, I've found there's so much potential to make this process easy, efficient, and valuable for both you and for clients. Let's close out our look at sales with several ways you can develop your own sleaze-free sales process.

Developing Your Sleaze-Free S.A.L.E.S. Process

You likely already have a sales process, though it may or may not be something you do consistently. If you've worked on shaping your business, you may have used my record/review/realize process to make it better. Diving specifically into sales, here are five big things I've learned to make your sales process more sleaze-free *and* successful:

S | Sell the prize, not the process.
A | Add value.
L | Lay out easy steps.
E | Explain in stages.
S | Safeguard your brand and business.

SELL THE PRIZE, NOT THE PROCESS

When you show up as their doctor and not their friend, it's important to remember what you're really selling (or prescribing) as that valuable solution.

When I worked with Adele to face my selling fears, she challenged me to clearly explain to her what I did. What I shared was all about what was included in my projects, how we worked together, what happened when, and so on. It was 100% *the process.*

After my lengthy explanation, she stared back at me. She pointed out, "Annie, it's like I want to go to the beach, and all you want to talk to me about is the plane!"

She was right. I'd talked in great detail about the plane: how it was made, how many seats it had, and how many drinks you'd be served on your way to the sunny shores.

But as she helped me to see, nobody cares about the plane *as much as they care about their destination!* In what you do, that's the transformation. After someone works with you to get your valuable solution, what changes in their life, business, or both? What is *easier?* Or *better?* What kind of person can they become (with your help)? That's what people buy when they buy a plane ticket somewhere. The promise of the sunny beach and how they'll feel when their toes hit the sand. The plane, while important, is a means for making that happen.

This is why now, in my consultation and marketing, I highlight the benefit. I focus on how having a Brand Story Solution can help you proudly market yourself and attract dream clients. I even have a simplified visual of this service that says this promise right at the top. The destination is clearly the focus.

In everything from how you sell your free consultation to how you market your services, always sell the prize, not the process. The process and the expert delivering it make it enjoyable and add to the experience, but they aren't what a prospective client wants *most.* Always remember to keep eyes on the prize.

ADD VALUE

As you know, my sales process begins with a complimentary consultation. This is a high-value offer of time with me and it's completely free. It's an opportunity to connect with prospective clients and help them find more clarity on their next step in their business. My goal in any consultation is to listen, assess their problem, and recommend the right next step to reach a solution.

That step might be getting a project proposal to work with me or a referral to another partner, or it may even be an action they should take on their own for now. I focus on making this consultation time valuable and clarifying. Because it is those things and not an exercise in vanity, it's an easy thing for me to proudly promote. My time is in high demand, and my strategic thinking is valued by consulting clients, so inviting someone to have a free consultation with me is a valuable thing I can offer.

Moreover, at every stage that I can in my sales process, I look to add value to help my prospective client get closer and closer to solving the problem they're facing. Here are some of the ways I add value throughout the sales process:

- I set clear expectations on my scheduling page for free consultations *(what it covers, when it's the right time to do one, etc.).*
- I ask thought-provoking questions in my consultation scheduling form to help a prospective client identify the best solution.
- When someone signs up for a free consult, my email marketing system sends them a welcome email highlighting other high-value, complimentary offers I have like my free workshop series and elevator pitch templates.
- In my consultation, I make thoughtful referrals or recommendations about their next step.
- If I set a proposal meeting, I send a helpful, beautiful overview of the Greatest Story client experience in a PDF.
- I email the proposal and all examples following the proposal meeting.

Notice that none of this means that I do "free work" or highly customize what I do, as we talked about with "You're Not Unreasonable, You're Valuable" and "Your Most Valuable Solution for Their Crucial Problem" earlier in the book. It simply means that I've created a sales process that respects my prospective clients' time and helps move their big picture forward, whether or not we work together right now.

LAY OUT EASY STEPS

Make it *easy!* I've found so much in business can be solved by making thing simpler and easier. Having a sales process to follow rather than winging it each time makes it far easier for someone to say *yes* to working with you.

What can you do now to make your process as easy as possible for prospective clients to go through?

For example, I make it easy to:

- Know how to get an estimate from me or ask me questions about working together (set a free consultation!).
- Pick a time and schedule that consultation on my website in just minutes (click the big red button on my website).
- Share key info via a few thoughtful questions on the scheduling form.
- Gain clarity on what you need to do next (work with me, work with someone else, etc.).
- Better understand how I can help you solve your problem via live discussion.

- Schedule a live proposal for branding services.
- Officially book a branding project or consulting with me (just by clicking a link).

When you think of how things now, do people have to go three emails deep with you just to set an initial time to talk with you? Do you offer multiple ways to get an estimate (email, presentation, form, etc.)? Is it tough to get clear information about what you do? How hard or easy is it to just say *yes* to working with you and pay for your services?

Laying out easy steps, like so much of what we did in operations, is about getting to that awesome yes easily and quickly. Whatever you can do to smooth out these steps, especially investing in a scheduling tool, could really power your sales process and get ideal clients working with you faster!

EXPLAIN IN STAGES

When working with clients, even and especially at this early phase, I've found that information overwhelm can happen quickly. If someone's new to what you do *and* they're stressed about something in their life or business, they don't have a lot of time to become an expert in your process or services—*nor should they need to.*

That's why a lot of the art of sleaze-free sales comes down to explaining things breadcrumb-style: offering what people need to know *as they need to know it.* This is why I don't put a lot of information on my website about my services, but I do explain more live during a consultation. Then, I put more detail in a proposal. Finally, the most detail appears in a contract, the point at which a client is 95% committed to the project and ready to focus on this level of information when I explain it in a contract review meeting.

Breadcrumbing information for prospective clients can guide them easily through the sales process and smoothly into working with you. This way, they won't get bogged down in the details because you'll add them through each of your strategic steps—building upon their knowledge and interest rather than hitting them over the head with it on your website or first conversation.

SAFEGUARD YOUR BRAND AND BUSINESS

In our time in operations, I preached the gospel of boundaries and bad-fit clients. You can stop most of them from happening by safeguarding your brand and business right here in your sales process. In fact, after you reframe sales as service and realize you don't have to "pitch yourself," you may discover that the toughest part of sales is actually saying *no* or *not right now* or *not this project (especially if it can't pass "Wendy's Will of Rights").*

Though I've already broken down many best practices around this in operations, let this "S" reinforce to you how valuable it will be to both you and anyone you might work with to "qualify" or assess how good a fit it is for you to work together. After all, bad-fit clients are expensive and best-fit clients can sustain your business *forever.*

I do several things in the sales process to attract ideal clients and repel bad-fit ones who'd be happier with other partners. To safeguard my own brand and business, I take care to:

- Ask questions about budget and timing in the short questionnaire when a prospective client schedules a free consultation.
- Respond transparently to live questions about investment, turnaround, and other ways I work with clients during my free consultations.
- Recommend other partners or solutions if I sense I am not a match for someone's needs, communication styles, expectations, or all of the above.
- Present my branding project proposals as live meetings only, to ensure all context is communicated and questions are answered.
- Require a signed contract, pre-scheduled project timeline approval, and non-refundable deposit to work together.
- Host a mandatory 15-minute contract review to ensure all expectations are clear and that I can be a partner up-front, not a policeman later.

These touchpoint and moments of transparency have helped steadily ensure that I work with dream clients who value the prize, the process, and the partner. It begins with the sleaze-free, successful sales process and blossoms with just as thoughtful a client experience.

—

If you practice S.A.L.E.S., you may also discover the same: better clients, more *yeses,* and increased confidence as you grow your business. Suddenly, sales can become one of your favorite things to do, because it brings you more money and more of what you love. That's a pretty good deal if you ask me.

YOUR SALES "KEY C" CHECK

As you considered how to improve your sales process, we explored:

- How to be in demand, not demanding.
- Offering a clear call to action (like a free consultation).
- Selling as the doctor, not the friend.
- A sleaze-free S.A.L.E.S. process.
- Selling the prize, not the process.
- Adding value along the way.
- Laying out easy steps.
- Explaining next steps when appropriate.
- Safeguarding your brand and business.

With these aspects in mind, take 10–15 minutes to reflect on and answer the questions here in the book, in your *Establish Yourself Companion Workbook*, or in your own notebook. Though these questions are intended to help you find clarity about what feels uncertain, the very first question will allow you to give yourself much-deserved credit! You're on your way.

WHAT'S WORKING

What's *one* thing you're really proud of about your sales process and meeting new prospective clients?

COURAGEOUS CONFIDENCE

What's *one* thing you wish you had more courage and confidence about in sales?

CRUCIAL CLARITY

What's *one* thing you need more focus and clarity on?

CONSCIOUS CONSISTENCY

What's *one* thing you need more consistency with?

CONTINUED COMMITMENT

What's *one* thing you want to commit more to when it comes to selling?

Now, which *one* of the these things feels most urgent to you?
List that one in the form of an action step here.

MY MOST VALUABLE ACTION STEP FOR **SALES:**

For this step, **are there any professionals and/or tools you may need to make that top action step happen?** *List your thoughts on this here.*

positive
shift
Brand Story Guide

CLIENT EXPERIENCE

Welcoming and Working with Clients

So much attention can be spent on marketing and sales that it can be easy to forget the most incredible engine of all for driving new business: doing great work for our current clients and empowering them to become our most vocal and loyal advocates. The art of welcoming and working with clients is something that doesn't get enough airtime in the world of business advice given its enormous growth potential for your practice.

Becoming a well-referred business by fostering an ever-growing list of happy clients could grow your practice forever, even if you never do a stitch of traditional marketing again. And it'll ensure exponential success when you pair that stellar reputation with great, strategic marketing. To gain this immense value, all you need to do is apply what you've learned so far and intentionally brand your client experience every step of the way.

The Value of Branding Your Client Experience

In Step One: Embrace Your Story, we explored the power of branding and its ability to help you confidently present yourself as an expert. We looked at creating a toolkit of messaging and visuals that would help you communicate and translate that value to others. But you shouldn't save it for just your marketing. Your branding toolkit can positively impact every part of your client's journey with you—from them first hearing about you to the most recent email you sent them—because branding your client experience and branding your overall business have much in common with each other.

You may remember that your brand is defined as how people think and feel about your business. Though you don't get to fully control that, you can impact it with things like your logo, your website, and your tagline (elements of your brand identity).

Your client experience is similar and lives as an embedded part of your overall brand. If your client experience is how clients *experience* working with you, then *branding* that experience by having thoughtful processes, adding your logo and colors to all your documents, sending gifts, and more can elevate it and make it more valuable. Though you'll never be able to fully control your clients' experience of what you provide and their impressions of working with you, you can play an active role in shaping these elements.

That's what branding a client experience is all about and why it's so important. If you put strategic thought into the quality, ease, and enjoyment of someone's time working with you, it will bring more consistency to that experience, provide clearer value, and be easier for you to deliver over and over again.

Looking like a total professional and having a seamless process will add significant value to your work. Adding value then allows you to charge more for your services than those who don't. It'll increase your clients' satisfaction and confidence in you (and in referring you). It'll add to your credibility and grow awareness that what you offer is high quality in process, delivery, and results.

Why is this so beneficial? We know this instinctually when we think as consumers instead of business owners. When I think of people I've worked with, I've found exceptional client experiences to be very rare. Most people I've hired to help me or have considered hiring have had little to no client process (and it drives me a little nuts!). I don't enthusiastically recommend those partners as often as I rave passionately about those who do! The people who do good work make it easy for me to work with them, and have a professional process turn me into an instant fan and brand evangelist every single time.

I currently send about two to three referrals to every month to one partner simply because I know how fantastic they are and I recommend them without hesitation! It isn't because their marketing is great (they do very little of it, in fact). It's because I feel valued as their client *and* I love the process of working with them. Ensuring your business is just as referrable is simple, straightforward, and something you can emulate today. And when you look to brand your client experience, let's look at what tools would help you the most.

As we explored branding together early on, I recommended that you create (or work with a professional to develop) a go-to branding toolkit that helps you share your brand story. I've found that the better you know your brand story, the stronger your client experience can ultimately be.

So within a toolkit like that—at minimum—you need these four simple, yet impactful branding assets to provide a smooth, professional client experience:

1. A professional logo
2. Specific brand fonts
3. Specific brand colors
4. The tone of your business

Having these four elements defined can elevate, visually and emotionally, a well-thought-out process. When they receive a document and your logo is at the top, and it feels like *your* brand, rather than just a random Word document, your clients will feel cared about. They'll feel like they're working with a professional who's at expert status. That's what deploying these four tools can do for you.

While the first three in this list are fairly self-explanatory, let's spend a moment on tone. This is really about what your business is providing to clients. *How does my business make them feel? What vibe does it give off?* This understanding, paired with visual assets like fonts and colors, can take your average thank-you note and make it something uniquely branded to you and what you do. It can make your clients feel appreciated and confident in you.

Take, for example, Mary Macdonald of Personal Path Financial Planning. Her business is all about possibility. *What might be possible if you could budget for that new car, vacation, and so on?*

Her stationery, shown here, brings that possibility to life. When she welcomes a new client with a handwritten note, they get this inspiring Dale Carnegie quote: "We all have possibilities we don't know about. We can do things we don't even dream we can do." She literally communicates and inspires possibility with just an inexpensive notecard.

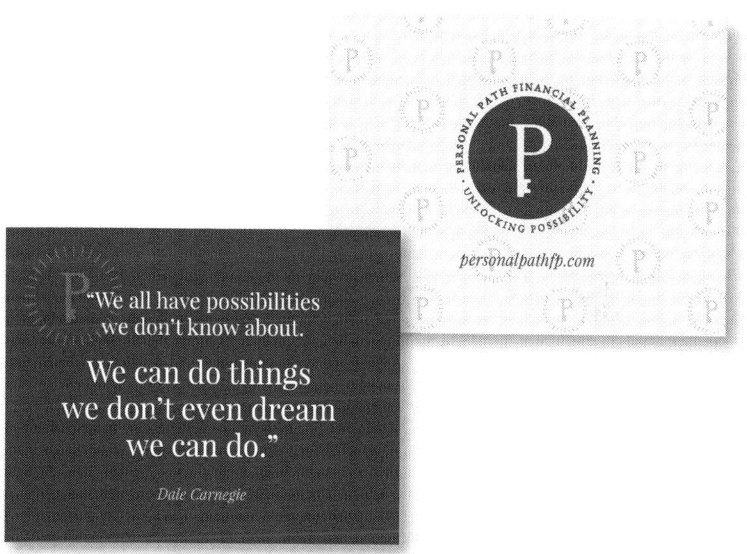

With the exact same format of stationery, Tim Barnes and Luke Ehresman of Gazelle business management software communicate a completely different tone. Their business is all about partnership and how they, as fellow musicians, are there to help you support and grow your practice. As many of their clients are older solopreneurs, Tim and Luke often have to send notes regarding illness or loss to spouses. Their stationery is about being one team and conveys "Individually, we are one note. Together, we're a symphony." That's a lot of caring customer service on simple paper, right?

Stationery is just one way that you can brand your client experience and bring that credibility and emotional connection to all you do for clients. Business cards, client gifts, even branded emergency chocolate M&Ms can all add to the experience of working with you. What matters is how it reinforces your brand story, presents you as the expert, and delivers value while you work to provide a valuable solution.

It's also important to realize how branding is not just for thank-you notes or client gifts, it's for *everything* you do. If you don't already, one huge way to up your game is to take the time to "brand" all of your documents and emails—everything you send to clients. You'll immediately look like the pro you are if you take a few minutes to create a digital letterhead template with your logo, info, and branded fonts/colors. Suddenly, you'll be ready to send branded invoices, proposals, contracts, resources, and more to your clients with that letterhead on standby.

Moreover, you can brand your email signature to reinforce your story and make you easy to refer (your clients can just copy the info and email it on when they refer people). You can even brand ecards! Use your brand tools to send birthday cards, holiday cards, or even branded ecards via Amazon and other retailers.

Part of offering an "above and beyond" client experience is creating a smart system that you establish and use regularly. Think through your process, add those branded touches in templates, then rinse and repeat. Not only does it make it easier for you, it makes you look like the expert when everybody else is sending basic Word document proposals in Times New Roman!

One big place you might use these four branding tools comes at the very beginning of your official client experience—the moment when someone has just committed to working with you and now needs to be welcomed properly.

Warm Welcomes Matter: Well-Timed Client Gifts

When you've hired someone, when are you both the most excited and most nervous about working with them? *The beginning!* Specifically, it's that time between when you've paid a deposit and seeing them contribute something of value that naturally creates some anxious anticipation. Depending on what you offer and if you have a waitlist to work together, you may not be able to deliver immediate value to a brand-new client. This is where a warm welcome can work wonders!

First, just being aware of a welcome being necessary can have huge impact on your practice. I've paid other consultants thousands of dollars only to receive a welcome postcard in the mail three weeks later (or nothing at all). I've hired lawyers who didn't even state the word *welcome* in an email to me before I was deep into their process. By simply knowing it's important and valuable to you to welcome people, you're strengthening your client experience and making yourself that much more referrable later.

I believe your welcome process for clients should cover two key areas: one, a welcome email and two, a welcome gift. Both of these, when deployed together, speak to that moment when someone has just booked you and before you've had the opportunity to provide value through service. They assure your clients that they've made the right decision in hiring you while requiring very little "work" on your part (my favorite type of business activity: *high impact, low effort*).

A WELCOME EMAIL

Going back to what we discussed in operations, email templates can be a lifesaver here. Following your booking steps (at the end of your sales process), it's critical to send a welcome email (literally with the word *welcome* in it!) to establish your official working relationship.

This email might introduce key documents like a questionnaire, provide contact information, link to a project home base, or give access to a project calendar—maybe even all four. But at minimum it states your intention: "*Welcome! I'm so excited to work with you, and here's our very first step!*" Simple, easy, but so powerful to ensure your clients feel valued and cared about as much as they did in your sales process. It's a moment of reassurance that shouldn't be overlooked.

A WELCOME GIFT

I also recommend sending a welcome gift. This is even more pivotal than a final thank-you gift at the end of a project or engagement. Why? Well, because at the end of a project, you've hopefully delivered a ton of value and transformation. A final gift can blend into what you've already provided. However, a welcome gift is a strategically valuable step! It allows you to almost instantly give your client something wonderful to maintain all the fantastic momentum you've been building up in your sales process. Here are some of my favorite best practices for welcome gifts:

- Mail or email as soon as possible post-booking.
- Choose to send something related to your business.
- Select a gift that they (and/or their team) would definitely enjoy, use, and/or value.
- Strive for thoughtfulness versus expense.
- Mail a handwritten card, even if you email a gift (like a digital gift card).

For years, all I sent was a small, 3x5" kraft notebook with "Your Next Chapter" hand-stamped on it. I included a library-themed enclosure card with a short welcome note. Each one cost about $10 in materials and shipping. Though inexpensive, I can't tell you how many of my clients still have that little journal tucked away in their offices.

In 2021, I upgraded my welcome gifts to bigger, more branded journals, a branded red pen, and that same enclosure—this time with a custom, real wax seal that says "Greatest Story Creative." It's elevated, but the spirit is the same and the cost isn't that much more. When you open the box, there's a sticker that says "Welcome. Let's brand your greatest business!"

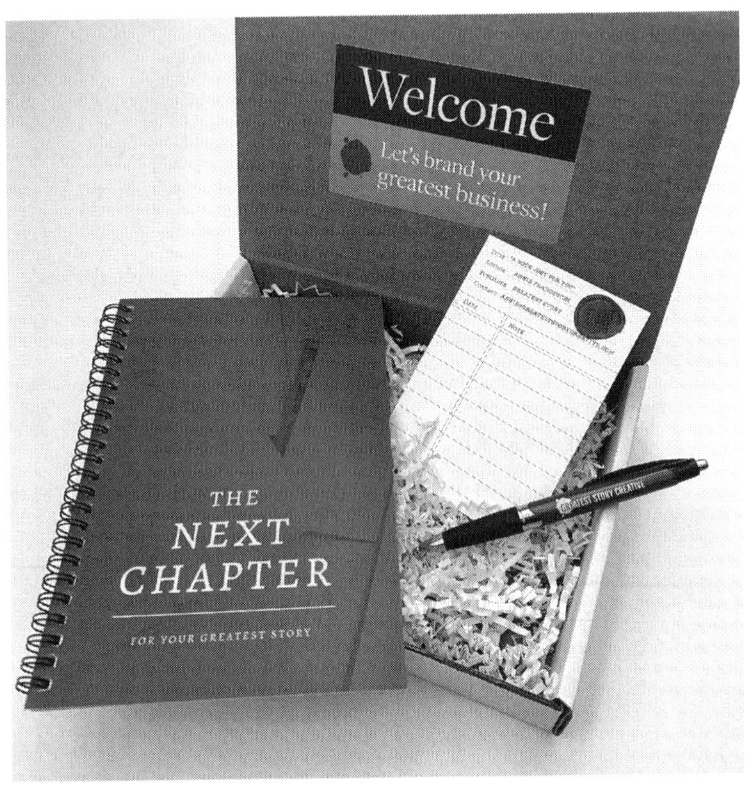

Photo by Annie Franceschi

Whether it's a $10, $30, or $100 gift, doesn't really matter. Gifts like these illustrate what a warm client welcome all about: creating a moment of joy for someone who's chosen to invest in you. It quickly assures them that they've made a wonderful decision and investment in themselves. It signals that their lives, their businesses, or both are about to change, and that's something to celebrate!

—

With a bit of intention, an email template, a branded welcome gift, and a quick trip to the post office, you can set every project up for success right now. Simple as that.

So from there, how do you continue to keep that good juju going? You keep branding what you do—in process and professionalism.

The Thought Behind Smoothly Working with Clients

Having a poor client experience can have a lot of unintended impact. For me, a bad client experience left me crying at Target.

It was a Sunday in January 2021. My then-11-month-old son, Leo, was scheduled to start attending daycare the very next day. We'd been lucky to keep him at home for nearly his entire first year of life (and the first year of the pandemic) thanks to help from family. But with a new year beginning, it was time for Leo to meet new friends his own age and it was time for me to have enough mental health space to run my full-time business. We were sending him to a small school that thankfully we'd been able to visit prior to the virus crisis, but nevertheless there I was, bawling my eyes out by the cribs at Target.

Admittedly, I likely would have been upset about such a major change for us regardless, but when I think back on it, the reason I felt so stressed and anxious at Target was because I had *no idea* what to expect for Leo's first day. Leo's school had no formalized welcome process whatsoever. I didn't know what his first day would be like, nor what to pack, nor what should go in his lunch. In the absence of any sort of "first-day checklist" or any guidance from the school, I was left to anxiously wonder and worry as only a new mama can: *Will he be OK? Where will he sleep? What if he can't sleep?* Of course, this quickly spiraled into *I'm a terrible mom. What the heck am I doing? I can't do this!* Hence the tears at Target.

Monday came, and I cried when I met with his teacher at the door. She turned out to be lovely and reassuring about my concerns. She kept me posted on his adventures throughout the day. Since then, Leo has thrived there and become an enormous fan of that hit new song "The Wheels on the Bus."

But here's the deal. So much of the pain I experienced could have been avoided *if* the school's director had simply made a document that was shared with parents about what to expect on the first day. Just one document, made one time in an hour or less, could have kept me (and likely other first-time daycare parents) from tears at Target. It would have helped me feel immensely better about my investment and the school I'd chosen for my son. It would have given them a reusable tool to easily answer the same handful of questions they likely get dozens of time every year.

While this is an excellent example of why a welcome process is really significant, it also underscores how important it is to be thoughtful about how you work with your clients in general. To be effective, you should pour intention into every step—from the very first to the very last—thinking about each from being in your clients' shoes. If the school's director had strategically looked at the systems in place, maybe she would have realized that they weren't providing any key info to new parents to help them acclimate to daycare. She could easily fix that and avoid situations like what happened to me, and she still can *if* she ever asks for parent feedback. The same can go for you and your clients.

If you've created strategic systems, including a welcome email/action steps you do when a client starts, you're already setting yourself up to be successful with everyone you work with to the extent that's in your control. Once you've welcomed someone, your job then becomes to provide deliverables, create space for transformation, or otherwise fulfill the promise of your valuable solution—the service that your client invested in.

While that can have a lot to do with you doing executional work or providing coaching, a lot of it can also be streamlined to run smoothly—so that work or coaching can be as successful as possible. Like with so many tips I've shared in this book, having your processes clearly defined for how you deliver or facilitate services is critically important. When it comes to client work, I'm a strong believer in email templates and answering questions before they are asked. Doing so will also ensure that clients know what's going on, stay confident in your abilities, and get you anything you need to be successful (like input, content, and other materials) in a timely manner. Some of the many ways you can provide smoother client experiences, establish healthy boundaries in your working relationships, and keep people well-informed are activities like:

- Reviewing your preferred methods of communication in the contract review phase.
- Putting office hours in your email signature.
- Providing a client portal that links to all documents they need (contract, invoices, files, etc.).
- Sharing links to book meetings, like consulting sessions.

- Creating a project calendar and/or sending official meeting invitations for milestones/meetings.
- Hosting an online workbook or shared word-processing document to track goals or progress.
- Providing questionnaires via forms or documents.
- Writing out email templates for every phase of your process or program, so you never forget to share something with a client.
- Linking to a frequently asked questions document or list on your website.
- Providing an end-of-project checklist that sets your clients up for future success.

Of these things, two stand out as incredibly pivotal to keeping my client experiences running as well as they can:

1. Share next steps.
2. Keep your word.

SHARE NEXT STEPS

If you've ever worked with someone who doesn't have a good client process, you already know how agonizing and stressful it can become when you don't know what the next step is. *Where's that logo that person was designing for me? Where's my website? When's our next coaching session? Are they even working on my project!?*

Having been on both sides of the fence, what I've observed is that many business owners work very hard for their clients, but they are often not as great about communicating the process and where they are in it. The result: They work hard but clients are left in the dark about turnaround time, next steps, and more. This creates an atmosphere of unintended anxiety and concern. While it may not always lead to crying at Target, I've been there as a client more times than I care to count, and it's made projects that should have been awesome feel weighed down by clunkiness and unnecessary stress.

The reality is that if you've worked hard to have a plan, don't skip that key step of making sure that your clients also know the plan. I recommend that you have a simple way to always make sure that your clients know the next step. I post my client's next step to their private home base, note it in a post-meeting email, and even mention it live before we wrap up any conversation. A client who knows the plan is more likely to be a happy client, and you won't have to waste time putting out unnecessary fires that got lit while you were away working hard for them.

KEEP YOUR WORD

Akin to sharing next steps is the enormous brand value in keeping your word. To me, this means committing to consistency, sticking to your timelines and shared processes, under-promising on value, and over-delivering. You likely know this from having been a client: A client who trusts you will be a happy client.

Nothing erodes client trust more than constantly moving deadlines, being disorganized, or not replying regularly to client emails or phone calls. Everyone gets busy and has things come up, of course. The key is to communicate as soon as you can when they do, and if you have to reset a deadline, do everything you can to hit it that second time.

If you work to optimize your practice by embracing your story and shaping your business, you should be ready to translate these things in your work with clients easily. Having processes means that you can be more organized, work more easily, and deliver when you say you will. This will even create bandwidth for you to provide bonus value and delight clients throughout your working relationship. Strategy, as it always does, will maximize the effort you put into it and give back to you tenfold or more, making you a joy to work with and an incredible client experience to refer.

CLIENT EXPERIENCE

Reviews and Building Lifelong Client Relationships

In translating your value, you've been learning how to confidently sell your value, warmly welcome your clients, and keep them happy and satisfied throughout your work together.

Now, after you've provided significant value to a client, you get another incredible opportunity. It's one that's often overlooked: the chance to turn that person into your lifelong fan, a repeat customer, and a secret weapon for making your business better. The key to game-changing fans and feedback comes from solidifying your relationships through client interviews, applying their insights, and staying top of mind as time goes on. Here's how to put this into action, one client at a time.

Get More Fans and Feedback by Interviewing Clients

My all-time record for asking one client to write a review for me was *20* back-and-forth emails. Maybe you've been there, too. In the early years of my business, I understood that reviews were powerful, but I had a lot of trouble getting clients to spend time to write one.

One day, it finally dawned on me: For my business, many clients hire *me* to do their writing! They're busy business owners, and writing is not their strong suit. It felt like a lot to ask when I'd request a few words about their experience by email, so I asked myself instead, *How can I make this easier for these people, especially those who don't like to write?*

The answer: interview them. In 2017, I began interviewing each of my clients live at the end of every project, recording their responses and typing them up. I'd take the top three or four sentences, and provide them as a quick summary if they'd like to post it as a review. Suddenly, a cumbersome ask for a client was a moment of customer service—a chance to answer questions, provide value, and ensure they had received a satisfying client experience. And overnight, reviews got posted because I'd made it easy and they were pulled from the client's own words.

At the time I started this, little did I know the incredible power a simple 10-to-15-minute client interview would soon bring into my business. Not only have client interviews led to dozens of five-star reviews of my practice online, they've shaped the growth of my business exponentially, too. They've empowered me to proactively resolve project issues, deliver the highest-quality customer service, and even sharpen my marketing, so I can focus mostly on what works and let go of what doesn't.

If you don't already do this as part of your process, I encourage you to go ahead and conduct a series of five to 10 client or customer interviews via phone or video chat this month. I'm not talking about surveys; I'm saying conversations that can massively influence your business and your marketing going forward.

Here's why it's so valuable to interview your clients directly:

- **Objectivity and familiarity:** Your clients know your service from a different perspective than you do, so they are a fantastic source of objectivity that you need to better understand your messaging.
- **Brand affinity:** Their words reflect how they *feel* about your business.
- **Insight into your marketing:** Their words reflect how they *talk* about your business when they recommend it (or don't).
- **Insight into untapped opportunities:** They may see opportunities for your services that you can't see.
- **More reviews:** The easier you make it to give you a review, the more you'll get—plain and simple.
- **Customer service:** If you provide a live opportunity to value someone's client experience, you can smooth out any issues, apologize if needed, and provide solutions whenever needed.

Here's who you could interview:

- **Past clients:** Even if it's been a while since you worked together, there's great value in reconnecting. (It may even lead to new business by getting on a past client's radar.) If you worked with several people at a company, interview them together or separately.
- **People you've partnered with as collaborators:** Though they may not be clients, your key partners will have great insights about you and what you do that you may not already have.

- **5–10 people (the more, the merrier):** I recommend talking with at least five to 10 people so you can get a sense of an average.

Having done this now for more than four years, I've refined how I do it to make it as easy, productive, and valuable for clients and for me as possible. If you struggle to get written reviews from your clients or wish you had better insight from them, you may want to practice my Fans & Feedback process. Fans & Feedback™ breaks down to the easy-to-remember abbreviation, **F.A.N.S.**

F | Follow a system.
A | Ask thoughtful questions live.
N | Note feedback to fix the future.
S | Share and stay top of mind.

In this section, I break down each step as a story so you can fully explore the value of how client interviews work and can easily be applied to your business as you find relevant.

FOLLOW A SYSTEM

Systems save the day, and adding one around interviewing your clients will keep you doing them consistently enough to ensure they add value to you and your business in all the ways they can. *For inspiration, here's what my client interview system for my Brand Story Solution currently looks like:*

- Every branding project has a 30-minute "End of Project" Interview, scheduled along with other project meetings.

- There's an agenda for the meeting.
  - Answer any of the client's questions about the project (10 min).
  - Share the next step service solution I offer (if relevant) (5–10 min).
  - Interview the client about their experience (10–15 min). *I record this as video or audio.*
- Transcribe the interview and put the top three to four sentences together as a short summary.
- Follow up with a short summary sent by email with links to spots where a client can post a review.
- Share as quotes on social media, on website, and to mailing list.
- Stay top of mind by posting relevant content online and to my mailing list, sending emails to check in with past clients over time, and keeping past clients posted when those they referred reach out to me.

This type of flow works great for project-based work, but if you have long-term or continuous client engagements, you can definitely follow a system like this too. One of my coaching/consulting clients who works with people on monthly retainers now does a quarterly check-in call to see how things are going. This call allows her to have a high-quality touchpoint with clients and learn more about their needs over time. My client recently shared that the quarterlies have been eye-opening: Every single client has shared that they love her and want to give her more work to do, but they aren't sure what else she could take over for them!

This is the kind of insight I love about client interviews: growth potential. A simple quarterly check-in call has highlighted a huge business opportunity. Now, if my client can make recommendations to her clients of other ways to use her well, they'll glad pay her *more* to accomplish those tasks. This is a totally profitable exercise that pays off almost immediately, and it's *free* to do—gotta love that.

Once you embrace *your* system to follow, the next aspect to consider is what exactly to ask your clients when you interview them.

ASK THOUGHTFUL QUESTIONS LIVE

Once you're following a system overall for getting client feedback, it's important to ask a clear, consistent list of questions—and to ask them *live.* Hosting a live conversation, versus asking for someone's thoughts by email, creates an opportunity for a dialogue that you can't have otherwise. Not only that, it makes a more efficient use of your clients' time and skill set by only asking them to discuss their experience rather than write about it.

I recommend coming up with a standard list of questions to help you understand the client's experience, key marketing insights (like why they hired you!), and the toughest question of them all: "What can I do better?"

Why You Always Have to Ask Some Form of "How Can I Do Better?"

I finally got over the fear of asking this question when I thought about it from the other perspective: how my clients might feel if I did. I thought back to my wedding. One of my own wedding vendors never followed up with me for feedback on my experience. I remember being really frustrated by that because there were a few things I wanted to share with that person, but I didn't because they never asked me. There were things that may have been cleared up and things this person could have learned from our experience to improve their business for future clients. I often think of it as a loss for both of us. And importantly, it's also the major reason I didn't recommend that particular vendor passionately to others.

I started asking this tough question because I never wanted my own clients to feel that way about me or my work, even if I hadn't done a perfect job in their eyes. One day, I did have my worst fears happen in a client interview. While yes, it was terrifying, it was also a perfect example of the third step of F.A.N.S.: noting feedback. Let's look at why.

NOTE FEEDBACK TO FIX THE FUTURE

Once, I asked my client about their experience during a Zoom meeting. She paused. It felt like forever. She finally spoke. "Actually, I'd hesitate."

Ouch. Well, it hadn't been the easiest experience for either of us—but certainly not for lack of intention. But this was the moment I'd always dreaded: asking for feedback, and actually getting the good, the bad, and the awkward.

Here's the thing: I'm glad I was brave in light of those fears and asked these questions. Because after my client's gut punch, I got an opportunity. She gave me the valuable opportunity to ask about and listen to her client experience—what went well *and* what could have gone better. Though she was happy with the final branding, she felt the process to developing it was rocky and stressful. For context, I'd thought this specific project was going to be me working just with the CEO, but it turned out to be an entire small team that all provided feedback, which required a lot more email back and forth, revisions, and really just things that my process wasn't designed for at the time.

Through asking her questions about what happened, I got to better understand her perspective and show her that I respected it. For my part, I also got a chance to provide some context back to her to better explain parts of the process and demonstrate that I could listen and take her feedback to heart. Though it was tough to hear, this feedback was beneficial for helping me and my business grow in many ways.

For one, it helped me to understand that my process was a much better fit for solopreneurs and two-person teams, and I began to niche down more to those types of ideal clients. For another, her feedback empowered me to see specific ways to improve my process, like clarifying the number and names of stakeholders up-front. Generally, it helped me make my work and client experience better for the next client.

In the moment, it also allowed me to practice professionalism, show my client that I genuinely cared about her experience, and clear the air—ensuring that she felt heard and listened to. It crystalized for me a truth: Unhappy clients are unhappy whether or not you ask them for their feedback, so always offer the conversation if you hope to fix it.

Lastly, because I'd provided the opportunity for feedback, my client and I were able to see and respect each other's perspective, leave the project as friends, and even become referral partners! Though my client didn't feel my business was a good fit for teams like hers, she graciously shared that she thought it was a wonderful one for my favorite types of clients (coaches, consultants, and solo service business owners). Since then, she's referred me several times to people that are more in that wheelhouse. In the end, it all worked out.

But what if I'd been too afraid to ask her to the meeting? What if I'd gotten defensive in the conversation when the feedback wasn't all positive? I can imagine that if I hadn't asked for the conversation or been gracious when it happened, not only would I have lost referrals, I would have damaged my personal brand and my business brand for quite a while for this client and those in her network.

This conversation is just one of the many reasons that I've done a client interview at the end of nearly every branding project since 2017. Having done more than 50 of them, I can tell you confidently that your clients sit in the critical blind spot of your business. They experience it from a totally different angle than you ever will—and because of that, their feedback is gold. Yes, the good, the bad, and the awkward.

There's so much that I've gained from client interviews that has helped me grow as an entrepreneur and grown my business. I view it as an essential activity that not only protects my brand and reputation, but creates lifelong fans and referrals, and makes the business better every time.

That's what noting feedback is about: taking everything your clients share with you to heart. Not every client will take you up on this experience, but when they do, they have such tremendous value to share with you from every angle—both in ways you may expect and in ways that will surprise you.

Besides fixing relationships and closing projects on a high note, here are the many ways that noting client interview feedback has powered my business for years:

- Shaping my services and marketing to translate my value more accurately.
- Creating smoother processes and removing hiccups.
- Enhancing and elevating client experience.
- Providing peace of mind.
- Offering encouragement and validation as I grow.

—

If you embrace client interviews using the Fans & Feedback process, you'll discover that the feedback part may be even more valuable than the fans. When you're in business, especially if it's just you, it can be isolating. Having a system that allows you to have productive, powerful, and, yes, even sometimes-difficult conversations with your clients will keep you consistently moving forward in ways you can't even imagine right now.

When you open yourself up to that feedback opportunity, as scary as it is, that's as rewarding as it can become. I can't wait to see the impact it has for you.

When put your client interview system in place, ask the right questions live, and note key feedback, the final step is all about what you do with it to fully inspire and keep those lifelong fans.

SHARE AND STAY TOP OF MIND

As you work your way through F.A.N.S., you take an initial or existing client relationship and fortify it for the future. This may mean that when you wrap up work with a client, it's really the beginning of one of the most valuable relationships you can have in your greatest business—*if* you nail the final step: **share and stay top of mind.**

This is a twofold strategy, and the first aspect of it is sharing. The way I got into client interviews was wanting more reviews for my business and needing to make that process easier. We all know as consumers how powerful reviews can be. So I encourage you: If you take the time to interview your clients thoughtfully and take their feedback to heart, don't skip the step of sharing their review back with them.

The final stage of the client interview process is to circle back to a client, share that short summary and/or a transcription of their interview, and invite them to *share* it as a review. Many will, especially if you make that as easy as cutting and pasting their own comments and clicking a quick link. But the sharing doesn't have to stop with that moment.

You can take that client interview and share parts of it on social media. You can turn it into a case study on your website or a client success story for your email list or podcast episode. You could pair it with visuals of your work together or highlight it in your newsletter to publicly congratulate your client on their progress. Of course, in some situations, you may need to anonymize a client's words—but in any case, you are also invited to share it well and share it widely, too.

Because when you also share your client's stories in various ways, especially in their own words, it creates some of the most captivating marketing ever with very little work on your part. And it allows you to do the second piece of this final step: stay top of mind with them.

The people who've already worked with you and loved the experience can emerge as your biggest advocates. They can stay that way forever *if* you intentionally stay top of mind with them and continue to invest in that relationship. You'll have some of the best, most high-value referrals from past clients if you commit to staying top of mind with them. While they may have loved working with you initially, the ball is in your court to stay on their radar, to continually support them, to cheer them on, and to ensure they feel awesome about being your fan well into the future!

Here's what staying top of mind with your clients might look like:

- Sharing clients' success in stories, in presentations, and online, and tagging them in your posts.
- Emailing them every few months to sincerely check in on how they're doing.
- Asking them regularly if there's anything you can do to support *them.*
- Attending their events, liking their posts online, and subscribing to their newsletters (and writing back when you get them).
- Making thoughtful referral partner and other networking introductions for them.
- Hosting events just for past clients to network with each other.
- Keeping them posted when people they refer set consultations with you.
- Sending a gift or thoughtful thank-you when those they refer book your services.
- Teaming up to do a workshop, interview, or other collaboration opportunity together to share audiences.

Much of this can be systematized so you'll actually do it. Steps like automated emails or email templates to remind yourself to check in regularly can keep you top of your clients' minds and inboxes for the foreseeable future. And that's not just a valuable thing to do for all your past and current clients, it's a powerful relationship-building mindset in general. I go into more detail on this soon when we get to "Simplified Systems for Magic Marketing."

For now, you've successfully considered the entire Fans & Feedback process (F.A.N.S.), the culmination or key checkpoint for your work with clients. Let's consider what action would be most valuable to improve your client experience going forward.

THE NEXT CHAPTER

YOUR CLIENT EXPERIENCE "KEY C" CHECK

As you considered how to optimize how you work with clients, we explored:

- How (and why) to brand your client experience.
- Using your professional branding toolkit to elevate your services and work together.
- Well-timed welcome gifts.
- How to smoothly work with clients.
- Why client interviews can game-changing (Fans & Feedback).
- Key aspects of a client interview system.
- The value of applying client feedback.
- Why and how to share client reviews.
- Staying top of mind to maintain strong client relationships over time.

With these aspects in mind, take 10–15 minutes to reflect on and answer the questions here in the book, in your *Establish Yourself Companion Workbook*, or in your own notebook. Though these questions are intended to help you find clarity about what feels uncertain, the very first question will allow you to give yourself much-deserved credit! You're on your way.

WHAT'S WORKING

What's *one* thing you're really proud of in terms of how you work with and serve clients?

COURAGEOUS CONFIDENCE

What's *one* thing you wish you had more courage and confidence about when you consider your client experience?

CRUCIAL CLARITY

What's *one* thing you need more focus and clarity on?

CONSCIOUS CONSISTENCY

What's *one* thing you need more consistency with?

CONTINUED COMMITMENT

What's *one* thing you want to commit more to when you serve clients to make their experience a stellar one?

Now, which *one* of the these things feels most urgent to you?
List that one in the form of an action step here.

MY MOST VALUABLE ACTION STEP FOR **CLIENT EXPERIENCE:**

For this step, **are there any professionals and/or tools you may need to make that top action step happen?** *List your thoughts on this here.*

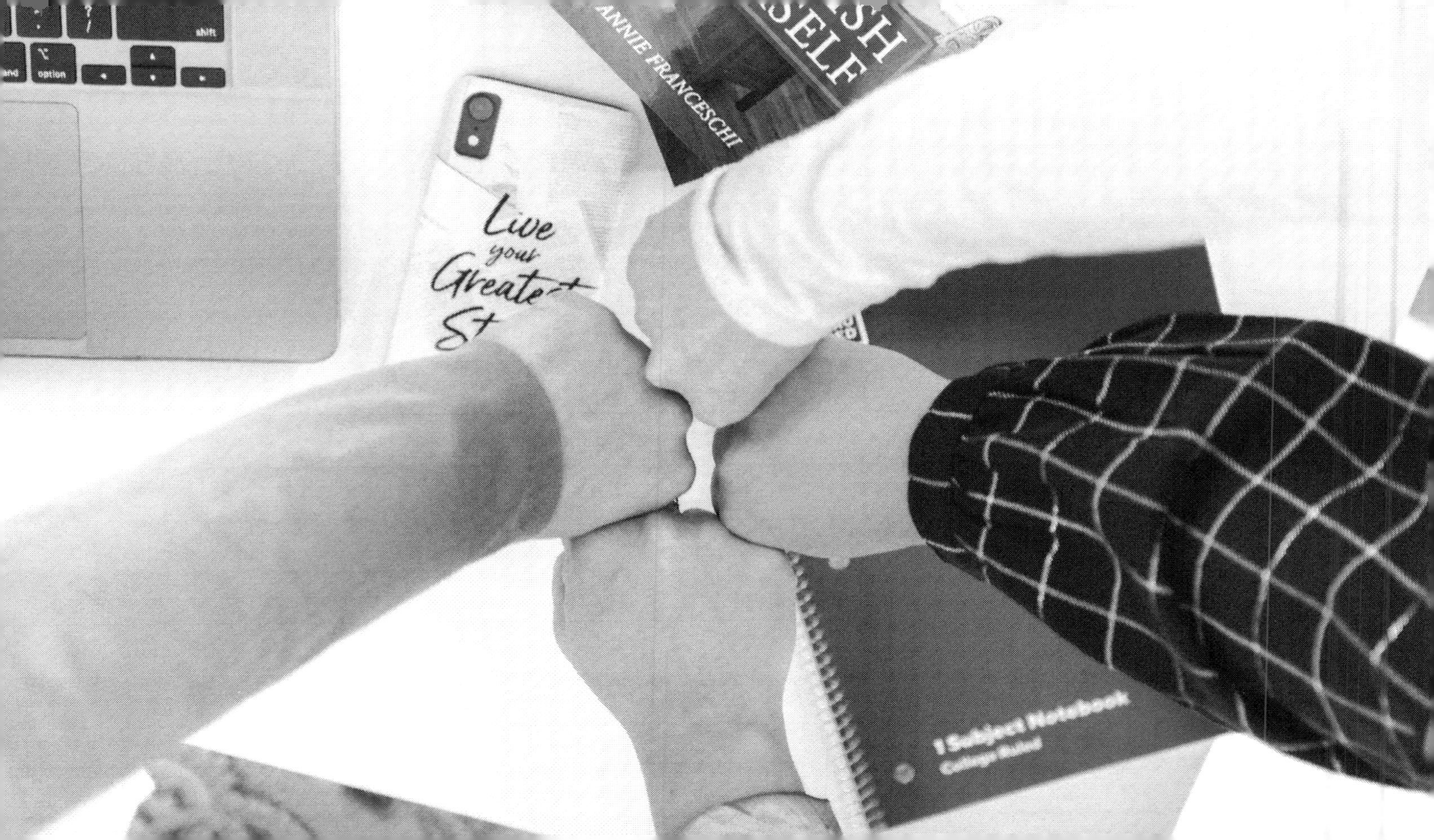
ANNIE FRANCESCHI
Live your
1 Subject Notebook
College Ruled
option
shift

Referral Relationships

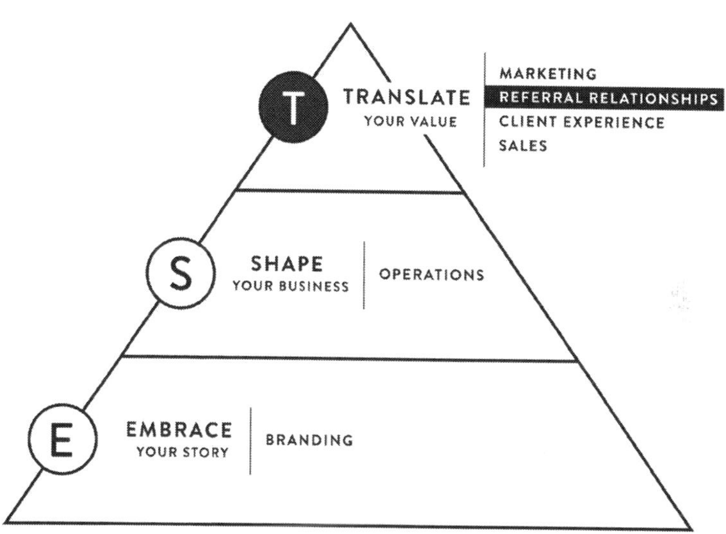

The art of fostering and keeping relationships can bring your business ideal clients, visibility opportunities, PR interviews, and more. It doesn't get its time to shine in the spotlight of business development enough. From where I sit, relationships drive *all* revenue for service business owners. All of it.

Before you object and think of that person who googles you, then buys your service—yes, that happens—but exponential business growth (in ideal clients, podcast interviews, major opportunities, etc.) only happens if you develop, build, and sustain relationships with others. You may look at some entrepreneurs' successes online and wonder, *How are they collaborating with so many big people? How are they reaching multiple six figures? Is it Facebook, or their newsletter, or all the things they post on LinkedIn?*

If you really look at the reasons behind such success, it's ultimately due to relationships. The conversations that happen in direct messages, virtual coffee dates, and in-person lunches—those are what you don't have the visibility to see when you observe people thriving in their online businesses. But whether you connect with someone via a chat box or an email or at Starbucks, the old-fashioned nature of "talking to people" *always* factors in.

As I've shared throughout the book, in the early years of my business, I nearly burned out trying to use social media and all the shiny object tactics to grow my business. I networked, but I didn't do so with intention or strategy. I wasted my time in "tactic tornadoes." After I almost gave up on everything in 2016, I pivoted and decided to invest in what made the most common sense but wasn't commonly taught: strengthening relationships with both my clients and those in my network who came into contact with potential ideal clients.

On the relationship front, it took time to see results, but those results continue to astound me. Currently, most of my business is via referral or past clients. That means that the majority of the time, a past client, a partner, or someone in my network has already sung my praises to someone before they've met me—and they often arrive with a crucial problem, believing I might be the exact right person to solve it. Moreover, many past clients return happily and easily for ongoing strategy, consulting, and creative support. And now, when I launch a new workshop, service, or offer, I have an engaged network of people ready to consider it, buy it, and/or help me get it in front of my ideal clients.

To have this kind of support takes a meaningful investment of your time and energy. It's often inexpensive or free to do. If you practice intentional relationship building—both with your clients and with referral partners in your network—over time, it will take on a life of its own. Like a tree that begins as a little seedling poking out of the ground, if you stay the course, you'll be relaxing in the shade of its leaves for the entire lifespan of your business.

Now, I know we've all "kissed some frogs" when it comes to networking. There was a time when I'd spend hours doing 1:1s that never went anywhere or abused my time as free consulting. While I definitely have some best practices around that now, I've found there are three big factors when creating connection that lasts and grows your business (and the business of those you connect with). Here are three elements that make the most of your time, show respect of others' time, and add value to both of your lives and businesses:

1. Being **clear**
2. Being **considerate**
3. Being **committed**

In this area of business, let's dive into each factor and best practices that support them.

T
S
Share Your Business
E
Embrace Your Story

REFERRAL RELATIONSHIPS

Be Clear (Not Creative)

Crucial clarity is essential to realizing your greatest business. It shows itself in two major ways when networking: one, clear focus about the nature of your networking, and two, clarity in how you communicate what you do to others. If you have clear goals about the types of relationships you need to build, and you're incredibly clear in your conversations with new people, you'll be well on your way to the connections that will grow your practice into the future.

If you ever worry about "standing out" or the pressure to not be "boring," let what follows be some permission for you. I've learned that your success as a brand and a business is far more related to being clear than it will ever be about being "creative." In this section, I pass on my client-generating strategy of practicing simple awareness. I also give you key branding tools like CHIPS™ that you can use to grow relationships that will grow your business.

Why I Traded "Standing Out" for Understanding

As I've touched on throughout this book, for years I chased creativity and learning about all the get-rich-quick marketing of any and every business. I hated the hard sales pitches, the $27 templates, the over-marketing, and the intense focus on "converting people." I also really despised being a "demanding" business. I cringe every time I think about it.

I kept wondering for so many years: It is *me?* Am *I* not good enough? Have I not done enough to sell myself and what I do? Well, it took me trying "all the things" to realize that "all the things" just didn't work for me. I later learned, they often don't work as well as you think for the people that sell you that story because, all too often, followers *don't* equal figures.

After burning out on what I was told to do, and getting permission from myself through my work with Adele, I keyed into the only and best qualities that have worked for me to translate my value especially through relationships: crucial clarity and conscious consistency.

Focusing on these factors has meant that I can stop trying to be so *creative.* Instead, I've embraced simplification. I've worked on simplifying my business processes and offerings in my Streamlined Service Value Ladder, worked with a more specific audience, stopped worrying about my email list and blogging so much, and focused on what had been working well without all the bells and whistles. Instead, I've become old-fashioned and focused strongly on what I call a "simple awareness" strategy.

I've embraced the value of repetition for memory, though I used about worry about feeling "fresh." Now I keep a focus on making every element of my branding, marketing, sales, and operations clear and consistent. My goal has become to ensure everyone I already know clearly understands what I do and for whom (and could remember it)—and that's *it!*

To this day, I don't worry about making sure that all people I meet know that I worked for Disney, or that I've been doing this work for eight-plus years, or that I have advised hundreds of entrepreneurs. Nope. I've just doubled down on simple awareness. Because though most people don't give it much attention, simple awareness is more than enough to drive a service-based business to success.

Here's what it looks like for me, and what all great service businesses do—regardless of how great or frequent their online marketing is.

MY COMMONSENSE BUSINESS GROWTH PLAN

- Believe in yourself.
- Make your business great.
- Treat people well.
- Do good work.
- Serve those who need (and value it) most.
- Make sure everyone knows what you do.
- *Repeat.*

If you can do this consistently, it can be more than *enough.* Because here's the thing: There's *so* much noise out there—online and offline, overflowing our inboxes and our brains. The worlds of what we do are filled to the brim with insecure entrepreneurs (much like who I used to be) who are constantly changing their tactics, dressing up their work, and making things way more complicated than they need to be. A natural instinct is to think, *Gosh, there's so much out there! I've got to find a way to stand out!*

Having been there, tried it, and seen it bomb, I'll tell you: **It's not about standing out. It's more about *understanding.*** Most service-based professionals get a majority of their business via referrals and word-of-mouth. Yet, when my consulting clients ask me for referrals to other types of business partners, I come up short more often than I'd like because, even though I'm well-connected and established in my area, many business owners I meet and know are so unclear and/or so general about the problems they solve, the solutions they offer, and whom they serve that I don't know *who* to refer for *what* . . . so I don't refer them.

Ever been there when trying to refer somebody? I'm betting you have multiple times, and for the same reasons. And I don't want that to happen to you. I want you to be enthusiastically referred by as many people who know you, have worked with you, or have just met you as possible.

Donald Miller teaches in his book *Building a Storybrand,* "If you confuse, you lose."[24] I add, "If they're aware, they'll share."

Could all of the people on your email list and in your network pass a pop quiz about you with only one question on it: *What do you do and who for?* Well, if they couldn't today, imagine if they *could!*

The average person's network is about 250 people. What if even just 100 of those people confidently knew the most crucial things about you and your business? If that were the case, then you'd become a card in their deck—easy to refer and connect when people in *their* network have that exact problem, need your solution, or have a question about your category. It would also keep them aware that you might be a solution for them! That's how networking connections could turn into new clients.

That's what I want to teach you about clarity and consistency in referral relationships, and what we're about to explore in more detail, including my helpful mnemonic CHIPS. This approach is what's worked for me for years and allowed me to simplify everything I do in my business, work less, and make substantially more money!

If you focus on a simple awareness strategy in all that you do to translate your value (marketing, sales, networking, etc.), then deliver excellent client experiences that delight current and past clients, here's what happens (and what has happened to me):

- Nearly everyone referred to you actually needs something you offer. *(More than 90% of those I meet with in complimentary consultation calls are fits for something I offer.)*
- Nearly everyone referred to you already knows that they have a problem *(so you don't have to convince them and come off like a sleazy sales guy).*
- You never, ever have to pitch yourself again—because people come to *you* to set a free consultation or to email you for more information.
- You don't have to stress about the latest marketing tactics online or offline.
- You can do simple, streamlined marketing that drives awareness, in a style you enjoy doing that plays to your strengths *(such as a regular speaking series, a fun newsletter, an interview video show or podcast, etc.).*
- You don't have to have thousands of people on an email list or following you on social media to be profitable and make six figures or more annually.
- You become well-known as an expert at something.
- You get asked to speak or be interviewed for relevant opportunities (aka *opportunities that shine a light on your expertise and the main problem you solve, and put you in front of audiences that make up your ideal clients).*

Let's take a closer look at this strategy as it plays out in building and strengthening referral relationships. If you go all in on choosing clarity, not creativity when networking, you have to start with a tough test: letting go of creative job titles.

Creative Job Titles Don't Connect, They Confuse

When I teach my workshop, Branding with Annie, live and in-person, I always invite the attendees to go around the room and share briefly about what they do. However, I always challenge them to do so in a specific format: tell us what you do in a short, simplified way that a fifth-grader could understand.

If you've gone to just about any networking event or business seminar, you know that the invitation to "tell us about yourself" can easily turn into hearing a five-to-10-minute life story from someone that leaves you little to no idea what they do. And suddenly, you've lost 30–45 minutes of your seminar time to speak just "going around the room."

When this happens, I've observed that many grown adults can't follow those directions. People do better with this if you are specific. So, since I only have about five minutes of my presentation time to devote to awareness/networking of who's in the room (whether in-person or virtual), I teach everyone my best strategy for doing this: leading with your key category and describing what you'd do in a way a fifth-grader could understand it. You're not allowed to give your elevator pitch, only the general description of what you do.

I explain what a mistake it is to use one because ***creative job titles confuse more people than they connect with them.***

When you only have seconds to connect with others, as you do in networking instances like this one, by choosing some creative job description, you risk not being relevant to those who might want to work with you or refer you. Yet, even when I explain this, I still have at least one person who insists on using their creative job title/or their pitch. Here's my favorite story that happened at Branding with Annie:

We go around, and everyone's sharing their fifth-grader job description. We arrive at a woman who answers, "I'm a failed mathematician." *What?* It definitely got a laugh. It got a reaction. You could feel the confusion that filled the room. We awkwardly moved onto the next person.

That "failed mathematician"? She's actually a great mortgage broker. I'd known her via networking and she's awesome. She had come to her profession after having studied to be a professional mathematician but had left that path to pursue helping people buy their dream homes. She loved this very creative description of herself because she imagined that it piqued curiosity about her story. It always gets a reaction, so she was afraid to let go of it, even when I'd directly challenged the room to choose clarity over creativity.

She's the perfect example of why I make that challenge. Because what if sitting next to her had been a real estate agent needing a new mortgage broker relationship? And what if across the room had been a closing lawyer? Or even someone who was thinking of buying a new house? These valuable people would have absolutely no idea to go up and talk to this woman after my workshop based on what she shared. And just like that, so many profitable opportunities are missed due to the security blankets of creative job titles. *And let's be real: Even if people had a math interest, they probably wouldn't connect with her since she was a "failed" mathematician, right?!*

Here are a few other favorites I've heard while networking over the years,

- "I'm a plastic surgeon for mobile apps" *(actually a mobile app developer).*
- "I'm a space exchange guide" *(actually a real estate agent).*
- "I'm a trailblazer for women" *(actually a life coach).*

In seeing this happen time and time again, I've come to realize that people hold really tight to their creative job titles/descriptions because they think their key to success has to be creativity/standing out (so they let go of understanding).

You might easily think, *There are a million mortgage brokers, life coaches, business consultants, and so on . . . so how will anyone see that* **I'm** *different? That what I do* **is** *different from just anyone? How will they pay attention to me if I don't instantly grab their attention?*

Well, after I traded being creative for being clear, I became a lot more well-known and trusted in my field. *Yes,* a lot of people do branding, even in my local area. But I'm top of mind for a lot of people I know because I stay the course. Because I'm not afraid to associate myself with the understandable category. And I'm not trying to put such a spin on what I do that I miss profitable connections with possible clients and referral partners.

But you may wonder: Can you ever use a creative job title to brand yourself? Yes, but you need to treat it more like a tagline than a job title. You may see some big influencers and people who give themselves creative monikers. Keep in mind that this strategy places a huge financial and time investment burden on them to *educate* their audience on what their moniker *means,* making it easier to immediately understand and connect it back to its larger professional field.

So for you, there may actually be a time and place to brand yourself as something like "The Brand Boss" or "The Leadership Magician" or something like this, but that belongs as part of your marketing—not how you describe yourself when networking. It can't exist without context, because reactions don't equal revenue.

Reactions Don't Equal Revenue

Even if you don't use a creative job title, it can still be very tempting to talk about what you do with an emphasis on "getting a reaction" and trying to focus on your hook—*aka* how you stand out from everyone else.

As you know now, I used to be pretty in love with my multi-passionate business version of Greatest Story Creative (that was really four businesses in one!). One of the reasons I loved it was because I'd *always* get a reaction from people when I talked about it. Do you get a reaction from people when you pitch your business or describe your job title? It's a great feeling, *right?*

Well, I'm here to tell you something that I've learned the hard way: **Reactions don't equal revenue.** Having someone think you're cool and having them invest in your services are often two completely different things. Our desire and hopes to "get a reaction" can sometimes blind us to that difference.

Here's how things used to go for me when Greatest Story Creative was a business with four "arms" (weddings, events, business, and everyday).

Someone would come up to me while I was networking.

They'd ask me, "What do you do?"
And I'd be like, "I'm a business storyteller."
And they'd reply enthusiastically, "That's *so* cool!"
But in their head, they were thinking, *I have no idea what I would hire her to do for me but, like, that's interesting. That's so cool and original, though. Awesome.*

Meanwhile, I'd be thinking, *Wow, great reaction!*

Then fast-forward, I'd never hear from that person, nor would they refer me for things. When I stopped and thought about it, the disconnect actually makes a lot of psychological sense. While they thought what I did was interesting, they didn't get how it could help them (the possible hero/client!) solve a problem that mattered to them or others they know. It was creative, but it was also confusing. It lacked context.

In short, I was creative, but I wasn't *relevant.* It got a reaction, but it never led to revenue. That's what I want you to get. I want you to deliberately choose clarity over creativity *every single time*—for this reason especially.

If I were to speak to that same person now, here's how the conversation goes if I stay focused on what I do best (branding for service business owners) in my dramatically more streamlined version of Greatest Story. Same person; I just answer differently here.

They ask, "What do you do?"
I reply, "I do branding for coaches and consultants."

"Oh? Cool. I've been thinking of starting a consulting practice."

Now I'm invited to share more of how I can help (a solution).

I respond: "Awesome. I often help new consultants tell their story by writing their clear marketing message."

Now they're thinking, Yes! I'm so stuck on my story. Maybe she can help me!

That person may ask for more info, or email me later, or book a free consultation on my website because I've put an easy-to-find big red button to do just that. But they're more likely to act. And that's what you want when you're translating your value to others: *action,* not reaction. It's about action, not applause.

I know it seems counter-intuitive to do, but when you flip the situation, you get it from that perspective. You're a busy person, and while you're impressed by many people, you're only going to pay attention to those who can help you and add value to your life and/or to those you know (your network). You've got a bazillion tabs open, so unless someone is specifically relevant (not super creative) you won't remember them and you won't act.

How do you do this well? You start with the first two keys to unlock more ideal client referrals.

The 2 Clear Keys to Unlock More Referrals

Building on this, and informed by a lot of ineffective networking I've done and a lot of effective branding work I've done for clients, I've come to believe there are two major keys you need to unlock more referrals to your ideal clients and get people in your network to look out for you strategically:

1. Your category
2. Your hook

As I just shared in my example of "Reactions Don't Equal Revenue," when I led with "business storyteller" in the exchange, I disconnected myself immediately from a possible client. That's because I led with the *spin,* not the category. If you start with spin, ideal clients and referral partners will *spin* away from you.

Like we can cling too closely to creative job titles, we can also be so worried about standing out that we try to talk about what's different (our key twist) *before* we introduce what makes us relevant (our key category). To effectively get referrals to ideal clients and pique their interest when you meet with them, you have to know both and use them in the right order to forge a real connection. Let's define these terms.

YOUR CATEGORY

Examples: branding, business consulting, life coaching, virtual assistance, wellness consulting

This category needs to be something just about anyone (even a fifth-grader) would easily understand. It's likely boring, but it's clear. For example, even if you absolutely hate calling yourself a "life coach," if life coaching is the big "encyclopedia" that your approach would fall under, you need to embrace the term for its usefulness. If your business were a Russian nesting doll, you have to always name the biggest doll as your clear category. Of course, what you do that makes you so wonderful, valuable, and unique is a much smaller doll in the set.

The reason for this is simple: You need to connect something boring to what you do because boring can clearly communicate. Boring is searchable. Boring is easy to refer and to explain to others what you do. It gives people an instant frame of reference to determine if what you do is relevant to themselves or their network. Without it, it's all reaction with no action (and no revenue).

A lot of people resist this because they're adamant that what they do isn't your typical "life coaching" or "business consulting." But that's where the hook comes in. However, if you never share your key category, I'd argue you're leaving a lot of possible connection on the table in your quest to be unique and perceived as special. *What good is it to be unique if it can't connect you to the people you can help most?*

The key category is called a "key" because it has the power to unlock possibility and potential in your business. You have to accept that, because people are busy *(I know you are!)*, they don't have a lot of free space in their minds to remember everything about your work and how great it is. You're lucky if they remember one or two things about you and your business. So when networking and building strategic partner relationships, I encourage you to make those one or two things your category and your hook, in that order.

I say in that order because the right category can and should unlock every revenue-generating activity you offer: from your highest, most-valuable solution service to your area of expertise to speak as a paid speaker or on a podcast for visibility.

YOUR HOOK

Examples: telling your story in a clear marketing message, helping you get to inbox zero, producing amazing virtual events, fixing your presentation slide design, guiding you on how to become a bestselling author on Amazon

This is probably something you're used to using or thinking you have to constantly use. Your hook is the thing you're known for that can unlock everything else you do. It isn't *everything* you do, but it functions like a key that unlocks and leads to other ways that you help your clients. Ironically, it's a great strategy to help you stand out *successfully* and become more memorable.

What if you're not sure what your "hook" is or should be? Ask your network! Ask your favorite past clients and your best referral partners what they think of you most for.

However, your hook is the smaller of the two keys. It's helpful but, as you can see with mine, it doesn't unlock every aspect of what I do the way that boring old "key category" can.

The trick is to think of the category and the hook as a dynamic duo. Like Batman *and* Robin, both are important, but when you use one without the other, you're leaving opportunity on the table. A category with no hook doesn't present you as an expert at anything. Using a hook with no category? That's way less relevant for most people you'll meet, and you run the risk of others not understanding that you can help them.

What else could help you get more people referring you to ideal clients? Well, you need to put all of your brand "CHIPS" on the table.

Put Your Brand CHIPS on the Table

As we just explored, knowing your category and hook can be critical to communicating what you do when networking. To take it further, I've created an easy mnemonic to help you drive consistent awareness around your network and ideal client referrals back to your practice *and* make it easier to market, brand, and create services for your business. My method is called CHIPS, and it has a lot to do with helping others clearly and quickly understand what you do.

My working theory is this: If you can clearly communicate what you do to everyone you meet, you'll get way more referrals to your perfect-fit clients, ready to invest in you. The more people who know and understand what you do and who you do it for, one, the more referrals you'll get, and two, the more likely those referrals will be an amazing match for your services and your price.

Most people know and have influence over 250+ people, so you want others to think of you as a "card" in their deck—ready to play the minute they connect with or spot your perfect client! The best way to become that card to others is to borrow a poker analogy: put all your chips on the table when you talk about (or write about) what you do. If people easily understand your key elements, they'll be more likely to remember and refer when the time is right. Meet your simple brand CHIPS, the five biggest connection drivers of your practice:

C | **Category**: the clear official professional field you work in
H | **Hook**: what you're most known for in that field
I | **Ideal Clients**: a brief, universal description of your ideal clients' "occupation"
P | **Problem**: the #1 most crucial problem you solve for ideal clients
S | **Solution**: your #1 most valuable solution to that problem

For an example of this in action, here's how I've defined my brand CHIPS:

Greatest Story Creative
Category: Branding
Hook: Helping you clearly tell your story
Ideal Clients: Coaches, consultants, and service business owners
Problem: Unclear, inconsistent marketing that doesn't capture their value
Solution: A three-step Brand Story Solution (clear marketing message, consistent visual brand toolkit, and compelling website)

And here are several other great examples I've developed strategically for different types of businesses, varying in the types/scopes of clients they serve.

Work-Life Directions, founded by LaRae Jome, PhD
Category: Career counseling and mental health
Hook: Helping you navigate all aspects of working life with career counseling that's inclusive of mental health
Ideal Clients: Mid-level career professionals
Problem: Feeling lost and stuck in a current job and career path

Solution: Mental-health-inclusive career counseling to give you the tool to break past work-related struggles, clarify needs and goals, create an action plan, and confidently move forward on your best next career steps

Sales Savvy, founded by Liz Rossilli
Category: Sales consulting
Hook: Teaching you how to confidently, genuinely cold-call prospects and turn them into clients
Ideal Clients: Women B2B service providers (such as coaches, photographers, and designers)
Problem: Slow or inconsistent sales
Solution: Signature outreach system to create a smart sales plan and the confidence to put it into action

Rader Co., founded by Marcey Rader
Category: Productivity and health
Hook: Helping your team drowning in email
Ideal Clients: HR leaders and executives at biotech, pharma, accounting, and innovative organizations
Problem: Fear and guilt of employee burnout (resulting in low retention and low performance)
Solution: Individualized productivity tools, healthy habits, and coaching accountability to help every employee create sustainably balanced lives, effectively moving the organization forward as a whole ("Keep good people to keep moving forward")

No matter what types of clients you partner with, if you define *your* CHIPS, you will immediately gain a clear, consistent means to communicate what you do when you network. You'll never have to worry again that someone won't "get" what you do—because it'll be simplified and shared smartly. You can easily put this information in an email and send it over when you network, solidifying and clarifying what you do.

You'll also be able to use this approach as a super powerful reminder of crucial clarity for yourself of what to focus on and market awareness about. One of my favorite things to do is to print out my CHIPS and put them up front and center in my office. Before I consider creating a new marketing freebie, or a workshop, or adding a service, I consult my CHIPS. *Does this new thing make sense for where my focus is?* This mnemonic has saved me precious time and focus many a time since inventing it, and that's been a profitable endeavor.

A powerful tool for simple awareness, your CHIPS can help you make stronger connections to people because they keep you from worrying about telling the whole story. Instead, they help you consistently communicate what's most crucial: the key info new people and busy people have room for in their heads.

The reality is that no one has time to become an expert on you, but they do have a bit of brain space to remember what's most important. So hand it to them—clearly, not creatively.

EXERCISE

Create Your Best Referral Bio

FREE RESOURCE

If you need help with this, I have a free tool/training on CHIPS called **"Your Best Referral Bio."**

This is a plug-and-play template that includes three elevator pitch scripts for things like sending emails to referral partners, messages on LinkedIn, and posting online.

Get your free copy now at greateststorycreative.com/referralbio or find the link in your *Establish Yourself Companion Workbook.*

REFERRAL RELATIONSHIPS

Be Considerate

In life and in business, relationships are always a two-way street. Yet as your business grows, you get busy and it's easy to lose sight of caring for the vital relationships that can build your business. While clarity is important, just communicating what you do won't create meaningful connection if you aren't an active, thoughtful partner to others.

With a bit of extra thought and some systems *(right?),* you can make your referral relationships more authentic and valuable to both of you when you focus on being considerate. Let's look at how to up-level all of your business relationships with conscious care.

Become Easier to Refer

The email subject read, "MARKETING MELTDOWN!" I braced for impact. This was from a past branding client. *Ack—what happened?*

Well, it turns out, my client Sheila had worked with a company that I referred her too. A few months later, her project had blown up. She'd come to me wanting my help to untangle things through consulting. I was happy to help her, but truly I was so embarrassed and felt somewhat responsible for the mess she was in.

The company I'd referred to her was a group I'd personally interviewed to proactively ensure they had a great client experience and process. So I was incredibly disappointed to hear Sheila was having a terrible experience—one, because she wasn't getting results, and two, because I'd had no head's up. The company never thanked me for the referral nor for booking this client, so the very first time I'd even heard they were working together was this SOS distress call.

Why hadn't the company let me know they were working together? *Thanks, Annie, for connecting us!* Why hadn't the company given me a head's up it wasn't working out? *Challenges happen sometimes in client experience, but why was I blindsided?*

The whole thing was unsettling and led to another disappointing choice: to stop referring that company altogether. Not only does that mean the company loses potential business, it impacts my value and resources, too.

I wish I could say this was an isolated incident, but it's not. Unfortunately, I think things like this have become somewhat widespread in the service business community. I don't want you to be in this spot, as the person referring or the one receiving a referral. But avoiding this, and having strong strategic partnerships and excellent referrals, all come from working on being easy to refer in the first place.

Do you think you and your business are easy to refer? I have a hunch that many people think they're easy to refer, but in my experience, the majority *are not.* Here's why.

"Thanks, Annie!" I'll occasionally see this little message in an email or on LinkedIn, as I'm referring a potential client to another business owner. That's usually the beginning and end of a lot of entrepreneurs' "referral" process. Unfortunately, I can't tell you how many times, how many referrals, and how many *years,*

I've referred possible, current, and past clients to other business owners and then only ever receive a quick "Thanks, Annie!" in reply from that entrepreneur.

I've probably sent tens of thousands of dollars' worth of possible referred business to people. To some partners, I've even shared multiple referrals in a year. You know how much of that business anyone thanks me for beyond (sometimes) a quick "Thanks, Annie!"? Very little.

Too often, here's what's happened on my end:

- The person that I referred goes on to work with that business owner and I never hear about it (aka *the business owner never thanks me or lets me know).*
- I hear about it when that person comes back to me, furious about a bad client experience! *(Side note: This is also typically my first time hearing that they're even working together!)*

In more than eight years as a business owner, a small percentage of the people that I've sent referrals to have responded by doing one or more of the following:

- Sent a thoughtful email or handwritten thank-you note for a single referral or multiple ones
- Sent a physical or digital gift
- Sent me referrals as well

To reference Adam Grant's book on reciprocity styles, *Give and Take,*[25] I'm generally a "giver," but my "matcher" tendency definitely comes out when I send several referrals as a referral partner. I try not to keep score. I do always refer when I am trying to help someone get the support they need. However, it's hard not to keep score when the scoreboard begins to grow with my number and the other person's stays at zero.

What's the effect of this? Why is it important to be a great referral partner? After all, there are many ways to get clients. Well, the effect for me is that I've stopped referring many people. *A lot* of people! I won't recommend someone if I'm not confident they can do a great job. It's disheartening for me.

What too often happens is that I meet someone who seems incredible and sounds like a great fit for what many of the ideal clients I work with need, and I start sending referral after referral and sharing resources with those people. I do this because I want both the business owner and my clients to succeed. I want my client to have the right solution to their problem. In some cases, I even give up possible business to ensure my prospective client gets their best fit possible.

This said, after five or more referrals, if it seems like all I'm doing is growing someone else's business for them, I stop. If I hear about bad experiences from those I've referred—client or otherwise—I stop. If I'm not given a head's up about major challenges working with someone who's a current client of mine, I stop. Long story short: If my referrals turn out to be a totally one-sided affair that risks upsetting clients, I stop.

I bet that if you frequently refer someone but never hear from them, you likely stop, too. So, why does this keep happening?

This stems from the problems that come with a business that isn't thriving and is potentially headed for burnout. I've found that too many entrepreneurs have one, a scarcity mindset; two, a disorganized business; or three, both. Things aren't working, so they are desperate for referrals, but they don't give many in return, especially if our services overlap. Additionally, maybe they don't have a system in place to consistently thank others and share appreciation. And perhaps most simply, they aren't asking or capturing information from new leads to understand where they came from or who referred them.

What I wish more business owners would pay heed to is this: build, deliver, and appreciate. If you are not thoughtfully ***building*** referral relationships, ***delivering*** great client experiences, and ***appreciating*** the referral givers in your network, you are getting less of them than you could be, which means fewer clients, less revenue, and less growth. This also hurts your brand for the long run.

So what do you need to ensure you're being a great referral partner and you're getting as many perfect-fit referrals as possible?

Two big things to become easier to refer:

1. Be great.
2. Be caring.

Be *Great* at Serving Those Who Are Referred to You

When someone sends you a referral, they are lending you some of their clout. They are endorsing you, so they are involved. It's critical that you then deliver and take the best care of that person that you can. To do this well, you need to have a well-organized business with a polished client experience that offers opportunities for dialogue and feedback (i.e., so much of what we've already walked through in this book).

Of course, not every project will go smoothly, but if you serve someone who was referred to you, you have a responsibility both to your client and the referral partner to do the best job possible. *And if you hit a snag, be sure to keep the person who referred that client in the loop so they don't get blindsided with a meltdown email!*

Be *Caring*: Treat Your Referral Partner *as a Partner*

While not a literal partner in your business, anyone who consistently sends you referrals (or has the potential to) is a strategic partner of your business. One amazing strategic partner can bring you all the clients you need in an entire year, if you play your cards right and are *considerate* of that relationship. No matter how your business is doing financially, never take this for granted, whether it's two referrals or 20.

What are ways to be a considerate referral partner?
What if I don't have enough business to refer back?
Do I have to give an expensive gift?

- Keep people posted on the process. *(This person set a consultation or emailed me, they booked a project with me, etc.)*
- Thank those who send you referrals in a thoughtful (read: multiple sentence) email or handwritten thank-you note *(even better if you have devised a referral process).*
- Consider sending a digital or physical gift if the client books your services.
- If the project goes awry, let the person who referred you *know* so they have some context for how the referral went.

- Make sure that those who refer you know that you value them. Show them your appreciation regularly (and send them referrals too, if you can/are in a spot in your business to do that).

If you can't mutually send referrals for whatever reason (perhaps you don't have enough business, you offer too similar services, etc.), be sure to send a significant gift proportionate to the amount of business you've been sent by them. *In short, let people know you care and value them.*

Now, I've told you a lot about how I've stopped referring many people because they were not great or considerate (or some combination of them). But what about those I know who *are* great and considerate? Well, I refer them enthusiastically and constantly! Take one of my partners, in particular. Though she only became a branding and consulting client of mine in 2020, I've referred and/or connected her to at least 50% of her all-time clients. Most people I send her way come pre-sold because I've already sung her praises so highly.

I do that because I know what she does extremely well and I can trust that she's a professional with a good process. She consistently keeps me posted on how referrals turn out and thanks me, often with a thoughtful email and a little gift, so I know she values the support.

It doesn't have to be complex or expensive to be a good referral partner and someone who's really easy to refer, but it does take intention. So if you're learning anything from this book, I hope you see that pouring some strategy into what you're doing will take you far toward reaching your greatest business.

MASTER
YOUR MONEY NOW
Brand Story Guide

REFERRAL RELATIONSHIPS

Be Committed

Clarity, consideration, and—finally—commitment will create the connections and relationships you can confidently count on to grow the next chapter of your business. Relationships by their very nature take time. Just one coffee date or quick exchange of messages won't bring you ideal client referrals. Only commitment will ensure the work you do to meet others now will matter to you both later.

The Power of Staying in Touch and Frequent Networking

In my Fans & Feedback process, I shared that the S of "F.A.N.S." is all about sharing and staying top of mind. I broke down ways you could intentionally stay on clients' radar and continue to build on your relationship.

A similar best practice holds true with referral partners and new connections in your network. It's essential to stay top of mind for your relationship to grow and stay healthy. If all you do is chat once or twice, you will soon disappear into a sea of everyone else they meet. Staying in touch becomes something worth investing your time and attention in.

For referral relationships, it becomes that much more important to provide value in the process of staying in touch. We just talked about importance of reciprocity and appreciation, but here are many specific ways you could intentionally stay on someone's radar and add value to their lives and businesses while doing so. *(You'll notice this a bit of a twist on the list I shared about staying top of mind with clients. This uses the same skill set!)*

Here's what keeping up with (and adding value) to your referral relationships might look like:

- Emailing people every few months to sincerely check in on how they're doing
- Asking regularly if there's anything you can do to support *them*
- Attending their events, liking their posts online, and subscribing to their newsletters *(and writing back when you get them)*
- Making thoughtful referral partner and other networking introductions for them
- Referring ideal clients to them
- Hiring them for consulting or projects, if you need their help
- Hosting events just for past clients to network with each other
- Keeping them posted when people they refer set consultations with you
- Sending a gift or thoughtful thank-you when those they refer book your services
- Teaming up to do a workshop, interview, or other collaboration opportunity together to share audiences

Whatever you do, do it regularly. Use systems like calendar reminders, automated emails, and a to-do list to ensure that you really commit to your relationships for the long haul. Because I consistently check in with and support my referral partners, most of them I've had for years and they've each sent me multiple clients. I've taken care to hire them when I need them, like their posts, introduce them to my clients, and collaborate when I see great opportunities.

The joy of doing it this way is that you truly get to help one another. You create a new connection, and that relationship only deepens over time if you take care of it. *The plant grows if you water it, right?*

Moreover, don't forget about frequency. If you don't have a lot of strong referral relationships or as many clients as you'd like, it really makes a significant difference how many (or few) networking calls you have.

To give you an example, I coached one of my clients privately for 10 months, working against a specific, year-long growth plan I'd recommended. At multiple trainings, group calls, and private sessions, I encouraged my client to make building referral partners a huge priority because she had few clients and needed more awareness in her network in order to gain more. Since her practice was quiet, I recommended that she set virtual coffee dates with at least 20 people a month (five per week). By 10 months, if she met with five people a week, she'd be at around 200 meetings—200 new connections that she could establish and begin fostering.

While this would be a lot of time spent networking, the thought is that the first 20–30 conversations/new connections give her some momentum, clients, and so on, and then she could cut down on networking. When 10 months had passed, I checked in to see how many she'd completed in time that we'd been working together. I got this response: "3. No referrals yet."

Unfortunately, with just three, I don't think there will be any referrals anytime soon. Meeting just a handful of people one time is highly unlikely to make a difference in growing anyone's practice. The odds just aren't in your favor. If she'd spent only one month doing five per week (20 new connections), I'd be willing to bet she would have gotten at least one referral, new connection, or other opportunity because frequency matters.

Relationships take time to build (months and years, not days and weeks). Moreover, developing and finding good ones take frequent action. If you want to work on building referral partners to help you fill your practice with more clients, I strongly recommend networking often with high-quality people whose practices are thriving and complement yours in some ways (i.e., they share ideal clients but provide them with different services).

In terms of how many to aim for, I use this graph with my clients to show them that if their business is down, their relationship building and meeting new people time needs to increase accordingly. This is pulled from my Referral Networking Guide, an overview of best practices for setting one-on-one meetings with new people to foster referral partner relationships.

HOW MANY NETWORKING 1:1S TO DO PER WEEK
TO BUILD AWARENESS

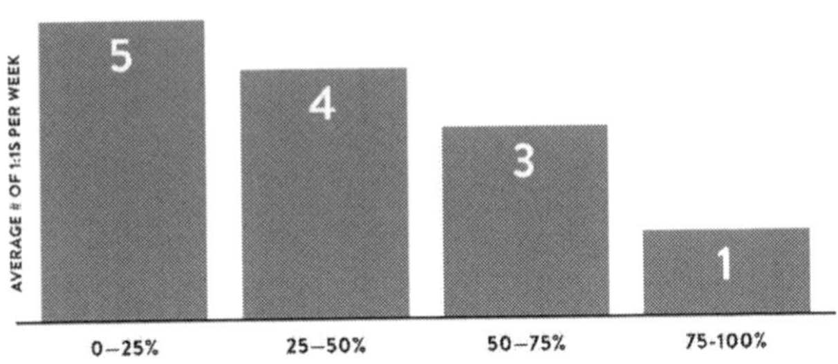

Start at the Percentage of Desired Clients/Revenue You Currently Have

The beauty of something like this is that you can easily increase or decrease depending on how busy clients are keeping you. I have one or two virtual coffee dates a month on average, because things are consistent and steady, and networking takes time away from other things. It's still worthwhile to do even when I'm at my busiest, though, because it's a big-picture approach. Investing in relationships takes time but it pays off, so start as soon as you can and remember those best practices including staying in touch long after that first get-together with someone new.

The last thing I want to share with you about referral relationships is the part I'm always practicing: keeping people posted on the newest things I'm doing. If you tend to keep upcoming things in your business to yourself, you want to hear this gem too.

Do They Know What You Know?

If you're somebody like me who can worry about "bothering people," building referral relationships can take a lot of mindset work. You may also miss opportunities you'd get simply if the people you know *knew* about what you're up to.

How many times have you created a new workshop, or course, or service—and then told only a handful of people about it? Then watched it flop? If I'm really honest with myself, this has happened far too many times for me. Even though I've reached so many levels of my greatest business, this has been an area I tend to struggle with: actively keeping the people in my network personally posted on what's new.

While I've moved beyond the "bothering people" mindset in a sales/consultation perspective, I'm still actively working on overcoming it when it comes to telling my network and clients about things. To keep myself more accountable, I devised a simple client-generating awareness checklist called **"Do They Know What I Know?"**

I print this checklist and keep it nearby, reminding me every so often to ensure that I'm actually letting people know what's going on in my business. After all, if others don't know, the business can't grow right? While I can spend hours on marketing, too often I forget to simply let people know what I'm up to! (*That* is marketing, too.)

I revisit this checklist every three to six months to double-check that I'm keeping my network aware of what I'm up to, how they can support me, how I can support them, and what I have going on that might be valuable for them (or someone they know!). Every single time I do that, I create awareness that can generate clients and develop strong, ongoing relationships. Talk about an easy win all-around!

In having this accountability document, I find that I'm reaching out to current clients, past clients, referral partners, and even my mailing list far more often. I'm getting thousands of dollars in sales and more than 10,000 eyeballs on my free templates just from sending a couple of emails. I'm booking more consulting than ever and getting better referrals than ever, simply because I'm actively letting more people know about that *new* thing (the new program I created that follows the Brand Story Solution, the free workshop I'm hosting, or the new consulting service I have).

I'm willing to bet that if you sat down and thought about it, many of the people you work with and network with have no idea what's new in your world—and, if they did, you'd have an influx of sales and opportunities from very little effort. So, as you commit to strengthening your new and existing client and referral relationships, I encourage you to commit to yourself and the value of what you offer—to let people know about it.

If you've put in the work of being clear, consistent, and committed to great referral relationships, make the most of them. Let people help you, too. That's what relationships are all about.

EXERCISE

Let Your People Know What's New

Create your own "Do They Know What I Know?" client-generating awareness checklist, taking inspiration from the one on the following page or use the one included in your *Establish Yourself Companion Workbook.*

Take 20–30 minutes to fill this out, checking boxes only if you're confident that group of people is aware of each item on your list.

I challenge you to pick one key element and one group who is not aware, and let them know! Send emails, pick up the phone, and connect with those people. Contact at least 10 people in the group—individually, sincerely, and personally—and watch what happens next. If you get through that, I challenge you to pick another group. I have a hunch you'll marvel at what starts to happen from here, just from these simple awareness actions.

And hey—be sure to revisit this exercise regularly, like every three to six months. There's likely something new people will need to know about then, but they will only hear about it *if* you tell them!

"DO THEY KNOW WHAT I KNOW?" CHECKLIST

KEY ELEMENTS OF MY BUSINESS	REFERRAL PARTNERS	CURRENT CLIENTS	PAST CLIENTS	LINKEDIN NETWORK	EMAIL LIST	FRIENDS AND FAMILY
My newest offer/program						
My new free gift/lead magnet						
My most valuable service						
What I do/what my business does						
Who I help (my ideal clients)						
What field I work in (my category)						
The #1 problem I solve for ideal clients						
My new course/training						
Write in your own below!						

YOUR REFERRAL RELATIONSHIPS "KEY C" CHECK

As you considered how to initiate, build, and strengthen referral relationships, we explored:

- The value of relationships to growing all businesses.
- Trading "standing out" for understanding.
- Ditching creative job titles that don't convert.
- Why reactions don't equal revenue.
- The two clear keys to unlock more referrals.
- Putting your brand CHIPS on the table when networking.
- How to become easier to refer.
- The power of staying in touch.
- Actively letting people know what's new in your business.

With these aspects in mind, take 10–15 minutes to reflect on and answer the questions here in the book, in your *Establish Yourself Companion Workbook*, or in your own notebook. Though these questions are intended to help you find clarity about what feels uncertain, the very first question will allow you to give yourself much-deserved credit! You're on your way.

WHAT'S WORKING

What's *one* thing you're really proud of when it comes to your current business relationships and referral partners?

COURAGEOUS CONFIDENCE

What's *one* thing you wish you had more courage and confidence about with your relationships and goals for relationship building?

CRUCIAL CLARITY

What's *one* thing you need more focus and clarity on?

CONSCIOUS CONSISTENCY

What's *one* thing you need more consistency with?

CONTINUED COMMITMENT

What's *one* thing you want to commit to more on the business relationship front?

Now, which *one* of the these things feels most urgent to you?
List that one in the form of an action step here.

MY MOST VALUABLE ACTION STEP FOR
REFERRAL RELATIONSHIPS:

For this step, **are there any professionals and/or tools you may need to make that top action step happen?** *List your thoughts on this here.*

GREATEST
STORY
CREATIVE

Marketing

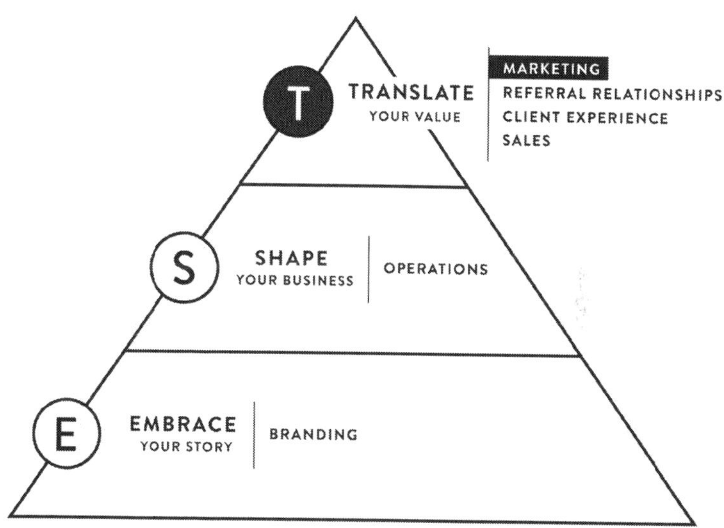

At last, here we are. Together, we've walked through best practices and systems inspiration from branding, to operations, to sales and client experience, to referral relationships, and now we're finally at marketing. Here's the beauty of this: If you've been thinking about or taking action on optimizing the other five areas we've journeyed through, you've already been optimizing your "marketing"!

If you've been prioritizing embracing your story, shaping your operations, and translating your value into sales, client experience, and relationships, then creating compelling, effective marketing now should be as easy as topping a high-quality cupcake with delicious, beautiful frosting. Because you haven't fixated on the frosting and you know exactly who your ideal clients are, present yourself as an expert, and have a profitable business set up for success, traditional marketing strategies can now allow you to swing open those doors and invite your best-fit clients to take part in all you have to offer them.

As we explored when I shared about the interdependent relationship between branding and marketing, for all its bells and whistles and attention, marketing is simply action. It's about getting eyes and ears on your business to invite ideal clients to connect with you. That kind of *action* is something you can invest in throughout how you shape your business and translate your value.

We've already covered many ways to do exactly that. In fact, if you foster stellar client relationships and partner relationships and a high volume of them, you may never truly "need" to have a traditional marketing presence. For example, one of my clients' businesses is thriving so well on just referrals, optimizing her operations, and maintaining the quality of her work that she can't ever seem to find the time to fully maximize or do traditional marketing. Of course, she doesn't *need* to! This said, I'm still excited for her to optimize it soon by putting simple systems in place to use marketing to help her grow that much more.

That's what I want traditional marketing to be for you: an important tool for sure, but one of many tools you have at your disposal for inviting your best-fit clients to work with you and invest in your high-value solutions. That's it. Marketing doesn't have to be your full-time job. You don't have to live on social media to be successful. You don't need to be everywhere, trying every new app and tactic. In short, you don't really have to worry so much about it, if you put some sexy strategy into *how* you're going to do it consistently going forward.

So with this in mind, let's finish our journey of finding reverse revenue and growing your greatest business. Together, let's explore why marketing can be such a bear to conquer in business, some of my secrets to taming the beast and putting things on autopilot, and the hard, honest truth about the instincts you need to fight to make sure your marketing and branding actually work for the long haul.

REVERSE
L REVENUE
THE EST. YOURSELF WAY
BRANDING OPS MARKETING
THE TYPICAL WAY

MARKETING

Avoid Tactic Tornadoes with Sexy Strategy

Ask any coach or consultant what they think about marketing their business, and the word *overwhelm* will come up. After I personally almost burned out on traditional marketing, I was able to both simplify and increase the effectiveness of my own by doing two things: one, realizing why most traditional marketing can be a trap and two, getting hyper-focused on common sense marketing strategies that would work best for me (while leaving the rest behind).

Together, let's better understand why marketing can feel like (and too often is!) a complete waste of time. Then, let's explore the kind of thinking you can embrace to keep yourself from falling down that black hole again.

Social Media, Tactic Tornadoes, and the Black Hole of Internet Marketing

If you've ever spent time worrying about or working on promoting your practice on social media or in a marketing email, you've probably gotten into what I call a "tactic tornado."

A tactic tornado happens when all your time, energy, and self-worth get wrapped up in marketing—trying to somehow, some way, reach internet fame, attract a wealth of ideal clients, and, most especially, get thousands if not tens of thousands of followers! *Then* you'll be successful. *Then* you'll have made it. You're just one more post, one new app, one "viral" meme away from getting there!

If you're like me, and you've never wanted to live your whole life on social media, that just doesn't happen for you. Instead, you keep trying things and listening to the people who have hundreds of thousands of followers sell you on strategies that promise overnight success, tons of fans, and more—if only you post on Instagram every day. Or create webinars with sales funnels. Or make a TikTok with business tips. Or set up a room on Clubhouse, even if you have no idea what the heck that is. *(Or maybe you just stay on the sidelines, keeping your business a secret, because that tornado looks pretty scary!)*

Soon, you can get caught up in a tactic tornado, and before you know it, you're down what I call "the black hole of marketing." It leaves you feeling lost, burned out, and stuck, with zero return on investment on your time, money, and resources. It makes you think that no one cares about what you do, nor wants to hear what you have to say. But you don't have to stay in the black hole, nor do you have to get caught in another tactic tornado. You don't have to avoid marketing yourself for fear of getting swept up in this either.

Every business owner finds themselves there at one point or another. Years ago, I got stuck there for time after chasing all the free marketing resources and wasting time writing posts for social media and Facebook groups. After the tactics I thought I *had* to follow failed, I then spent thousands on a marketing consultant who appeared to have mastered the level where I wanted to be.

So I followed her advice, even though some of it felt "icky" and inauthentic in ways to me. Then I watched anxiously as I got no results. She recommended that I take a series of videos intended as free content and instead bundle them as a "product." She had me create an entire sales funnel, then nobody bought it *(because it should never have been a product)* and the launch completely bombed. She had no answers as to why, and ultimately I felt hung out to dry. Feeling rejected and deflated—like I'd never find a confident, effective way to market myself—I thought I might give up or take up permanent residence in the black hole. I hated feeling like I was good at what I did but nobody cared about it, and I'd never "make it" in the world of online business.

But then I was lucky to encounter someone who freed me and my mindset from my black hole: author and viral marketing consultant BJ Mendelson. I caught a talk he gave at Social Media Week Chicago titled, simply, "Social Media is Bullshit."[26] *Yes!*

BJ believes "social media is bullshit" in the sense that social media and even online marketing are not for *everyone, every business, or every ideal client!* In his talk, he tells a story about how a woman came up to him after a talk in tears. She was feeling both shame and relief to hear his perspective. She'd spent so much time and money on social media marketing, only to see no return, and it left her deeply doubting herself. His permission and admission about social media emotionally freed her.

Honestly, his perspective freed me, too. It got me thinking that social media and online marketing are dynamic ways, but definitely not the *only* ways, to market my business. It seems simple to write, but in today's world, in which everyone is online all the time, and pushing you to have an email list and post on every social media channel, and encouraging you to share what you had for lunch too, it's hard to imagine. It can feel like how others have achieved success has to be *your* game plan, to the letter.

When I started to consider there may be other ways, it helped me to look at marketing my business more creatively. It allowed me to look at Greatest Story Creative through a lens of *What's gotten me clients so far? Who are the types of clients I want to work more with—and where have those types of people come from?* Really, what's the data I can pull from?

Those key questions helped me to take stock of my growth so far and one, give myself credit for the effective marketing I'd done, and two, focus on what was working *best.*

I decided to make some changes that felt a bit scary then but have served me well and consistently to this day. Here's what I told myself, in case you might want to give yourself these permissions in your marketing:

- Stop worrying about what other people are doing.
- Stop caring about follower count or how many people are on my email list.
- Stop pursuing marketing I hate doing, like being on every social media platform, having to post all the time, and chasing the latest apps and trends.
- Never again sell something to my email list that I don't 100% believe in.
- Do more of marketing activities I love doing like speaking in-person and on video, and do them regularly.
- For all marketing activities—those I want to do and those I need to do to be credible and visible online—make sure I have a system to do them clearly and consistently, and delegate where necessary.

Once I put these rules into action, everything shifted. Before, I was spending hours each week trying new tactics, posting online, and chasing the tactic tornado of it all. After I committed to my marketing strengths and values, things changed.

Soon, we look at how you can systemize and structure your content marketing similarly. For now, I encourage you to think outside your box and consider letting go of what you think you *have* to do to be successful at translating your value through traditional marketing. Why? Because:

- Your marketing should (and can) play to your strengths.
- Your marketing doesn't have to be all about social media.
- There are many ways to be consistent about how you do your marketing.
- Marketing can be a simplified, effective tool that grows your business without overwhelming you.

Systems and virtual assistants can be your friends for staying away from tactic tornadoes and getting out of the black hole. But it starts with letting go of wanting to be like everyone else. It begins with thinking how you can be the best, most valuable version of yourself in your business.

I trust you can do that, and I'm excited to see what you come up with for your simplified marketing *strategy*. That is the magic word behind avoiding these tactic tornadoes in the first place.

Strategy Is the Sexiest "S"

Especially in marketing, often I feel like nobody wants to talk about strategy. They love to talk and teach tactics all day: the new app, the new Canva template, the this, the that. But never the *strategy.*

Well, if you want to move the needle, I really want you to consider the sexiest "S" of them all in business: strategy. Before you try the latest new app, or platform, or webinar trend, stop and consider your strategy. What are your CHIPS?

Think about your strategy first—before you go create that amazing podcast. *Are your ideal clients (the people who you really want coming through your doors, are a joy to help, need your biggest solution, and can afford you) listening to podcasts?*

If *they're* not listening to podcasts, what in the world are you doing thinking of creating a podcast? Ask the question up-front and save yourself months of money, time, and resources figuring out how to host a podcast that will never have the right audience you want to attract.

Consider your data—what's worked and what hasn't. Double-down on what you've enjoyed and what's brought in clients, and let go of what you hate and what hasn't worked—even if it's what everyone says you *have* to do to grow a business!

From branding to operations to marketing, strategy is something that gets really overlooked because tactics pop up constantly and are the shiny objects. For marketing, setting a strategy takes time, reflection, perspective, and sometimes even paying an expert or two to help you come up with one, depending on the area of business. But it's so valuable to stop in your marketing planning to set down your goals and needs—to know exactly what you want to accomplish, whom you want to get in front of, and where they actually hang out looking for someone like you, online and offline.

Though most people don't realize this, doing less marketing but doing it with a strategy will have a better payoff than trying to do everything—especially every new thing—without stopping to really think if it makes sense. It's so much better to tell yourself, *I am not going to waste my hard-earned time and money on every single marketing strategy. I'm going to do one or two really well, and that's going to bring in people I love to help.*

One of my favorite social media experts is Andréa Jones of OnlineDrea, Inc. Though she's built her own mini-empire of a business helping coaches and consultants grow on social media, you know what she recommends as the best way to start? Being on only *one* platform. That's it. Even the social media expert will tell you to be smart, intentional, and don't overcommit. *Catch her interviews on Branding with Friends for more gems.*[27]

So as you consider how to bring more confidence, clarity, consistency, and commitment to your marketing, pause and ask yourself, "Is what I'm thinking of doing really strategic? Does it serve my ideal clients? Can I do it without burning out? Is it an opportunity or will it create a tactic tornado?"

With this strategic thinking by your side, you are ready for to employ two other sexy "Ss": *simplified systems!*

MARKETING

Simplified Systems for Magic Marketing

A simplified system is the ultimate expression of a smart strategy. When you've taken the time and perspective to define what's important to you about marketing (and what isn't), the next step is to put together simplified systems to help you do specific, focused marketing that aligns with your values, plays to your strengths, and allows you to share about your business clearly and consistently.

As you consider what types of marketing you most believe in and fit your business best, I share with you the types of systems that have kept me out of tactic tornadoes and brought me more ideal clients than ever. I share the strategic approach that's helped me more than quadruple my revenue and consistently elevate my expert status all while doing *less* (but better) marketing! Now, *that's* what I'd call magic.

Let's see what magic you might create as you embrace a more systematic approach to marketing your business . . . if you're willing to fully commit to it.

Create Consistency Containers

Tactic tornadoes capture us when we treat our marketing actives are just one tactic followed by another. Then, when we hop from thing to thing (blog writing, to LinkedIn posting, to free webinars, etc.), it becomes nearly impossible to build enough momentum and consistency to get known for anything or see results.

This is why I've come to believe in and create what I call "consistency containers." Beyond building strong client and referral relationships, everything I do to market my business to new people and stay top of mind with those in my network currently fits in one of a handful of consistency containers.

Consistency containers are essentially systems, anchored by a type of on-strategy content that I actually like to create. They are systems that I can easily follow to market my business well. They leverage a few, mighty strategies that I know will actually work for me, because they were inspired from the data I've learned about my clients and business growth—all the things I've tracked in operations and client experience. They allow me to spend as little time as possible on marketing, to ensure the time I spend is productive, and to give me ways to delegate many parts of the processes to my virtual assistant and automation tools like an email marketing platform.

Consistency containers keep me focused, grounded, and out of the tornadoes and the black hole. They keep me playing my hit song long enough that just about everyone I meet quickly learns what I do, the right fits connect with it, and my practice continues to grow with ideal clients and profitability.

What makes for an effective consistency container?

- It acts as a content marketing system of inviting value that attracts your ideal clients.
- It's anchored by one specific, on-brand form of content (in other words, a monthly workshop series, a podcast, an email newsletter, a video series, a blog, a social media tips series).
- It's a form of content that you confidently know your ideal clients already engage with (e.g., don't start a blog, unless you know your ideal clients read and value blogs).
- It's something you would enjoy doing as a business owner.
- It showcases you as an expert and highlights the problems you solve and the valuable solutions you can provide to ideal clients.
- It's shareable in one or more ways.
- It's manageable to produce/create from a time, resources, investment, and mindset perspective.
- It's easily repeatable for you to produce/create.
- The creation process can be partially delegated to team members and/or automated.

THE 2 ESSENTIAL TYPES OF CONSISTENCY CONTAINERS

For a service-based business solopreneur practice like yours or mine, part of the art of nailing marketing is not overextending yourself. When it's just you in your business (save for a few contractors or a VA, etc.), marketing can become a time-suck.

So if you don't already have something like a consistency container in motion for your marketing, I recommend starting with just these two:

1. A signature email marketing consistency container
2. A social media consistency container

Using examples from my practice, let's look at each of these and why they might be valuable to put into action in your business.

A SIGNATURE EMAIL MARKETING CONSISTENCY CONTAINER

It took me about two years in business to realize that having an email list is important to your growth as a business for the simple fact that it allows you to "own" your list. Even if you have 100,000 followers on LinkedIn, what happens if LinkedIn changes their rules or algorithm? How do you reach those people? Having a means to directly reach people who are interested in your expertise and solutions is what an email list is fundamentally all about.

Now, many marketers will loudly encourage you to think *only* about your list, insisting that having thousands of email addresses ready to buy from you should be your sole focus. That can make sense sometimes, as it's often reported that email lists typically convert into sales/clients at a very small percentage, such as 1—3%). However, in my experience, this can be a black hole many disappear into!

So as I share my own story and best practices with email marketing, consider that for the majority of my eight years in business, I've had fewer than 1,000 people on my mailing list (and zero for the first two years!). Yet, at that level, I've still experienced the rewarding business success that I'm sharing throughout this book. Additionally, many of my clients and colleagues who make six figures and multiple six figures have similar-sized lists *(and some, no list at all!)*. So while list size can be impactful, it also really matters who's on it and what consistent value you're providing to them—enter the Signature Email Marketing Consistency Container.

I started my own mailing list in 2015 as a weekly newsletter I called "Skip to Action!" I wrote this weekly faithfully for years and syndicated the articles as blog posts. However, I stopped years later when I didn't see results or get clients from it. My newsletter/blog content also didn't fit many of the rules I've set forth for consistency containers—especially about needing to enjoy doing it.

While I'm known as a writer, I really hated having to write *every* week—60 to 90 minutes every single Wednesday. While I've heard anecdotally that people loved what I wrote, "Skip to Action" never once directly turned into a client. An hour or more a week, 52 weeks a year, and crickets. I have more than 100 blog posts, and you know how many clients that's gotten me over the course of years, even though they're SEO-optimized? Two. This was, at worst, a recipe for burnout and, at best, a complete waste of my time.

Thankfully, I stumbled into my entire consistency container strategy to remedy this. In reviewing my historical business data and refining my brand, I identified that my best clients had first learned about me from speaking events (not social media!). So I knew that speaking was my strongest (and most favorite) way to attract new clients.

However, though I love speaking to associations, conferences, and groups as marketing, I don't love the chase that it requires. Pitching myself to speak can be exhausting and lead to inconsistent speaking dates and results. It also can take away valuable focus on the core work of my business.

To get around these challenges, I came up with a new strategy to ensure I could regularly attract my ideal clients. I decided that I'd speak once a month about branding through my own well-branded event series. I'd still take external opportunities to speak, but by creating my own series, I'd be able to consistently show up live, have something of value to offer, and connect with prospective clients—both those who knew me already and wanted to know more, and people who'd just discovered me via my website, social media, or a recommendation.

In May 2017, this vision became Branding with Annie, my workshop series on branding best practices for my ideal clients (coaches, consultants, and service business owners). Today, it has hundreds of alumni, has led to several dozen clients, and has directly generated tens of thousands of dollars in revenue—all from doing something I already love and doing it in a strategic, repeatable way.

Historically, my entire approach to Branding with Annie has been a consistency container system. With adding my Establish Yourself programs and this book to my business now in 2022, I've shifted to a more on-demand format that keeps Branding with Annie alive and still gives me the opportunity to teach it live in-person or on Zoom occasionally, as it makes sense for my future business growth *(check out the latest on this at brandingwithannie.com).*

This noted, for more than four years, I've successfully hosted Branding with Annie just about every month using these practices:

- Each workshop provided regular content I can promote to my email list to keep them engaged with who I am, what I do, and how I can help them.
- Every presentation followed the same clear format with a welcome, best practices, invitation to set a free consultation with me, and live group consulting.
- The topic rotated, each focusing on an element of my branding process/solution.
- The same eight or so topics were presented each year and have been easily repurposed as presentations for external groups when those opportunities arise.
- The workshop typically happened on the same date/time every month.
- I created email templates to announce each event and to follow up afterward.
- My virtual assistant easily set up every new date in my scheduling system, updated the event's standing webpage, and scheduled posts to promote it on my social media profiles with less than five minutes of direction each month from me.
- The ticket signup was automated, providing a confirmation to attendees.
- My email marketing system tracked who attended which event, so I could easily communicate with all Branding with Annie alums with the click of a mouse.
- It's been easy to refer to others, and many past clients, current clients, and referral partners have sent people

they meet to Branding with Annie because they know it'll be high value and give them a chance to connect with me.

- It has always included a clear call to action to my sleaze-free sales process: signing up for a free consultation.

Because I created it one time as a system, I can easily get professional help and employ automation to the process to make it happen. Moreover, because I loved doing it and it attracted my ideal clients, Branding with Annie has been my signature email marketing consistency container for five years. It's become a big thing I'm known for, and it's only become more rewarding with time as I've stuck with it, elevated it, and shared it with more and more people.

A workshop series like Branding with Annie is just one way you could bring in a signature email marketing consistency container strategy to simplify your marketing. Your version of signature content might be an incredible podcast where you bring on guests to highlight your expertise. It could be an email newsletter of case studies where you showcase how you've solved clients' problems and give actionable tips to your ideal clients. Truly, it's something you'd love to do regularly (such as monthly or bi-weekly) that fits all the rules of the consistency container.

To give you another example, my maternity leave inspired another consistency container that didn't require me to run it live the way Branding with Annie does. When I was planning my maternity leave to be from December 2019 to April 2020, I saw that I was about to have a huge gap of time that I'd be closed for client work. While I wouldn't be working, I still needed to stay top of mind with everyone in my universe, especially prospective clients waiting for my return.

So I rethought my email marketing strategy, this time channeling the joy and consistency that Branding with Annie brings me. I asked myself: What could I do that would help me grow more (so I wasn't just advertising to my existing audience)? I thought, *What could I create easily, that'd be fun to do, that I can delegate the large majority of, and that would get me in front of new audiences?*

Speaking again! It always comes back to speaking for me because that's what comes most naturally and what feels easy. My thought was if I could just speak for 30 minutes or an hour, then my VA could do the rest and I could create awesome, valuable email list and blog content forever. So that's exactly what I did. I kicked the traditional "newsletter" to the curb and instead devised a content marketing system around a business interview video series that I call "Branding with Friends."

Branding with Friends is currently a YouTube series in which I interview experts on areas of business that relate to branding such as SEO, LinkedIn, trademark law, and more. The episodes are 25–30 minutes, they come out monthly, and all I have to do to produce one are invite an expert by email and host the interview recording (about 45 minutes) about 12 times a year. From there, my VA can do the rest using templates, emails, and a process I took an afternoon to create prior to my maternity leave. All I have to do is send her a few details to customize, and she captions it, posts it, makes it a blog post and email newsletter, and sends the guest expert graphics and words to be able to promote it to their audience! She'll even be able to syndicate it as a podcast in the future.

Because it's a system and I have fun doing the parts that I personally do, it's thriving. Now on our 27th episode, 27 guest experts have shared what I do as a branding expert with their audiences. That likely adds up to tens of thousands, if not a hundred thousand, of new eyeballs on what I do—and it's a hell of a lot more fun and exciting than writing a boring newsletter once a week!

I never have to stress about Branding with Friends the way I did every single Wednesday when it was time for another newsletter to go out. And maybe the best, most unexpected part are the relationships I've been able to build with complementary partners as a result. Now, I know 30+ more incredible, inspiring people whose work dovetails beautifully with what I do and whom I help. Branding with Friends allows me to network with them, give them value and a spotlight, and share audiences, attracting more ideal clients and opportunities to what I do—not too shabby for what started as a maternity leave solution!

Other signature email marketing consistency containers I have in my business are free templates (to opt in to my mailing list), an evergreen nurture sequence that sends my best tips (pulled from repurposed content from those old blog posts), and even the *Establish Yourself Companion Workbook* you may be using as you work through this book!

Branding with Friends and these other systems are just a few ways you could have email marketing consistency containers in your business. For you, it might be a newsletter with helpful quick tips on your expertise (if you like to write and your ideal clients like to read!). For one of my clients who's a life coach, her system is both a freebie (a free meditation series) and an evergreen email sequence that sends you a new meditation every few weeks on autopilot.

However you choose to do it, having an email list and staying in touch with them every other week or every month will only help you to foster those new connections, solidify client and referral partner relationships, and keep your business growing by staying top of mind and top of people's inboxes.

A SOCIAL MEDIA CONSISTENCY CONTAINER

Like BJ Mendelson, I tend to think social media is bullshit for many businesses. At the very least, it just isn't as important to having a profitable business as so many make it out to be, especially relative to the time that can be wasted on it. I'm tired of all the business shaming going on if you don't have a million followers and the often-incorrect supposition that followers equal dollars.

That's why I treat social media as a credibility builder and an example to my clients of branded consistency. For the business, I'm only on LinkedIn personal/business and Facebook because I know those are the top platforms for my ideal clients. (I use Instagram too, but mainly for fun and fostering referral relationships, less for attracting clients.) On LinkedIn and Facebook, I post on-brand, strategic content several times weekly—not because it brings me a million clients, only because it shows that I have an active legitimate business where I'm an expert.

Having actually interviewed my clients, I know they are women in their late 30s to early 60s, and they often hate (!) social media, especially for business, like I do. For looking for experts like me, most of my ideal clients were on LinkedIn or Facebook if they were anywhere at all. They came to me often via referral, but I'm sure verified my legitimacy by looking at things like my website and consistency on places like LinkedIn and Facebook.

For these reasons, in 2017 I decided social media had a place in my business for providing credibility and consistency, so that's all I expect it to do. As I shared in "The Business-Changing Magic of Tools and Apps" section in Step Two: Shape Your Business, I do a batching content strategy and use a brilliant automation tool called SmarterQueue that can automatically post for me on a weekly basis. Because I can easily schedule posts to repeat in a series over time, the whole process only requires that I create new content for my social media for an afternoon or two once every year or so. That's how a social media consistency container works in my business.

I encourage you to simplify your social media this way too. Whether or not you use SmarterQueue specifically, I recommend devising an easy system to one, create your content, and two, post that content as easily as possible. I break this down how to do this using your brand strategy in my simplified marketing training, "Power Your Marketing." Batching this content does take a bit of time to set up initially, but in my experience, it's so freeing to only worry about social media an afternoon or two every year or so—versus every single day wondering, "What should I post?!" Set it, forget it, and trust you look awesome and on-strategy online.

—

As you're considering putting the two most important types of consistency containers into place to reset your marketing, the next questions become: What should you talk about? How much value should be free versus paid? This is where many coaches and consultants get lost, so let's cover that before we wrap our discussion of simplified marketing systems.

Why and How: Free Value vs. Paid Value

In 2020, one of my earliest branding clients came back to me with a big problem: She was doing a ton of marketing but none of it was working. Since our work together, Jenny had hired experts, done coaching programs, embraced what she thought might be a differentiator—but nothing was converting. Through Establish Yourself–centered consulting, I was able to take a closer look, diagnose why this was happening, and give her a roadmap on how to fix it.

Though many factors were contributing to this stuck moment, a huge element had to do with free value. With a Facebook group of about 50 members, plus a monthly workshop series that only about 10 people attend regularly, Jenny was a coach who was giving away tons and tons of free value and super serving a small audience. She was hosting hot seats, facilitating free transformations, and essentially solving problems. There weren't any marketing activities in place to get her practice in front of new eyes. She was constantly solving problems for the same people yet almost never talking about her offers, thereby removing any incentive for them to invest in her powerful skill set and solutions.

Jenny, like many of us at one time or another, had heard the best practice for your content marketing is to give it all away. *Give away your value and show people what you can do!* Well, I don't think that's the whole story—not for effective marketing for a coach or consultant. I don't think people like us should primarily market our businesses like free samples at Costco. I've found this to be a very large black hole for coaches in particular, who can easily give away too much their coaching rather than charge for it.

So what should you give away as inviting consistency container content and what should be held as an investment your ideal clients make with you? Let's break it down.

Mostly *Why*-Focused, Problem + Solution—Centric: Your Best *Free* Content

If you are a coach, consultant, or other service business owner focused on a high-ticket offer and other consulting/coaching-like investments in your time but you struggle with marketing, I recommend making your high-quality, free content more *why*-focused and less how-focused. Here's why.

You've likely seen successful practices speak to multiple audiences, give away a ton of value, and still appear to be doing well. In those cases, I'd wager they are natural-born marketers and selling stars (or can afford to hire them on a full-time basis), and they are also carefully segmenting their audiences to speak to the more DIY crowd, versus those who need the high-ticket expert. It definitely can be done, but it's a tighter rope to walk if it's not your wheelhouse. If you're reading this book, you're likely not the marketing natural nor someone with a huge marketing team, so you have to carefully consider what you talk about in your limited marketing activities. Moreover, you need to do your marketing a bit differently than a company that has a lot of capability to speak and sell effectively to differing audiences with various needs.

When I began writing my weekly newsletter/blog back in 2015 and beyond, I made the mistake of writing too much *how* content *(how to do what I do, how you can design your own logo or write your own tagline, etc.).* I didn't realize then that this would never attract my ideal client who, by their very definition, has *no* interest in doing their own branding; they want and need me to do it. Focusing on the how not only provided the answers, it attracted the completely wrong type of client who had no interest in investing in my services.

Why-focused content is like what I offer now on Branding with Friends. While I pass on a lot of best practices and tips (I'll nickname this "high-level how"), the focus of that show is to educate my audience about the *why*—why branding is important, what it is, how it can help them fix their biggest problem of unclear, inconsistent marketing, why you need a professional to do it, why I'm a credible choice, and so on. These systems also always introduce what I do as a professional and provide a call to action of how to get that professional help from me—so it's not amorphous value that doesn't offer a next step.

Moreover, your why-focused content can be simplified to focus mainly on featuring the **crucial problem** you solve for ideal clients and highlighting the **valuable solution** you provide. Indeed, this all comes back to where we started in how you are choosing to embrace your story and branding yourself as the expert on something specific! As we explore shortly, this *why* content is really playing the hit song you created over and over, and over again.

When you showcase the *why,* you can't constantly give away the *how—aka* the transformation you provide to your paying clients. Rather, you can provide high-quality free content by focusing it on educating your clients and getting them excited about the *value* and possibility of that transformation. So, for example, instead of free hot seats, maybe you bring a client into your Facebook group to share their experience of working with you (or you do both *but* you don't forget to speak about your offer). Or maybe you provide a template that helps a client get started on the first step of their transformation, but it doesn't do all of the work for them. It just gives them a start and a sense of how valuable it'd be to have a professional's help to keep going.

Though I know it may seem a bit boring to focus all of your free content primarily on driving awareness and excitement around the main problem and solution you offer (and why it's so helpful), doing so is a much more commonsense, effective strategy than giving away your solutions for free, never talking about what you actually sell, and over-serving a small audience you already have.

Remember: Marketing is about action—getting eyeballs on what you're doing. You want each of your consistency containers to constantly and regularly remind people of your CHIPS—*aka* what you do, who you do it for, what problem you solve. If people see that, understand you have a solution, and perceive that solution to be valuable, they will be invited to take the first important step in investing in you: that clear call to action of a discovery call in your sleaze-free sales process. As we explore when we close out our focus on marketing, sticking to this can be hard, but it really can pay off.

Lastly, give away your *why*-focused content on podcasts, in interviews, and while speaking, if you're doing those activities to attract clients. If you're being paid to speak, give more *how*-focused content, for the reasons I outline in the following section.

***Mostly How*-Focused, Transformation-Providing: Your Best *Paid* Content and Curricula**

Keep your free content more focused on the *why (and the "high-level how"),* and in your paid content, coaching, consulting, and teaching, deliver *all* of the *how.* Here's where you can and should package your incredible value and knowledge to actually change people's lives, businesses, or both. That change is worth investing in, and people will want to do it if they know it exists. This is the space where you can develop and deliver more of your core teaching, dive deep into the transformational work you believe in, or create the deliverables your clients so desire.

So many of the coaches I've worked with, especially life coaches, too often confuse their marketing with their teaching/programs, and lose clients and consults as a result. They give too much of the *how,* but not enough of the *why,* up-front. Moreover, they are too shy to promote their offers—so they give, give, give—yet hardly ever discuss their service/offer or ask for the sale. Yet the thing is, when you first encounter an ideal client, that client wants one thing from you: to solve their most crucial problem. If you want them to invest in solving that problem, your marketing needs to be less geared toward DIY problem-solving and more geared to clearly communicating *why* you have the right, best expert solution—and *what* exactly that is.

At that time, your prospective client doesn't care or necessarily value the process and teachings you will take them through the way they will at the end of your work together, when a transformation has happened. And if you try to sling that in front of them all at once, they get confused, or their problem gets solved, or they just don't connect and never invest in you.

—

I often teach it this way: Marketing **meets** while programs **problem-solve.** Your marketing needs to meet ideal clients where they are *before* you work together. I often refer to this as marketing needing to meet, and programs needing to problem-solve. It's best to save your transformational-focused content when a client has invested in that solution. Keep your marketing mostly focused on the *why,* so you don't bleed over and accidentally overwhelm someone who needs to invest in your genius for their benefit.

Whether you're an under-marketer or an over-marketer right now, I encourage you to take stock of the marketing you've been doing or have been thinking of doing. Sort the types of content into *why* and *how,* then offer them as free or paid accordingly. Don't forget to regularly share/sell your offers as a next step from your marketing content. And if you have a ton of *how*-based content that's perfect for your ideal clients, note that you can bundle it into a digital product, a course, or even a coaching program that's ready to go and ready to be invested in at various levels of your Streamlined Service Value Ladder.

If you embrace these two categories—focus on the *why* in your consistency containers, then deliver on the *how* in your client experience and offers—you'll convert even more ideal clients, turn them into lifelong fans, and make a profit, all by tweaking your marketing mindset.

Now all that's left is the trickiest part of marketing, and that's all about making a continued commitment.

Stop Changing the Lyrics; Play Your Hit Song

When we were talking about embracing your story, I introduced the importance of playing your hit song and committing to your choices about your branding, your business, what you do, and who you serve. When you think about marketing your business, translating your value is really about committing to your main marketing message and visual assets as if they were your hit song.

But instead of a song, this is using your CHIPS and brand voice/visuals so often that your prospective clients begin to see you, recognize you, and get to know you well enough to become your raving fans. This process takes a lot of time and a lot of action, more than it demands perfection.

Stop and consider this, from Thomas Smith's *Successful Advertising,* a pamphlet written in 1885:

1. The first time a man looks at an advertisement, he does not see it.
2. The second time, he does not notice it.
3. The third time, he is conscious of its existence.
4. The fourth time, he faintly remembers having seen it before.
5. The fifth time, he reads it.
6. The sixth time, he turns up his nose at it.
7. The seventh time, he reads it through and says, "Oh brother!"
8. The eighth time, he says, "Here's that confounded thing again!"
9. The ninth time, he wonders if it amounts to anything
10. The tenth time, he asks his neighbor if he has tried it.

11. The eleventh time, he wonders how the advertiser makes it pay.
12. The twelfth time, he thinks it must be a good thing.
13. The thirteenth time, he thinks perhaps it might be worth something.
14. The fourteenth time, he remembers wanting such a thing a long time.
15. The fifteenth time, he is tantalized because he cannot afford to buy it.
16. The sixteenth time, he thinks he will buy it some day.
17. The seventeenth time, he makes a memorandum to buy it.
18. The eighteenth time, he swears at his poverty.
19. The nineteenth time, he counts his money carefully
20. The twentieth time he sees the ad, he buys what it is offering.

Thomas Smith knew what so many of us often don't realize: For your marketing to work and be effectively "seen" by enough people to grow your business, you have clearly and consistently "play your hit song"—not once, not twice, but 20 times or more.

One of the biggest reasons I see coaches and consultants fail is that they are constantly changing their lyrics without really consistently using them for a meaningful period of time. Even if they invest in brand messaging, visuals, or both, some never try them out longer than a few weeks. I've noticed that some business owners feel more comfortable and safe hiding behind their computers and websites, worried about each word and graphic being perfect. Unfortunately, this isn't taking action. It's obsessing over perfection, and it will keep you stuck.

Though your confident brand assets really matter to your business, what also matters is the action you consistently take with them over time. I wrote in my personal development book, *Permission to Try*, that "action beats talent." That's true for your marketing. What can you build with the best hammer if you leave it in the shed to rust? Your brand assets, message, graphics, and even your website—these are tools. They have the ability to tell your story in a way that your ideal clients will connect to. But they can't do that if you don't get out there and build anything lasting with them.

To gain lifelong fans of your work, you can't change your lyrics or your melody too soon because you don't see immediate results/impact. When you have new branding and marketing consistency containers to show them off, you need to "sing your song" for six to 12 months at least—loudly, clearly, consistently, in places where your ideal clients hang out—in order for it to be heard, seen, and connected with fully. The way to do that is to use your key branding materials and message so consistently that they *bore* you. While that's not fun, that's a sign that you've used them well. That's how to get out in the marketplace well enough to create momentum.

This all means marketing yourself well. It means setting up simplified systems to do that marketing clearly and consistently, without constantly changing your message and/or visuals. This means going ahead with your website, and quitting noodling all the words on it (*aka* changing the lyrics). It takes getting your business cards printed and getting out to use them. This is investing in connection (branding done professionally). Then it's investing in taking action to get it all seen (marketing that plays to your strengths and delegates where needed).

Using your consistency containers with the brand tools you have is how you drive simple awareness, become visible, be remembered, and get referred. But do your brand tools like your message, logo, or website need to be perfect before you can use them? *No, and they never will be!* Of course, the more professional they are, the better results you'll get. But perfection isn't what you're striving for here: It's about branding *and* marketing (connection *and* action, right?). There's a reason I didn't say perfection was required for success. Though I struggle with perfectionism myself, I've found it far more realistic and rewarding to strive to run a great business, not a perfect one.

The other thing to consider is that your brand identity and your marketing activities aren't everything about your business—but they're good to think about as your hit song or signature sound. If you can make a hit of that, then you can add complexity to your business and your offers that go beyond it. Your fans will be able to recognize that signature sound and become fans of the other things you have to offer, but only if you're willing to do the consistent work of establishing that signature sound in the first place. *(Side note: This is the type of work I'm doing today in adding the complexity of my Establish Yourself programs to the mix of what I do at Greatest Story. They are coming from my signature sound that I've established through branding. They can succeed because I've built them upon that hit song foundation).*

The reality is that *yes*, your brand visuals, message, website, and marketing strategies will likely evolve over time. My own have shifted with the years, as I've become clearer on my ideal clients and the work I want to do more of changes. But becoming known and establishing yourself does mean making a continued commitment to use your tools long enough to learn those things—to grow and get business enough to be able to evolve through success.

Too often, I see clients coming up with one new song after another, rather than doing the hard (and, yes, often boring) work of committing to playing that hit song—over and over—until your ideal clients have seen you enough for you to build a brand and stream of referrals.

So when/if you decide to have your brand professionally developed and set out to use those tools well for six to 12 months, remember to hang in there—even Journey gets tired of playing "Don't Stop Believin'." But if they didn't play it? Their fans would be furious. *They would stop believin'!*

So go get some fans who believe in you and don't give up on your hit song too soon. Practice confidence, clarity, consistency, commitment. Together, they will help you win the war of marketing and growing your business, if you're willing to trust and really use them. And as we discover in the end, these are the things that will make the biggest difference.

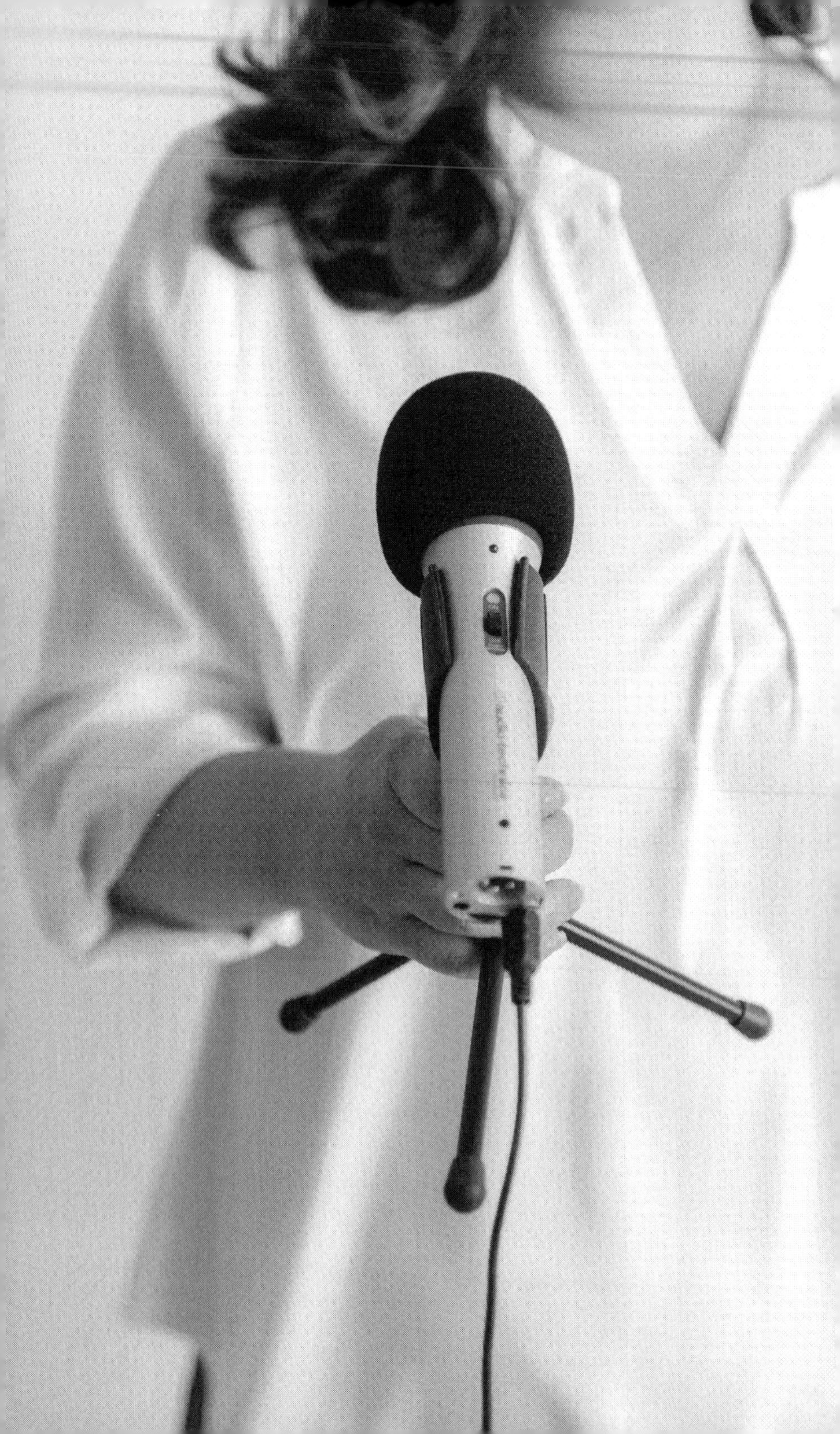

YOUR MARKETING "KEY C" CHECK

As you considered how to simplify and strengthen your marketing, we explored:

- How to avoid tactic tornadoes and the black hole of marketing.
- Why strategy is the sexiest "S."
- Creating consistency containers to simplify and strengthen your marketing.
- The why and how of free versus paid content.
- The hard, yet rewarding, commitment to playing your hit song.

With these aspects in mind, take 10–15 minutes to reflect on and answer the questions here in the book, in your *Establish Yourself Companion Workbook*, or in your own notebook. Though these questions are intended to help you find clarity about what feels uncertain, the very first question will allow you to give yourself much-deserved credit! You're on your way.

WHAT'S WORKING

What's *one* thing you're really proud of with your marketing?

COURAGEOUS CONFIDENCE

What's *one* thing you wish you had more courage and confidence about when it comes to marketing yourself and the work you do?

CRUCIAL CLARITY

What's *one* thing you need more focus and clarity on?

CONSCIOUS CONSISTENCY

What's *one* thing you need more consistency with?

CONTINUED COMMITMENT

What's *one* thing you want to commit more to on the marketing front?

Now, which *one* of the these things feels most urgent to you?
List that one in the form of an action step here.

MY MOST VALUABLE ACTION STEP FOR **MARKETING:**

For this step, **are there any professionals and/or tools you may need to make that top action step happen?** *List your thoughts on this here.*

EST.
ESTABLISH
YOURSELF

CONCLUSION

The Real Key to Establishing Yourself Now

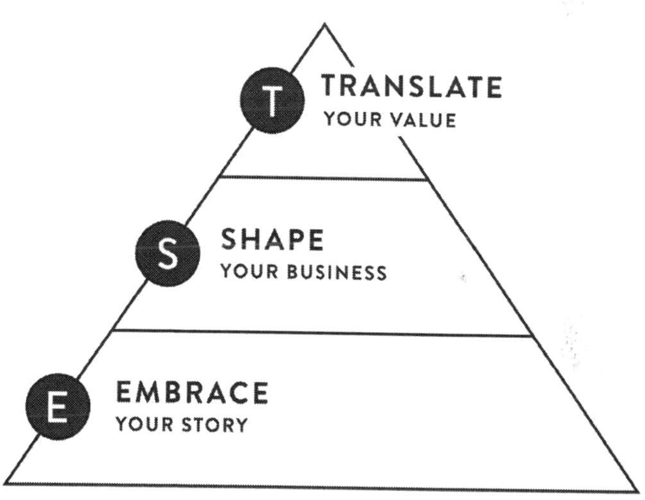

You've just explored the three steps to get to the next level of your potential in the Establish Yourself Framework:

Step One | Embrace Your Story
Step Two | Shape Your Business
Step Three | Translate Your Value

By journeying through the six essential areas of business (branding, operations, sales, client experience, referral relationships, and marketing), you've now had the opportunity to do a "Key C" check with yourself at every waypoint, identifying which specific actions have the potential to move the needle in your business. And in doing so, you've looked for how to maximize the Four Key Cs of unlocking *your* greatest business:

1. Courageous confidence
2. Crucial clarity
3. Conscious consistency
4. Continued commitment

When I first introduced these factors to you, I explained them as forming one key—a key that has the power to finally unlock the next level of your business.

Only when the Four Cs are *all* working together for you can you fully unlock the incredible business that comes from embracing your story, shaping your business, translating your value, and, overall, establishing yourself.

But what *really* creates that momentum? What gives you the confidence, clarity, consistency, and commitment needed to get there?

It's *you*. The key will turn only when *you* take action and turn it. *You* are the difference maker. Armed with the right key, you are the one who can and will turn it—the one person who will build a new incredible level of your business.

Now, it may take other professionals, tools, or both to help you get to that new place. Back in 2016, I had everything I needed, but it took perspective from Adele to help me see how to finally "turn the key." For you, it will be something (or someone) else. Maybe what you need is to connect with a coach or a marketing consultant, or get a branding toolkit, or create your consistency container, or just schedule some *time* to stop and work through the concepts in this book and the ideas you're dreaming up.

But whatever you need to do next, trust that *you* are the one who can and will make it happen. You always have been.

With that in mind, let's do one more "Key C" Check together, this time to help you identify your step-by-step plan and that very first action you can take next to grow your greatest business the moment that you put down this book.

Reveal Your "Greatest Business Plan"

Congratulations—perhaps without realizing it, every bit of work you've done through this book has actually helped you develop a blueprint perfect for growing your greatest business!

With your "Key C" checks completed in the six areas (branding, operations, sales, client experience, referral relationships, and marketing), you now have everything you need to know exactly what to spend your time, resources, and energy on next to get closer to build to new levels of passion and profit.

Here's how to find that *one* most critical action step, and, in the process, reveal your very own six-step "Greatest Business Plan." **Go back and transpose what you wrote under "My most valuable action step" in each area's "Key C" check.** You can do this by writing here in the book, completing the version in the printable *Establish Yourself Companion Workbook*, or using your own notebook. As you rewrite your steps, feel free to make any adjustments necessary now that you're looking at them with fresh eyes.

MY GREATEST BUSINESS VISION | *page 20*

My greatest business looks like

because

are deeply important and valuable goals for me.

MY GREATEST BUSINESS PLAN

To bring my vision to life, I will take action on these most critical steps:

1. **BRANDING** | *My most valuable action step, page 107*

2. **OPERATIONS** | *My most valuable action step, page 201*

3. **SALES** | *My most valuable action step, page 225*

4. **CLIENT EXPERIENCE** | *My most valuable action step, page 259*

5. **REFERRAL RELATIONSHIPS** | *My most valuable action step, page 303*

6. **MARKETING** | *My most valuable action step, page 343*

Now thanks to reverse revenue, not only do you have a solid, six-step plan to build your business to the next level, you know exactly what order to go in. Start with your action item on branding, then operations, and so on, working through and building upward.

Step back, smile, and celebrate with confidence that you know exactly what to do next—and in your notes for each section, you even may know who/what you'll need to do it! Now, all that's left for you to do to begin to establish yourself is to act on *this* one thing.

So, if you're ready to do that, gear up and enjoy my last kernel of advice for making your dreams happen: *pop the popcorn.*

Pop the Popcorn

As you think about taking that biggest next step to establishing yourself, there's one last thing you need to know for the journey ahead, and it has to do with food (because of course it does).

As a kid, I grew up in a house where hamburger had a helper, Pasta-roni was for dinner, and popcorn was microwaved. I'm betting you've had microwaved popcorn before and it's generally just okay. It takes zippo thought to grab a packet, unwrap it, and hit that handy "popcorn" button on your microwave. But is that as incredible as fresh, real butter-ed, perfectly salted, wonderfully golden, and not-burnt stovetop popcorn? Not by a long shot!

Several years ago, my husband, Gus, introduced me to a genius invention called the Whirley Pop™. It's a stovetop pot for making delicious, homemade (definitely *not* microwaved) popcorn! But the thing about a Whirley Pop, as I soon discovered, is that everything is in the art of preparation and patience.

To make unbelievably good popcorn, you need to diligently follow Gus's 14 steps:

1. Get your Whirley Pop on the stove.
2. Cut your tablespoons of butter into a bowl to melt (yes, in the microwave).
3. Get your salt ready.
4. Measure your popcorn oil.
5. Measure your kernels.
6. Get your bowl ready.
7. Pour the oil into the pot.

Jeez, still not even cooking yet! Just give me the packet, right? Wrong, my friend.

8. Turn the heat on medium and wait several minutes.
9. Okay, once you hear it sizzling, add your kernels.
10. Then put your butter bowl in the microwave.
11. Then slowly crank the Whirley Pop over the course of several minutes as the kernels start to pop.
12. Melt your butter so it's ready to go.
13. Listen for most of the kernels to have popped, then quickly take it off the stove and shake out into your bowl!
14. Top with your hot melted butter, salt, and other favorite seasonings.

Enjoy—in these 14 quick and easy steps! Ha!

It's a lot of work for popcorn, right? When I make it, I get stressed and impatient, waiting to put the kernels in—then waiting for them to pop. There's a long while when it seems like nothing's going to pop. I begin thinking that I'm totally wasting my time and should go back to that PopSecret situation.

> Then one kernel pops.
> Well, hey, then another.
> Then five, then 10.
> Then—it seems out of nowhere—the entire pot is bursting at the seams!
> It's sputtering oil left and right!
> Suddenly, I'm rushing just to get the pot off the stove, top it with butter, and serve it perfectly without burning it!

This is exactly what it's been like for me to grow my business by sticking to the hard work of confidence, clarity, consistency, and commitment.

2013 to 2018 was a season of getting all the ingredients out and ready, getting the oil going, and staring at the stove. The clients, the accolades, and the growth were like those sporadic kernels that popped here and there—leaving me wondering for months and years at a time: *Am I doing this right? Should I stick with it?*

In late 2018, I launched my first book, *Permission to Try,* and it became a bestseller. *A bunch of kernels!* Then in 2019, I finally became a six-figure business. *More popping!* In 2020, I made six figures again only working seven months after taking a five-month maternity leave. *Wow! Really popping now!* 2021 flew by and I had my biggest year to date financially, working 30 hours a week—including writing this book! *Pop, pop, pop, pop!!!* And here in 2022, I'm working to scale more, publishing this book, and doing all that I can to take great care of all the popcorn that's popped (so I can keep my momentum going and don't burn it all).

Right now, with *Establish Yourself* launching, I'm in prep mode, getting ready for my next "batch" of growth, which I'm betting will take just as much (if not more) patience, preparation, and sticking to the smart strategies that take time. That's the season I'm in.

Now, what if I'd given up in that five-year season of growth that was great but wasn't *exactly* what I'd wanted or envisioned? What if I'd taken what I was doing "off the heat" and began getting different pots and pans out to try making other things all at the same time?

In your season of business, you may be in that "getting the ingredients together" phase: trying to create the best website, the best service offerings, and so on. Or maybe you've put your marketing plan into action, but you're staring at all you're doing—nervous, wondering if that popcorn is ever going to pop.

The work of growing will always come down to popping the popcorn. Even though it isn't sexy and never will be. Even though it often takes years, not months, weeks, or days to achieve. You may think differently when you look at other successful entrepreneurs, but keep in mind even the renowned Steve Jobs once said, "If you look really closely, most overnight successes took a long time."[28]

> Creating a strategy is often fun, but sticking to one isn't.
> Clarity is important, but it can feel really boring.
> Consistency would be nice, but it's easier to try out lots of things instead.

If you do the work to believe in what you're doing and how you share it (embrace your story), build a thoughtful, intentional practice (shape your business), and commit to a simplified, smart marketing strategy (translate your value), then your only job truly is to hang in there and pop that popcorn.

There will be so many moments when you feel like you're waiting forever for the kernels to pop. But if you give up now, nothing will. If you don't have everything together (all the ingredients and the bowl ready to go), that popcorn won't pop, or it'll burn, and you won't be able to make your batch an epic one.

The way I see it, you have two options from here. One, keep microwaving your growth—going for what's easy (or promised to be). That's either avoiding marketing altogether or chasing the webinars with the overnight tactics, spending years trying to make your vision of your business a reality, but ending up with the burnt popcorn of a business—a mediocre practice at best.

Or two, you can trust that it's mainly your job to pop the popcorn. In this season, do your best and invest in having the right ingredients and tools to get you there. Believe in your story, value, and ability to make it happen. Hang in there when it feels boring, hard, and everything in between. If you continually choose courageous confidence, crucial clarity, conscious consistency, and continued commitment, the kernels are going to pop.

While I've never found a new marketing tactic that grew my business overnight, I have tested one that's grown my business over years and led me to the passionate, profitable work I'm beyond lucky to do. *And* it involves butter, so that's kind of a bonus.

Food and food metaphors can get you through just about anything. So, wherever you go from here, remember: Be the chef and create the perfect salad. Bake the best cake. Don't fixate on the frosting, and pop the popcorn. It's time to establish yourself and grow your greatest business like only *you* can.

Ready to
Establish Yourself?

Put your Greatest Business Plan
into action *with* Annie in the

Establish Yourself™
ACTION CLUB

THE ESTABLISH YOURSELF ACTION CLUB is an empowering group coaching program created just for you. From day one, get accountability emails from Annie, inspiring you to apply *Establish Yourself* to the six areas of your business. Maintain your momentum by joining Annie and other Action Clubbers live on Zoom for *Establish Yourself* "Ask the Author" sessions (hosted 11 times each year!).

At these events, grow in confidence by bringing your questions straight to the expert, getting feedback, learning new skills, and bonding with fellow coaches, consultants, and service business owners working to build their greatest businesses.

But that's not *all.* The Action Club also includes on-demand online access to **THE ESTABLISH YOURSELF VAULT:** a collection of every major Greatest Story Creative business tool, template, checklist, and resource mentioned in this book, far beyond what's been included for free in your printable *Establish Yourself Companion Workbook.*

This action-oriented, digital library covers all six areas of business and includes all of Annie's in-depth trainings, including ones on how to define your own brand strategy and simplify your marketing—*plus new templates, checklists, tools, and more as we add value in the future!*

THE ESTABLISH YOURSELF ACTION CLUB is your one-stop, value-packed growth program—designed to put everything you need to get to the next level right at your fingertips. It's true: The world's most epic business book club has arrived.

If you're ready to establish yourself, join Annie in the Action Club now!

greateststorycreative.com/actionclub

Visit the website for current details and terms.

Chapter Notes

1. "The 2018 State of Women-Owned Businesses Report, Commissioned by American Express: Summary of Key Trends." *https://ventureneer.com/wp-content/uploads/2018/08/2018-state-of-women-owned-businesses-report_FINAL.pdf.*
2. "Crucial." Lexico.com. *https://www.lexico.com/en/definition/crucial.*
3. Miller, Donald, with Dr. J.J. Peterson. *Marketing Made Simple* (HarperCollins Leadership, 2020).
4. Packnett, Brittany. "How to Build Your Confidence—and Spark it in Others." TED2019, April 2019. *https://www.ted.com/talks/brittany_packnett_how_to_build_your_confidence_and_spark_it_in_others.*
5. Brown, Brené. *The Gifts of Imperfection* (Random House, 2020).
6. "Embrace." Lexico.com. *https://www.lexico.com/en/definition/embrace.*
7. "Brand." Lexico.com. *https://www.lexico.com/en/definition/brand.*
8. Clark, Nancy F. "Act Now to Shrink the Confidence Gap." Forbes.com, April 28, 2015. *https://www.forbes.com/sites/womensmedia/2014/04/28/act-now-to-shrink-the-confidence-gap/?sh=78d14a6a5c41.*
9. Campbell, Joseph. *The Hero's Journey* (New World Library, 2014).
10. Miller, Donald. *Building a StoryBrand* (HarperCollins Leadership, 2017).
11. Patel, Neil. "Why Problem Solving Should Be the Only Value Proposition You Use." Neilpatel.com. *https://neilpatel.com/blog/problem-solving-value-proposition/.*
12. Assemblo. "Repetition Is Key: Why Frequency Makes Your Marketing More Effective." Assemblo.com, July 28, 2017. *https://assemblo.com/blog/repetition-is-key-why-frequency-makes-your-marketing-effective/.*
13. "Shape." Lexico.com. *https://www.lexico.com/en/definition/shape.*
14. "The 2018 State."
15. Achor, Shawn. "The Happy Secret to Better Work." TEDxBloomington, May 2011. *https://www.ted.com/talks/shawn_achor_the_happy_secret_to_better_work?language=en.*
16. Stanislavsky, Konstantin, and J.J. Robbins (translator). *My Life in Art* (Little, Brown and Co., 1924).

17. Smith, Mercer. "111 Customer Service Statistics and Facts You Shouldn't Ignore." HelpScout.com. *https://www.helpscout.com/75-customer-service-facts-quotes-statistics/.*

18. Clark, Dorie. *Entrepreneurial You* (2017).

19. "Unreasonable." Lexico.com. *https://www.lexico.com/en/definition/unreasonable.*

20. Neil, Dan. "When Cars Were America's Idols." *Los Angeles Times,* June 1, 2009. *https://www.latimes.com/archives/la-xpm-2009-jun-01-fi-gm-history1-story.html.*

21. Mohammed, Rafi. "The Good–Better–Best Approach to Pricing." *Harvard Business Review,* September–October 2018. *https://hbr.org/2018/09/the-good-better-best-approach-to-pricing.*

22. Coombe, Natalie. "How Much Does it Really Cost to Run a Business?" Blog post, NatalieCoombe.com. Date unknown.

23. "Translate." Lexico.com. *https://www.lexico.com/en/definition/translate.*

24. Miller, *Building a StoryBrand.*

25. Grant, Adam. *Give and Take* (Weidenfeld & Nicolson, 2013).

26. Blogintobook. "Social Media Is Bullshit Presentation By B J Mendelson at Social Media Week Chicago." November 8, 2013. YouTube video, 54:03. *https://www.youtube.com/watch?v=-W8fp5pyveU&t=1s.*

27. "3 Social Media Tips with Andréa Jones (Video)." Greatest Story Creative, January 29, 2020. *https://www.greateststorycreative.com/biz/ep1-social-media-and-branding.*

28. Iwerks, Leslie, director. *The Pixar Story.* Buena Vista Home Entertainment, 2007. 1 hr, 27 min. *https://www.netflix.com/us-fr/Title/70083532.*

ACKNOWLEDGMENTS

Gus and Leo—You are the two brightest stars of my greatest story. *You* are what make it great. I'm forever lucky to be wifey and mama. I love you. Thank you for all the smiles, snuggles, and support through everything and every day. And Leo, thanks for being the miracle that you are.

Sarah Potts—I mean, the book's dedicated to you! Thank you for shaping this book and my business in immeasurable ways and being the cheerleader that I've needed at every step. I'll always be grateful for you and I promise to continue to send you dinosaur memes/products on a daily basis.

Jodi Brandon—Thank you for being my partner/editor for round two of my author journey. This book is better for us having worked together before on *Permission to Try.* I value all your kind insight in the process, especially during the "messy middle" when I panicked about whether I had a weird table of contents.

Adele Michal—As I shared throughout this book, you helped me turn the key that I didn't realize I had. You're a gift in both my life and business, and I've been forever changed by having known you and having learned from you. Thank you for all you did, and all you do as a friend, coach, and client.

Faith Teasley—My photographer for life, here we are again. Thank you for capturing the spirit of the work I do and the life I live through timeless photography. It's an incredible bonus that you're also a treasured, loving friend to the entire "Leo Trio."

Janice Smith—I'm grateful to have found the "Greatest Story" of video in you, and inspired to call you a collaborator, friend, and client. Thank you for all you've done to help capture the story of this book in a trailer and beyond.

Hannah Carver—I never imagined a new networking friend would add so much value to my life and to this book. Thank you for your generous insight and vibrant joy about *Establish Yourself.* I'm so grateful for all the feedback, friendship, action, and your unwavering belief in who I am and what I'm doing. I just hope I can be that valuable a person to you for something big in your future.

My alpha and beta readers: Bonnie Artman Fox, Dawn Potter Sander, Darrah Brustein, Joann Vellara, Kate Rosenow, Liz Rossilli, Marcey Rader, Melissa Ternes, Nicole Case, Pamela Schultz, Rick Rocchetti, Tiffany Englert, and Wendy Gates Corbett—After spending more than a year writing this 300+ page book, I was nervous to send it your way. Thank you for sharing deep insights, encouragement, and feedback. I'm so grateful for the perspective you brought to *Establish Yourself,* and so inspired by the action you've already taken with it in your businesses. This is undoubtedly a stronger, more useful book thanks to your voices.

My amazing clients—Because of you, I get to have my greatest business. Thank you for entrusting me to do the most rewarding work in the world: giving you ways to see your own value, to brand and grow businesses you care about, and to tell your stories.

My treasured world of family and friends—Writing a book can feel like an existential rollercoaster, and so can running a business on my own. For being by me through it all, keeping me laughing, cheering me on, and loving me as I am, I'm deeply grateful. Writing a book and running a business is easier, better, and more meaningful with people like you in my life.

Dad—As I said in *Permission to Try,* you always want to hear what I have to say. Your unconditional belief in me and love for me have shaped who I am in countless ways. I love you and I'm exceedingly grateful you're my dad. And yes, you *can* read the book now.

Mom—I wrote another book so you have something new to brag about to your friends in heaven! You're on my mind and on my heart every single day. Your creativity and brilliance have shaped every page of this book, as they're forever a part of me. I love you. I miss you. But I breathe easier knowing that you're madly in love with your grandson, and watching over us all.

Minda—Dearest aunt and sweetest Mimi, you've been a loving light throughout my career and life as a business owner. Thank you for your big heart, joy, and how well you love our family.

Laura and Gina—Thank you for all the "lion taming" in the first year that I was writing this book. I may never forget sitting on the floor of the movie theater room suddenly remembering how hard the process is and wondering why the heck I was attempting to write a new book!? With your loving care of Leo Robin, you ensured that I had only one choice: *press on.* So glad I did, and so grateful to you.

Finally, to all who read and supported my first book, *Permission to Try*—This book wouldn't have happened without all that I learned from writing, publishing, and sharing *Permission to Try* in October 2018. Thank you for investing in yourself and in that little blue book: my pep talk for pivoting your career and giving yourself permission to do what scares you.

Grow your
Greatest
Business

ABOUT THE AUTHOR

Annie Franceschi believes that your life is your greatest story.

Annie is a branding expert, six-figure founder, former Disney storyteller, and bestselling author. In 2013, she quit a dream job at The Walt Disney Studios to start her own agency, Greatest Story Creative®. Since then, Annie has branded 120+ businesses, spoken for thousands, and published the empowering book *Permission to Try: 11 Things You Need to Hear When You're Scared to Change Your Life* (2018).

Today, through her Establish Yourself™ Framework, Brand Story Solution, and consulting, Annie helps coaches and consultants confidently brand and grow their greatest businesses.

Annie is proud to be a Duke University graduate, a lifelong Muppets fan, and a serial rewatcher of *The Golden Girls.* She currently lives in Durham, North Carolina, with her favorite person—her husband, Gus—and their favorite person—their son, Leo.

Connect with Annie

» *Free consultations for branding services and business coaching:* greateststorycreative.com
» *Speaking availability:* anniefranceschi.com
» *LinkedIn:* linkedIn.com/in/anniefranceschi

For More Permission . . .

Needing inspiration to get started?

Curious why I left a dream job at Disney?

Thinking of quitting a job?

(Or know somebody who NEEDS to!?)

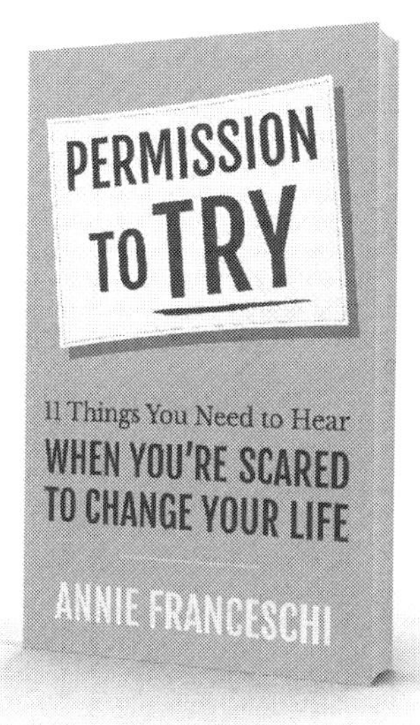

Discover my first book:
Permission to Try: 11 Things You Need to Hear When You're Scared to Change Your Life

Learn more and read the introduction now at
permissiontotry.com.

Share Your Story

When you reach your greatest business,
I'd love to hear your story!

Share your wins with me and the Establish Yourself community: *info@greateststorycreative.com*

ESTABLISH
YOURSELF
ESTABLISH
YOURSELF

Made in the USA
Columbia, SC
06 March 2022